ABACO: THE HISTORY OF AN OUT ISLAND AND ITS CAYS

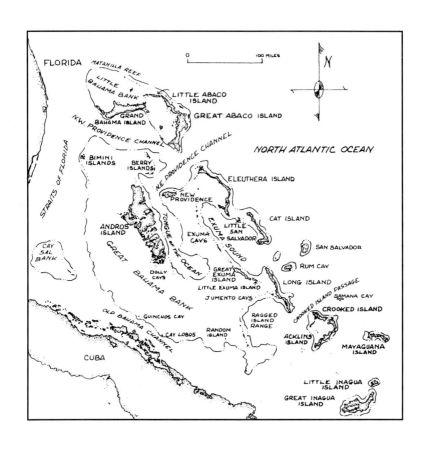

ABACO

THE HISTORY OF AN OUT ISLAND AND ITS CAYS

Second Edition

by Steve Dodge
Professor of History, Millikin University

illustrations by
Laurie Jones

cover painting by
Phil Capen

WHITE SOUND PRESS
1615 West Harrison Avenue
Decatur, IL 62526 USA

Voice: 217 423-0511
Fax: 217 423-0522

Second Edition

Cover illustration - The *Albertine Adoue*, the last sailing vessel to serve as Abaco's mailboat, was replaced by the *Priscilla*, a diesel-powered converted sailboat, in 1923. The cover painting by Phil Capen shows the *Albertine Adoue* at Hope Town in c. 1920.

ISBN 0-932265-34-0

Library of Congress Catalog Card Number:
95-060591

Published by

White Sound Press
1615 West Harrison Avenue
Decatur, Illinois 62526 USA

Voice: 217 423-0511
Fax: 217 423-0522

This book is dedicated to the memory of Byrle Malone Patterson of Hope Town, Abaco, who provided the kind of encouragement and inspiration every author thrives on when it was most needed, and to the author's wife, Marjorie Ann Dodge of Decatur, Illinois, who has consistently provided valuable guidance, help, and support.

PREFACE

Although the modern history of the Americas began in the Bahama Islands over 500 years ago when Christopher Columbus landed on the island of San Salvador, amazingly little is known about the Bahamas. Spain sidestepped them in the rush to the riches of Mexico and Peru, and the British later paid scant attention to small settlements on the islands of New Providence and Eleuthera because they focused their efforts on the greater resources of the North American continent. The British knew little about the Bahamas even after over a century of experience there. During the late 1780s inquiry was made, from London, regarding the number of acres of land in the islands. The response of the colonial government in Nassau was that they didn't even know the number of islands. One hundred years later, in 1884, the Annual Colonial Report indicated that previous geographic information regarding the islands was incorrect because a recent survey made by Lt. White of *H. M. S. Sparrowhawk* found that ". . . at least one half the bank hitherto marked as Abaco is covered with water." Another century has gone by since then, and the Bahamas have been accurately surveyed, but there are still great voids in knowledge of the islands. They are the nearest international neighbor of the United States after Canada and Mexico, yet many United States citizens know nothing of where they are located, and a remarkable number of well educated people confuse them with Bermuda (850 miles to the northeast) or Barbados (1400 miles to the southeast). All of this ignorance has been cheerfully accepted for several centuries, and rationalized by repeated references to the unimportance of the islands.

This book was written to fill some of the voids in our knowledge of the Bahamas, with full appreciation for the importance of that history as well as its relative insignificance when placed in the perspective of the history of the modern world. A friend and colleague once told me that writing a history of just one part of the Bahamas was "small potatoes" for an historian, and the National Endowment for the Humanities, in a grant application, wanted to know what contributions Abaco had made to western culture. My friend was right, and I didn't get the grant. It is obvious that Abaco is a small place outside the mainstream. It has contributed little to the momentum of the modern world. In fact, much of this history describes the impact of the modern world on Abaco rather than vice verse. The history of Abaco is important because it is unique. The insularity of the Abaco islands and cays forced their inhabitants to develop their own distinct society; they could not easily participate in the larger world beyond the watery horizon. The 10,061 Abaconians of today (1990 census) deserve to understand this special heritage, and other Bahamians will, I hope, be enriched by gaining greater knowledge about one of the major parts of their young nation of islands. I also hope that visitors to Abaco will gain a heightened awareness of the history of the Abaconians from this book—the first general comprehensive history of Abaco.

Two themes stand out. One is the extreme isolation of Abaco during the nineteenth and early twentieth centuries. The only contact with the outside world was by sailing boats which carried passengers and freight as well as mail. Passages to Nassau or to the United States were major expeditions. A second important theme is that modernization has been compressed in Abaco. Most of the world waited from 1807 to 1903 to move from the steamboat to the airplane. Abaco did not have a diesel mailboat until 1923, but it was supplemented by seaplane service about twenty years later, just after World War II. The automobile and the outboard motor, both of which were not introduced in Abaco until the 1950s, have transformed the lives of the Abaconians since that time—during the past forty years.

Researching and writing this book has been one of the great pleasures of my life. I have found enthusiastic supporters almost everywhere. I am particularly indebted to the staff of the Bahamas National Archives in Nassau, to the Wyannie Malone Historical Museum in Hope Town, to the Millikin University Library, and to many others who helped me by finding and providing materials or by granting interviews to me. It is commendable that Millikin University has provided its support for research on a small group of islands and cays located 1200 miles from its campus. It speaks well for the University, and its support for research and the furtherance of knowledge for its own sake. Many individuals have contributed to the two editions of this work. Cathie Whiting ran numerous errands in Nassau, Bill Reukauf helped during interviews, Vernon Malone, Dave and Phoebe Gale, and Richard Ruch made valuable suggestions for improving the manuscript for the first edition. My son Jon Dodge and eleven students in my Bahamas seminar at Millikin University, especially Adam Stanley, helped to improve the second edition. Vicki McElfresh compiled the index. Laurie Jones' illustrations add much to the value of the text, and Phil Capen's cover painting provides his visualization of the *Albertine Adoue*, Abaco's last sailing mailboat, tied up to the Hope Town public dock in *c.* 1920. Helen Nelson of Millikin University cheerfully and efficiently typed and retyped the manuscript in 1982, and then worked on the same material again in 1994. Many other persons, too numerous to mention here, have helped me, and I am grateful for their contributions.

If there are errors in this book, I am, of course, solely responsible for them. I view this work, now in its second edition, as a beginning rather than as an end. I hope it continues to whet the appetites of curious students and scholars in and out of the Bahamas, and that it will prod others to produce new historical works, so that we may all learn more about the history of one of the beautiful and unspoiled places of the world.

Steve Dodge

Millikin University
Decatur, Illinois
April 1995

CONTENTS

List of Maps and Illustrations

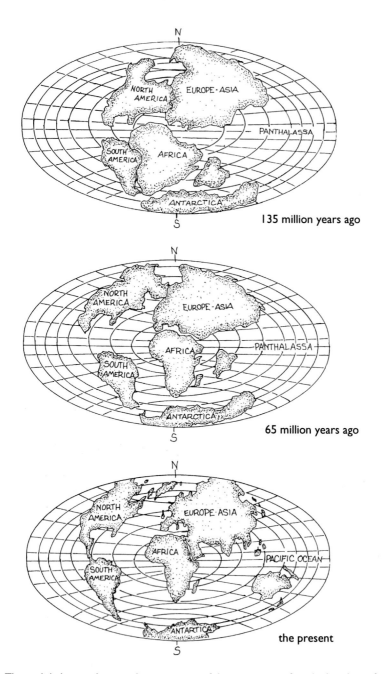

N

NORTH
AMERICA

EUROPE - ASIA

PANTHALASSA

SOUTH
AMERICA

AFRICA

ANTARCTICA

S

135 million years ago

N

NORTH
AMERICA

EUROPE - ASIA

AFRICA

PANTHALASSA

SOUTH
AMERICA

ANTARCTICA

S

65 million years ago

N

NORTH
AMERICA

EUROPE · ASIA

AFRICA

PACIFIC OCEAN

SOUTH
AMERICA

ANTARCTICA

S

the present

Three global maps showing the movement of the continents after the breakup of
Pangaea about 200 million years ago. The top shows the continents beginning to
move apart about 135 million years ago, the middle shows them further apart
about 65 million years ago, and the bottom shows the present configuration.

Chapter One —

Origins and Land

Two hundred million years ago the Bahama Islands did not exist, and all the present continents were part of the supercontinent Pangaea, which was surrounded by one great ocean. Pangaea rifted, or split, and North and South America moved westward from Eurasia and Africa creating the North and South Atlantic Oceans as they narrowed the ancestral Pacific (see maps at left). This movement of the continental plates was caused by the upwelling of new material from the interior of the earth which pushed the plates apart and created the mid-Atlantic ridges in the process. These ridges serve as evidence to support the plate or continental drift theory, and, when combined with other evidence, such as the amazingly close jigsaw puzzle fit of Northwest Africa with the east coast of North America, the argument is very convincing. Tectonic plate theory, regarded as a radical unsubstantiated idea as little as forty years ago, is generally accepted today.

Geologists now see the earth and its land masses as dynamic and evolving rather than static. When Pangaea rifted the continental land masses moved apart at the rate of about ten kilometers every one million years, or ten inches every twenty-five years—about the speed of the growth of a toenail. It took two hundred million years to create the Atlantic Ocean, and the enlargement of the Atlantic continues today, making it slightly wider each year. As the North American plate moves west it crunches and grates against the Pacific plate, causing a crumpling of the western edge of the North American plate which has resulted in mountains there. Also, as one plate pushes up against the other great tensions are built up which are periodically relieved as the earthquakes which occur from time to time in California. Tectonic plate theory not only provided a satisfactory explanation of the evolution of the earth, it also offered consistent and logical explanations for various existing phenomena. But the Bahamas presented a problem for tectonic plate theorists.

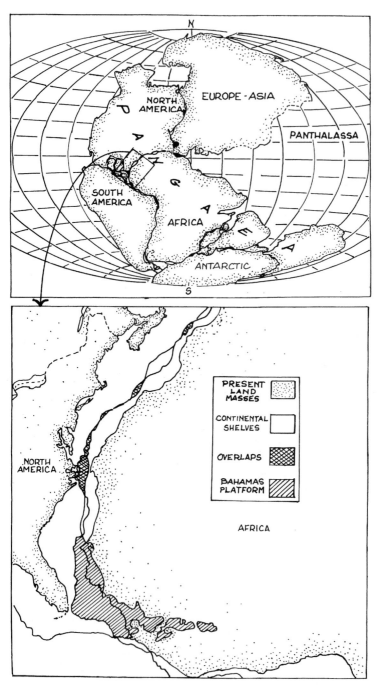

Supercontinent Pangaea rifted 200 million years ago (top). The meshing of North America and Africa is near perfect if the Bahamas platform is not considered (bottom). Drawings are after those in R. Dietz and J. Holden, "The Breakup of Pangaea," *Scientific American* (October, 1970), 30-41.

The difficulty was that the jigsaw puzzle fit of Northwest Africa and North America did not work if the Bahamas were included. The islands themselves account for only 5353 square miles of land, and are small enough to be considered negligible. But the Bahama Banks, which extend upwards from the floor of the sea one and one-half miles and are covered by only ten to forty feet of water, are much larger. Tectonic plate theorists include as "land" everything down to a depth of 1000 fathoms (6000 feet). Measured in this way, the Bahama Banks and Islands constitute a land mass of over 60,000 square miles—a major mass larger than present-day Florida, or Georgia, or Cuba. And with the Bahama Banks counted as land, the jigsaw puzzle did not work. It was therefore suggested that the Bahama Banks were not part of Pangaea, but were new land created after the breakup of Pangaea. Various theories have been put forward to explain the origin of this large new land mass.

The upwelling of hot basaltic rock which pushed the plates apart and formed the mid-Atlantic ridges also produced block faulting at the edges of the plates. This pushed some crust material upward to create new land masses. Block faulting resulted in a new land area at the trailing edge of the North Atlantic plate in the vicinity

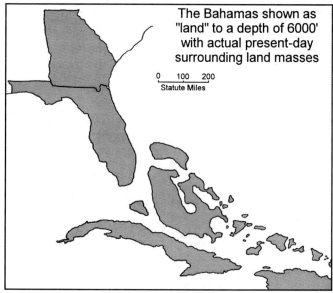

The Bahama Banks shown as "land" to a depth of 6000' with Florida, Georgia, Cuba and Hispaniols shown as they are today. The Bahamas actually were a land mass of the size shown above when sea level was lower than it is now during the Pleistocene and Pliocene Eras.

of the Bahamas, but as the plate moved west the rock beneath the fault cooled and shrank, so the land subsided and fell beneath the sea. One hundred forty million years ago it was covered by a shallow sea, and it continued to sink. But it did not disappear because new material was deposited from the sea at about the same rate as the land sank, so the area remained a large shallow region. It continued to subside, but this sinking continued to be offset by new deposits. Some may find it difficult to believe that sedimentary deposits could have created such a huge land mass, but test borings at Andros Island in the west central Bahamas produced relatively pure sedimentary calcium carbonate at 14,500 feet. The banks grew at the rate of 1"-1½" every 1000-1500 years for 140 million years to produce land masses which now tower 1½ miles above the floor of the sea. These numbers provide a startling perspective on how little of the earth's history has been coincident with human history. The banks are 1½ miles high, but have grown less than ½" since Columbus' voyage in 1492, and only 2" since the rise of ancient Greece.

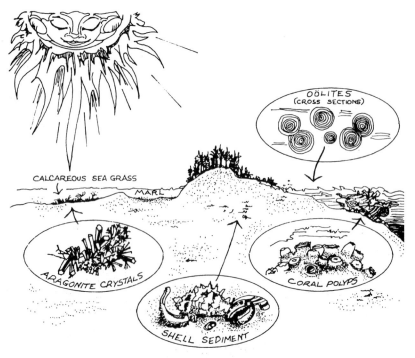

Five different methods of calcium carbonate formation built the Bahama banks and islands.

This long slow process involved at least five different methods of extracting huge amounts of calcium carbonate from the sea:

1) As the sun warmed and evaporated surface waters in the interior areas of the banks, calcium carbonate was precipitated and fell to the bottom of the shallow sea to form a white lime mud known as marl.

2) Marine organisms as varied as single-celled foraminifers and larger animals such as clams, conchs, and snails built shells of calcium carbonate and provided a second method for the buildup of material. When these animals died, their shells became part of the banks.

3) Oölites accumulated at the edges of the banks. These are formed when several layers of calcium carbonate adhere to a foreign particle such as shell fragment or fecal pellet. Oölites form in areas of tidal flow where particles are alternately suspended by current and then allowed to rest. The process is similar to the formation of a hailstone, but the result is about the size of a grain of sand.

4) Coral reefs grew along the edges of the banks where there was sufficient water exchange to support them. Reefs are created by coral polyps, small tube-like organisms which filter calcium carbonate from sea water and deposit it in beautiful reef formations. Because of reefs and oolites, the margins of the banks were built up more rapidly than the interior, forming a ridge or lip near the edges.

5) A fifth process involved the growth of calcareous algae and sea grass and its decomposition into very small aragonite needles.

These five processes occurred in different places at different times as conditions on the shallow banks changed over a period of one hundred forty million years. Their cumulative effect was to offset the results of subsidence by building immense raised platforms of calcium carbonate (limestone).

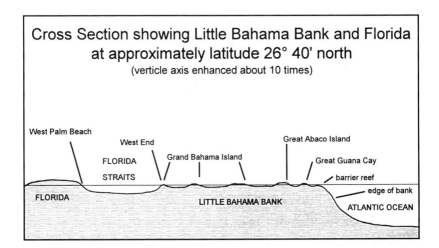

Cross Section showing Little Bahama Bank and Florida at approximately latitude 26° 40' north
(verticle axis enhanced about 10 times)

During the Pliocene era, which began about ten million years ago, and the Pleistocene Era, which began about one million years ago, glaciers periodically extended from the polar caps and formed over the northern and southern extremities of the continental land masses. During these ice ages an excessive amount of the earth's water was locked up in glaciers, and sea level was several hundred feet lower than it is at present. The banks were two rather large islands separated from Florida by a thirty to thirty-five mile strait. The banks dried, and they were exposed to sunlight and rainfall. The fresh water dissolved some of the sediments and eroded part of the banks, but in other places the fresh water helped to form calcite and cemented the sediments into limestone. Plants and trees grew and helped to hold the soil together with their roots. When they died, their decayed leaves and limbs contributed to the banks. Wind and wave action moved oölites into place around newly exposed coral and limestone formations to create beaches, and the relentless pounding of ocean waves broke up reefs and shells to create sand which combined with the oölites to augment the beaches. Winds blew the sand from beaches, and it was trapped by grasses and shrubs growing further inland and built dunes as barri-

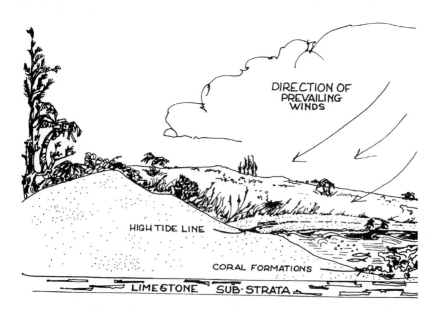

DIRECTION OF PREVAILING WINDS

HIGH TIDE LINE

CORAL FORMATIONS

LIMESTONE SUB-STRATA

ers facing the sea. Larger plants grew in the protection of the dunes. When the glaciers melted the sea rose again, sometimes to heights about one hundred feet higher than today, inundating all but the highest hills on the present islands. Sea level gyrated from ice age to thaw three or four times during the past ten million years, and the islands were alternately exposed and submerged. When the last of the ice ages finally ended about ten thousand years ago, the sea rose to cover the banks, but left the greater concentration of material along the margins of the banks exposed. These exposed land masses are the Bahamian archipelago as we know it today.

With the sea at its present level, Abaco has a land area of 649 square miles. It is about half the size of Rhode Island. Virtually all of the land has a limestone and coral base. It is soft rock which has been carved by the waves of the sea at the periphery of the islands and cays, dissolved by rainfall, and weathered by the prevailing easterly trade winds. Beautiful beaches of pink coral sand have added to the land area, and decaying vegetable matter has created pockets of soil above the limestone on the larger cays and on Great and Little Abaco Islands. Plants such as sea oats, bay lavender, and others able to withstand almost constant drenchings with salt spray, stabilize the dunes. Sea grape, long leaf blolly, buttonwood, and other scrub growth (to a height of about eight feet) abound in the shelter of the dunes. Mangroves, with their intricate root system which traps debris and retards erosion, help to build new land on the leeward side of the cays. On Great Abaco a huge pine forest grew in the soil on top of the limestone, and madeira (mahogany), lignum vitae, and other trees provided several generations of Abaconians with excellent boat-building lumber. Palmettoes, native to the islands, are found in abundance, and various kinds of palms, imported rather recently, now add beauty to the landscape.

The smaller cays lie three to six miles to the east and northeast of Great and Little Abaco and form a chain over 100 miles long. The protected waters on the bank between the cays and Great Abaco are about ten to twenty feet deep and are known as the Sea of Abaco or Abaco Sound. Most of the cays are protected from the open sea by one of the longest barrier reefs in the Western Hemisphere, which stretches from Elbow Cay to Walker's Cay, at the far northwestern end of the chain. The reef is comprised of staghorn, elkhorn, brain, star and other corals, and supports a wide variety of brightly colored tropical fishes as well as their larger predators. The queen conch inhabits large parts of the Sea of Abaco,

8

THE ABACOS

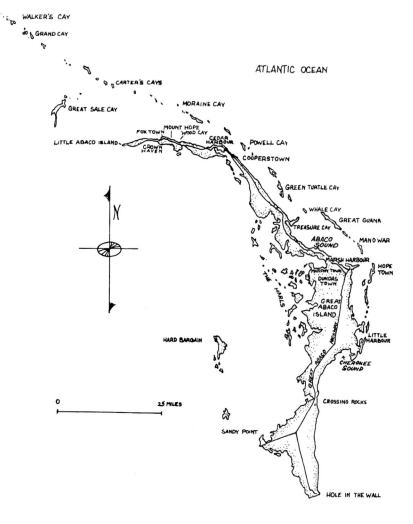

and the spiny lobster, known locally as the crawfish, is plentiful, especially in the northern parts of Abaco. The shallow, clear waters of the banks vary in color from white to brilliant green to blue in deeper areas. Local pilots read the depth of the water by color, and are not confused by patches of sea grass as are many visiting yachtsmen. Good natural small boat harbours are found at many of the smaller cays and at Marsh's Harbour on the "mainland" of Abaco.

Abaco lies just north of the Tropic of Cancer; its climate is generally salubrious. Summer weather prevails for eight months, and fall weather dominates during the other four months. Even during the summer temperatures rarely exceed 93 degrees, and the prevailing southeasterly breezes provide natural air conditioning. Abaco is far enough north to be exposed to successions of cold front passages during the winter months from December to March. These bring strong northwesterly winds and temperatures of about 58 degrees. Rainfall in Abaco averages about fifty to sixty inches each year, which is much more than the islands located further to the south in the Bahamas that receive closer to twenty-five inches per year. The fresh water percolates through the limestone of Great Abaco and, being less dense than salt water, floats on top of the salt water table creating a fresh water lens. Thus, Great Abaco Island has fresh water wells. The outer cays are too small for a useful lens to develop, and residents there collect rainwater from the roofs of their homes and store it for use in cisterns. Droughts were serious threats to existence on the outer cays during the nineteenth and early twentieth centuries, but in recent years the local ferry and freight services have alleviated this by carrying water from Great Abaco to the cays during long dry periods.

The western shore of Great Abaco is less well defined than the windward shore; the land slopes gradually and falls beneath the sea. In the bight formed by Great Abaco a large, very shallow area of lime mud called "The Marls" resembles a mire and has innumerable small islets, some of which are exposed only at low tide. There are no settlements in this area, but the shallows serve as breeding grounds for fish and crawfish. The region is lacking in the beauty of the windward side of Abaco, but it has great attraction for the naturalist. Some small islands, which lie further off the shores of Abaco to the west, are extremely isolated and life there is very primitive. One settlement, on Mores Island, is named Hard Bargain.

END NOTES

[1] The first geologist to suggest that the continents were in motion rather than fixed was Alfred Wegener of Germany in 1912. His theory was not well received. But by the 1950s Robert S. Dietz of California and Harry Hess of Princeton concluded, based on core sea floor samples and more accurate mapping of the ocean floors, that the floor of the Atlantic was spreading as a result of hot material from the earth's core rising to form the mid-Atlantic ridges and pushing the Americas away from Europe and Asia. They theorized that the continental plates "floated" on liquid material and were moved by convection currents. Most geologists now regard these theories as proved.

[2] The description which follows is a consolidation and simplification of the most plausible of these theories. For more detailed information see Robert S. Dietz and John C. Holden, "The Breakup of Pangaea," *Scientific American* 223:4 (October 1970), 30-41; Henry T. Mullins and George W. Lynts, "Origin of the Northwestern Bahama Platform: Review and Reinterpretation," *Geological Society of America Bulletin* 88:10 (1977), 1447-1461; Norman D. Newell, "Bahamian Platforms," in Arie Poldervaart, ed., *Crust of the Earth* (Geological Society of America Special Paper 62, 1955), 303-316; and Alan Stine, "Geohistory of the Bahamas," unpublished mss., p. 6.

[3] An alternative explanation is that the "basement" of the Bahamas was actually part of Africa and that the Bahamas plate rotated as it moved west. But this view calls for subsidence and sedimentary deposits also. See Mullins and Lynts (1977).

Chapter Two -

Lucayans, Explorers, and Pirates

The first inhabitants of the Bahama Islands came from Hispaniola or Cuba in about A. D. 500-800 and lived in the islands until the arrival of the Spaniards in about 1500—a tenure of 700-1000 years. After their demise due to slave raids and European diseases, the islands were empty for 150 years, and were then colonized by a few English Europeans in about 1650. This fledgling community developed into the modern Bahamas, a society which even today, with a tenure of about 350 years in the islands, has occupied the Bahamas less than half as long as the Lucayans. Despite the long occupation of the islands by the Lucayan Indians, they have left no mark on modern Bahamian society. They vanished, leaving behind only a few paragraphs that Christopher Columbus and other Spaniards wrote about them, numerous fragments of their Palmetto Ware pottery, and tantalizingly little other archaeological evidence of their 1000-year existence in the Bahama Islands.

They were already an island people before moving to the Bahamas, having migrated from the Orinoco River Valley in Venezuela to the coast and then to the lesser Antilles between 2100 B. C. and A. D. 600. Known as Arawaks, or, more correctly, as Taino peoples, they had reached Puerto Rico by A. D. 200-600.

They cultivated manioc and various other crops, and were governed by tribal chieftains the Spaniards called "caciques." The Arawaks have long been characterized as a gentle and peace-loving people who were pushed to the north by the Caribs, a second wave of migrants from South America who moved northward through the Lesser Antilles.

The Caribs were allegedly aggressive and more accomplished warriors in contrast to the docile Arawaks. The Caribs did not eat human flesh on a daily basis, but apparently practiced some ritualistic cannibalism. The name Carib means cannibal. So the traditional view is that the cannibalistic aggressive Caribs pushed the peaceful Arawaks relentlessly to the north. There undoubtedly is

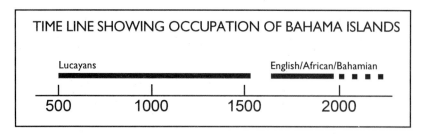

TIME LINE SHOWING OCCUPATION OF BAHAMA ISLANDS

Lucayans   English/African/Bahamian

500   1000   1500   2000

some truth to this, but recently some archaeologists have de-emphasized this simplistic dichotomy of good peaceful Arawaks and bad aggressive Caribs in favor of other reasons for the migration of the Taino Arawaks to the Bahamas.[1]

The Bahama Islands were pristine—they abounded in marine resources. A warmer climate than the Bahamas enjoy today, with more rainfall, had produced luxuriant forests of pine and hardwood. The islands were a very attractive place for colonization and development. The Taino Arawaks who settled the Bahamas are called Lucayans, from Lukku-Cairi, which means island people. They came in dugout canoes fashioned from large cottonwood trees, and established small coastal communities. The central Bahamas were probably best suited for them, and Long Island may have served as some sort of seat of political or religious authority. Duhos were special stools used by caciques, and half of all the duhos found in the Bahamas have been found within a 170 mile radius of southern Long Island.[2] The total Lucayan population was probably between 40,000 and 80,000[3] compared to about 250,000 in the 1990s. But if the two large cities of the modern Bahamas, Nassau and Freeport, are discounted, the population density of the Bahamas was not so very different in the 1990s than it was in 1492.

Duhos were ceremonial stools used by Lucayan caciques.

This Lucayan canoe paddle was found by Theodore De Booy in a cave at Mores Island, Abaco, in 1912. It was made from a single piece of cedar and was remarkably well-preserved. It is in the collection of the Museum of the American Indian in New York.

The lives of the Lucayans were simple; they cultivated a wide variety of crops, reaped the bountiful harvest of the sea, and occasionally captured some of the few land animals available to them on the islands. The single most important crop was bitter manioc, a starch tuber which required considerable processing because it contains hydrocyanic (prussic) acid. The Lucayans first grated the tuber, and then squeezed the poisonous juice from it. The resultant dried flour was then used to make pancake-shaped bread called cassava, which was the staple of the Lucayan's diet. It could be eaten immediately, or stored for up to six months. Cassava was their wonder food. It provided them with security and enabled them to live through droughts and storms which damaged standing

Lucayans lived in round houses called *canaye* made of posts and canes which were thatched with palm or other leaves. They baked cassava bread on griddles over an open fire.

crops and made fishing difficult. They also cultivated cotton and produced cotton thread. Every time Columbus mentioned trading with the Lucayans he mentioned balls of cotton thread.[4] This may have been their principal export product.

Michael Craton and Gail Saunders, in their new social history of the Bahamas, *Islanders in the Stream: A History of the Bahamian People* (1992), have said that the lives of the Lucayans were more fully integrated with the Bahamian environment than those of any other people who have inhabited the islands. They brought very little with them and adapted their life-style to suit their new environment. They did little to alter that environment, living in harmony with it.[5] It is no wonder that some Europeans, when they met these peoples, saw them as the epitome of the noble savage. When Columbus landed on San Salvador, two hundred miles south of Abaco, he described the Lucayans he encountered as handsome and generous: "they invite you to share anything they possess."[6]

Until recently archaeologists contended that the Lucayans did not migrate to the two northernmost islands in the Bahamas, Great Abaco and Grand Bahama. In some cases these were just wild guesses based on extremely limited survey work, but some archaeologists developed carefully reasoned arguments. Bitter manioc plants stop growing when exposed to temperatures of 50 degrees Fahrenheit and the leaves and upper branches die when subjected to 46 degrees Fahrenheit. Because both Abaco and Grand Bahama experience such temperatures for brief periods during the passage of cool fronts in January, February, and sometimes March, it was reasoned that the Lucayans would not, or could not, have moved so far to the north.[7] But there seemed to be elusive evidence that Lucayans had been in Abaco. When research for the first edition of this history was done during the late 1970s, various residents of Abaco said that there were Lucayan artifacts, such as drawings on cave walls, or engraved stones, though not one could actually be produced for examination.[8] During the middle 1980s two residents of Marsh Harbour, Abaco, whose hobby was bush exploring, found several Lucayan sites. These two, Ian Lothian and David Bethel, developed into skilled amateur archaeologists. They had identified 30 to 40 Lucayan sites by 1988, and were finding new ones each year. Other discoveries corroborated their finds.

The remains of a Lucayan Indian were discovered in Hope Town, Abaco, in 1990 when an excavation was made to build a cistern for a private residence. It was found about six feet below the surface, the skull was intact, and a small piece of Palmetto

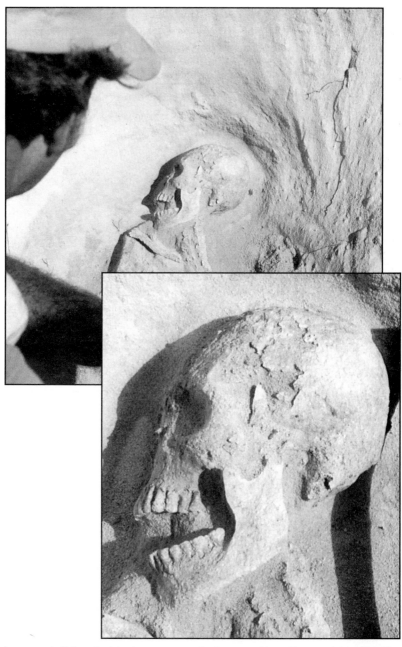

Lucayan skull found while digging cistern for house in Hope Town in July, 1990. The Florida Museum of Natural History determined that the skull was that of a Lucayan male about 30-35 years old who died about 600 years ago.

Ware Lucayan pottery was found in close proximity to the skull.[9] Analysis by the Museum of Natural History at the University of Florida (Gainesville) indicated that the skull was from a 30-35 year-old Lucayan male, who had died about 600 years ago. It was clear that the early surveys and reasoned conclusions reached by archaeologists were in error; Lucayans had lived in Abaco.

It also became clear that the settlements were extensive, and it was even suggested that the Lucayan population of Abaco may have been higher than the present population, which is about 10,000. These new discoveries soon generated interest in archaeological investigations in Abaco. Beginning in 1991 funding was secured to support some focused survey work and excavation in Abaco.[10] Most of this work has been done on three sites located a few miles north of Marsh Harbour—Rico's Hill North, Rico's Hill South, and Big Owl Cay. These sites were probably related and were probably all part of a single community. Paired sites (twin cities) were common in the Lucayan Bahamas, and the third site, a littoral location, probably served as a marine resource site for the other two. But these sites are unusual because they are inland rather than coastal. Most Lucayan sites were located on the coast in order to provide easy access to the sea.

Other factors also make these sites unique. The average number of rim styles of Palmetto Ware found on a Lucayan site in the Bahamas is from three to six, but a total of about thirty styles have been identified at each of these sites. Also, the incidence of decorated or incised shards (27% of 911 shards found in 1991) is much higher than what is usual. In addition, three very unique decorated shell barrettes were found, probably indicating the residence of a cacique of some importance. Further, the sites have been dated to about 1500; they are post-Columbian. What does all of this add up to? It could simply mean that some very creative potters lived in these sites in approximately 1500. But there is also a more fascinating explanation.

When Christopher Columbus visited San Salvador in the Central Bahamas, the day was marked by petty commerce rather than violence, but good relations between the Spaniards and the Lucayans must have soured when Columbus took seven Lucayans with him against their will, separating them from their families and villages. These first Lucayan captives were not taken as slaves, but rather as curiosities to show to the Spanish crown, and also to serve as guides. The Spaniards moved south out of the Bahamas, and established a permanent colony on Hispaniola. There they eventually made war against some of the resident Tainos, forced them to work, and sent some back to Spain as slaves. Far more devastating than this cruelty to the Lucayans were the diseases brought by the Europeans to which the Americans had no resistance. There truly were two separate worlds prior to 1492. Each was an independent ecological unit, and diseases which were endemic in Europe, that is, limited in their veracity because Europeans had developed antibodies to them, ravaged the vulnerable Americans. When laborers on Hispaniola died (the population declined from as many as two million to only 61,000 by 1509),[11] the Spaniards made slave raids into the Bahamas.

By this time the Lucayans had multiple reasons to dread the Spaniards. Seven men had been carried off from San Salvador against their will, and there may well have been some suffering as a result of European diseases in San Salvador even as early as 1492. By 1510 the Spaniards were raiding the islands and dragging the Lucayans off to Hispaniola where the indigenous Taino population had already been decimated by diseases such as measles and flu. Lucayans who escaped capture probably suffered from diseases. Some Lucayans were even carried to Spain—from November 1499 to March 1500 Amerigo Vespucci explored the Bahamian archipelago, and when he turned toward Spain he took 232 slaves with him.[12] When Ponce de Leon made his famous voyage through the Bahamas and to Florida in 1513, he found only one Lucayan Indian in all the Bahamas—an old woman living on Grand Bahama or Abaco.[13]

It is quite logical to assume that Lucayans who were fortunate enough to escape capture by the Spaniards would move further away from the Spanish base in Hispaniola to the northern Bahamas. It is also logical that they would have settled inland sites, which would not have been visible from the Spanish ships. The littoral site—Big Owl Cay—associated with Rico's Hill North and Rico's Hill South—is on the west coast of Great Abaco Island where the water is far too shallow for Spanish ships. The large number of rim styles could be the result of pottery carried to these sites from elsewhere in the Bahamas, but this is actually unlikely because Palmetto Ware was utilitarian pottery made in bulk because of its poor quality and limited life span. It was probably considered to be both disposable and replaceable, and therefore probably was not normally carried from one island to another. It is more likely that the multiplicity of rim styles is the result of various potters from

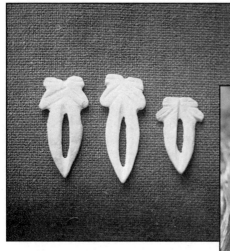

Shell barrettes (left) and shell jewelry with shards (below) found at Rico's Hill North on Great Abaco Island.

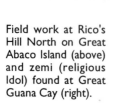

Field work at Rico's Hill North on Great Abaco Island (above) and zemi (religious Idol) found at Great Guana Cay (right).

throughout the Bahamas migrating to these sites in Abaco and carrying their traditions of pottery making with them.

The more fascinating explanation of the fact that Rico's Hill North, Rico's Hill South, and Big Owl Cay constitute an unusually large complex of inland sites with a multiplicity of rim styles and were inhabited in the post Columbian period, is that the Lucayans fled to Abaco to try to escape the Spaniards. These sites may be the Maachu Pichu of the Bahamas.[14]

Whether these sites represent the last stand of the Lucayans or not, some other very interesting information has been gained as a result of the recent digs. Hutia bones have been a common find in areas also yielding pottery shards, and all of the bones seem to come from hutia aged about one year. The hutia is an almost extinct cat-sized rodent which lived throughout the Bahamas, but is now limited to a small indigenous colony on the Plana Cays and a transplanted one in the Exumas. Some archaeologists had previously theorized that the Lucayans may have domesticated the hutia,[15] but Bill Keegan, in his recent book, rejects this idea because chemical analysis of Lucayan bones does not indicate that they ate a significant amount of meat from land animals.[16] The presence of these bones, all of similar size, seems to indicate that hutias may have been raised for slaughter at the optimal age and size. There is no definitive answer to the question.

These recent digs on Abaco have added significantly to our knowledge of the Lucayan Indians who lived in Abaco long before the first settlers of European and African descent arrived. It is hoped that more new knowledge will be gained in the years to come.

Columbus had landed in the Bahamas and sailed through the archipelago for about two weeks. He was intrigued with the people,

The Hutia, a cat-sized rodent, may have been domesticated and raised for food by the Lucayans.

who he described as well-formed, naked, and generous, and he engaged in trade with them. He marvelled at the beauty of the islands and the flora, but it was obvious that he had not found the riches of Cathay (China) and Cipangu (Japan), and he was clearly disappointed. When he asked about gold, the Lucayans pointed south, so Columbus sailed through the Bahamas to Cuba and Hispaniola. These were not China and Japan either, but they were larger islands and showed more promise than the Bahamian islands he had seen. Hispaniola became the site of the first European settlement in the Caribbean, and Cuba and Puerto Rico were soon colonized as well.

The Bahamas were smaller, less fertile, inhabited by poorer Indians, and surrounded by shallow waters with dangerous reefs which made navigation difficult. One of the explanations of the origin of the name Bahamas is that it came from the Spanish "Baja Mar," which means shallow sea. This would have been easily Anglicized to Bahama because in Spanish a "j" is pronounced like an "h" in English. [17] Although the Bahamas did not appeal to the Spaniards as a place to settle, the maps they produced indicates that they did explore the islands. Juan de la Cosa's map, drawn in 1500, indicates that extensive exploration had been done within eight years of Columbus' landfall on San Salvador. Juan de la Cosa's map is certainly not an accurate portrayal of the Bahama Islands, but it does correctly depict the Bahamas as a large archipelago stretching to the northwest from a point near the coast of Hispaniola. A very large island at the extreme northwestern end of the chain is designated as "habacoa." Although the shape and size of this island is not similar to the shape and size of Abaco (or any of the other islands in the northern Bahamas), the name "habacoa" continued in use and was later anglicized to Abbacoe and finally to Abaco (in Spanish "h" is silent). Julian Granberry, linguist and archaeologist, has explained that the Spanish Habacoa came from the combination of the Taino morphemes (small meaningful units) "Ha ba ko wa," which means "large upper outlier. " He says this name was first applied to Andros, but later shifted to Abaco (probably a map maker's mistake). The name "Lucayoneque" was often used on early maps to designate Abaco. Granberry says it was derived from the Taino morphemes "Luka ya ne ke" which means "people's distant waters land." [18] Some other explanations have been offered for the derivation of Abaco, [19] but these by Granberry are probably the best.

The Spaniards by-passed the Bahamas. They were interested in them only as a source of fresh Indian labor, and after the Lucayans

Juan de la Cosa's map, drawn in 1500, was the first to name an island "habacoa," a term which was later Anglicized to Abaco. This photograph was made from a hand colored lithographic reproduction of the map which was included in Jomard's Monumentes de la Geographie (1842). The photograph is reproduced here courtesy of the Edward E. Ayer Collection, the Newberry Library, Chicago.

were gone (as early as 1515 or as late as 1550), they probably considered the islands as obstructions to navigation and avoided them. Many Spanish ships were lost on the banks and reefs of the Bahamas; Michael Craton tells of seventeen ships which were wrecked in Abaco in 1595.[20] These wrecks have not been found. The Spaniards by-passed various other Caribbean islands as well. Spain ignored them and settled the larger islands, and then ignored the entire Caribbean in the rush to the riches of Mexico and Peru. This presented an opportunity for other European nations, who scrambled to colonize what Spain had shunned.

The first other European nation to take an interest in the Bahamas was France. A colony was established somewhere in Abaco in 1565. It was paired with a sister colony in Florida located near St. Augustine. The apparent goal was to establish naval ports on both sides of the Florida Straits, which would give them the ability to control traffic departing from Cuba or the Gulf of Mexico for Europe. A second ship from France sent shortly after the settlement was established could not find the Abaco colony, and no trace of it has been unearthed to date.[21] The Spaniards attacked and routed the French Colony in Florida after about three years. The French probably made another attempt to colonize Abaco in 1633, although the details are unclear. Cardinal Richelieu, Minister to King Louis XIII, granted Abaco and some other Bahamian islands to Guillaume de Caen, a French Huguenot (Protestant) in 1633. He was also granted the title Baron des Bahames. But the terms of the grant prohibited this Huguenot leader from settling Huguenots in his colony, and the grant was later withdrawn for political reasons. A second short-lived French colony in Abaco may have resulted from this, but the French did not gain a permanent foothold in the Bahamas.

It was the English rather than the French who successfully colonized the Bahamas, and it all started as a result of religious/political disputes. In 1534 the Christian churches in England broke away from the Roman Catholic church, not because of theological reasons, but because the pope would not grant King Henry VIII of England a divorce. Henry separated the English Church from Rome, and the head of his new "Anglican Church"—the Archbishop of Canterbury—granted the divorce. This occurred during the same years that the Lutheran and Calvinistic reformations were going on in Europe. The Anglican Church adopted some of the new beliefs, but numerous controversies arose. Some wanted the Angli-

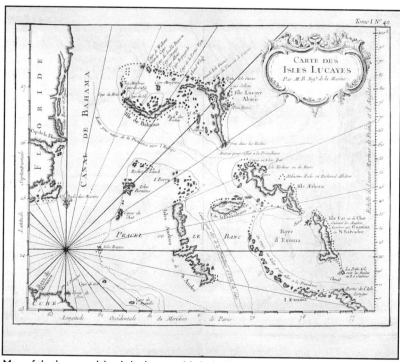

Map of the Lucayan Islands by Jacques-Nicholas Bellin, Paris, 1758. Reproduced with the consent of New York Public Library.

can Church to become more Protestant, while others wanted to move it back toward or into the Catholic fold.

The English government tilted first one way, and then the other, making various groups unhappy with each change. Some left the country. The Pilgrims went to Plymouth, Massachusetts, in 1620, and the Puritans, who wanted to "purify" the Anglican Church, left England to establish their "Zion in the Wilderness" at Boston in 1630. Some American colonies were not founded for religious reasons at all, but were nevertheless affected by the religious/political disputes in England.

Virginia was founded in 1607 as a business venture rather than by religious dissidents, and a small colony was established in Bermuda in 1609 when a ship on the way to Virginia was wrecked on Bermuda. The new colony on Bermuda produced tobacco, engaged in fishing and whaling, and flourished as a convenient port on the route between Virginia and England. Religious disputes which started in England spread to Bermuda.

In 1647 William Sayle, a former governor of Bermuda, decided that religious freedom for Protestants who were suffering under pro-Catholic leadership in Bermuda could best be gained by establishing a new colony in the Bahamas. A group of about seventy arrived in 1648 under Sayle's leadership and established themselves on an island they named Eleuthera, the Greek word for freedom. The fledgling colony was plagued by division and shipwreck, and struggled to survive during the 1650s. A second English settlement was established about fifty miles to the southwest, on New Providence Island, during the 1660s. Many of these colonists also came from Bermuda. This colony grew faster than Eleuthera, and soon became the main English settlement in the Bahamas.

Nassau was dominant, but it was not much of a capital city. It was common practice for European governments to "give" colonies to a private company or even to an individual as this was an inexpensive and risk-free way for the crown to extend its dominions. Sometimes it worked, and sometimes it didn't. The British government had given the Bahamas to Sir Robert Heath in 1629, but nothing had come of it. Now a colony existed, but the proprietor provided no leadership. As a result of very little control from England and the near ideal location of the Bahamas for preying upon Spanish shipping which passed through the Bahamas or the Florida Straits on the way from America to Spain, the new colony was soon dominated by pirates.

By 1713 there were probably one thousand active pirates living in Nassau; the town was overrun. Blackbeard (Edward Teach) was among them. Many other famous pirates—Charles Vane, Benjamin Hornygold, Stede Bonnet, and the female pirates Anne Bonny and Mary Read—operated out of Nassau and wreaked havoc on shipping in the Florida Straits. Some of the pirates styled themselves Governors, and some of the Governors conspired with the pirates. The line between what was legitimate and what was piracy was a fuzzy one. Many probably drifted into and out of piracy several times. During wartime governments commissioned privateers to prey on enemy shipping. When peace was made by European diplomats, privateers did not always cease their activities. This made them pirates. The attacks on Spanish and French shipping from Nassau soon brought reprisals, and the city was unable to defend itself successfully from a French and Spanish attack in 1703, and from a Spanish attack in 1706. Even when liberated from foreign powers and presumably under English control, Nassau was extremely difficult to govern.

Many have romanticized the colorful age of piracy. Blackbeard has been described as an almost invincible hulk of a man who wore the hair of his beard in plaits, packed six pistols on a special belt, and who went into battle wearing smoking slow-matches in his headband. He must have looked much like the devil himself. He reportedly had fourteen wives. He died as the result of a fight after tolerating five musket balls and three sabre thrusts. Bahamians themselves have enjoyed the fact that their history has this element of excitement. Streets, bars, entire cays, and various other things in the Bahamas are named after pirates. In Abaco, Matt Lowe's Cay and Stede Bonnet Drive in Marsh Harbour are named for pirates. Some have gone so far as to say that there is a bit of piracy in all Bahamians, and that modern Bahamians are proud rather than ashamed of this heritage.

Michael Craton and Gail Saunders, in their recently published and very excellent social history of the Bahamas, have added new dimensions to this segment of Bahamian history by pointing out some socially progressive aspects of piracy. Common seamen in the British Navy or in the merchant service were men who lived at the bottom of the socio-economic system. They were overworked and poorly paid, had few rights, were often punished severely for minor infractions of rules, and some had been impressed into service rather than choosing their jobs. A few fled this life of virtual servitude for piracy, where captains were selected by the crew and ruled by consensus rather than absolute authority granted by the Admiralty.

A good comparison of the freedom and relative equality enjoyed by pirates as compared to the lives of regular seamen can be gained by examining the system of sharing prizes or spoils. In the British Navy the Admiral received half, the captain got 25%, the other officers split 12½%, and the crew split 12½%. Pirates, on the other hand, provided one share for each seaman, 1½ - 2 shares for gunners, carpenters, boatswains, mates, doctors, and quartermasters, and 2 shares for the captain. Craton and Saunders contend that the pirates' more equitable system of allocation was probably as offensive to the establishment as piracy itself.[22] This new interpretation provides a different perspective on the Bahamian heritage of piracy. Indeed, the Bahamas was first settled by freedom-seeking religious dissidents and then soon became dominated by free, rough, and wild seamen. Some contend that all these early influences can be found in the modern Bahamian, or Abaconian, character.

The pirates menaced shipping to and from the east coast of North America and caused the governors of English colonies there to request action from London. The crown finally assumed responsibility for the government of the colony, changing its status from a proprietary to a royal colony, and appointed Woodes Rogers as the first royal governor. His most important task was to regain control of the colony from the pirates.

He arrived in 1718 carrying a general amnesty for all pirates from the English Crown. Many accepted, but Charles Vane, sometimes called Vane the Great Pirate, raised the skull and crossbones and fled from Nassau Harbour to Green Turtle Cay in Abaco. Woodes Rogers recruited a recently reformed pirate, Benjamin Hornygold, and sent him to "view them and bring me an account of what they were." When Hornygold did not return promptly, Rogers feared that he had joined Vane and returned to piracy. But after three weeks Hornygold reached Nassau and reported that Vane had attacked two ships bound from Carolina to London, the *Neptune* and the *Emperor*. He had stolen only provisions from the *Emperor*, but had taken the *Neptune* with its cargo of rice, pitch, tar, and skins. Vane escaped from Green Turtle Cay after detecting Hornygold. [23]

Abaco must have been a fine base for pirates. Ships bound south from the northeast coast of the United States normally sailed to the east of Abaco rather than bucking the Gulf Stream in the Florida Straits. Ships bound for Nassau usually made a landfall at Hole-in-the-Wall, Abaco, and then ran before the prevailing easterly trade winds to Nassau. Pirates could easily gain protection in the lee of cays such as Green Turtle, Manjack, Great Guana, Man-O-War, or Elbow, and after sighting a sail, could intercept the ship, and then return to shelter on the bank behind the cays. Abaco was surely used as a base by pirates other than Vane.

Evidence regarding settlements in Abaco prior to the arrival of the loyalists is contradictory. Dr. Paul Albury, in *The Story of the Bahamas*, contended that there were people living at Abaco. He believed that such a good place for wrecking could not have been uninhabited.[24] Woodes Rogers, when he first suggested the establishment of an assembly for the Bahamas in 1718, recommended one representative for Abaco, but in the same communication he listed able bodied men who could serve in the militia and did not mention Abaco. Perhaps the explanation of this apparent contradiction is that Rogers was optimistic regarding migration to the Bahamas and anticipated the settlement of Abaco. He believed that emigrants would come from Anguila and from Carolina, and wrote: "Numbers of those people I depend will be here from the knowledge they have of the Soil being so very Productive, that with little Labour almost every root, Plant or Grain will in small time ripen to perfection."[25] Within a year, Rogers apparently reversed his plan for expansion of settlement in the out islands and called for the evacuation of eleven settlers from Cat Island (150 miles southeast of Abaco) to Eleuthera, Harbour Island, or New Providence so they could not be captured and used as pilots by enemies of Great Britain. Abaco was not mentioned.[26] Roger's successor as Governor, George Phenney, did not list Abaco in a census report which indicated that 703 persons lived on New Providence, 129 at Harbour Island, 184 on Eleuthera, and 14 or 15 on Cat Island.[27] Penney was also very optimistic concerning the agricultural potential of the Bahamas, which, he contended, had not yet been realized, the "Present inhabitants being mostly Seafaring Men."[28]

Although there were many optimistic reports concerning the agricultural potential of the islands, most of them based on speculation rather than fact, Woodes Rogers probably reflected the real interests of the British government accurately when he explained that the value of the islands was based mostly on ". . . how much they are capable of annoying the Neighborhood."[29] Thus, no great projects were initiated by London to develop Abaco or other out islands. Knowledge of the out islands of the Bahamas was extremely limited, even in Nassau. Governor Thomas Shirley, in a description of the islands written in 1768, estimated that the size of Abaco was 273 square miles (the actual size is 649 square miles), and reported that Eleuthera was 437 square miles (actual size - 200 square miles). According to Shirley, only five islands were inhabited: these were New Providence (2350), Harbour Island (350), Eleuthera (400), and Cat Island and Exuma ("in all supposed to be 30 people who have lately gone thither to make a trial of the Soil and for the convenience of wrecking.").[30] The only substantial evidence of actual settlement in Abaco prior to the arrival of the loyalists is a letter from the former Spanish governor of the Bahamas which explained that refugees from Florida "have taken possession of Abaco Island, seizing the plantations which the people of Providence have there."[31] But it is quite possible, even likely, that these "plantations" were only seasonally occupied farms operated by absentee landlords. Although there is some contradictory information in the record, the evidence is clearly in favor of reaching the conclusion that Abaco was not settled prior to the arrival of the loyalists—pirates, transient wreckers, visiting fishermen, and seasonal farm laborers excepted.

END NOTES

[1] See William F. Keegan, *The People Who Discovered Columbus* (Gainesville: University of Florida, 1992), pp. 62-64.

[2] George A. Aarons, Interview with the author, Nassau, 9 August 1989.

[3] Keegan, p. 162.

[4] See Christopher Columbus, *The Log of Christopher Columbus,* trans. and ed. by Robert Fuson (Camden, Maine: International Marine Publishing, 1987), pp. 76, 77, 78, 81.

[5] Michael Craton and Gail Saunders, *Islanders in the Stream* (Athens: University of Georgia, 1992), p. 58.

[6] Samuel Eliot Morison, *Christopher Columbus, Mariner* (New York: Mentor, 1955), p. 43.

[7] See W. H. Sears and S. D. Sullivan, "Bahamas Prehistory," *American Antiquity* 43 (1), 3-25. Some continue to accept this argument despite overwhelming archeological evidence of extensive Lucayan settlements in Abaco. Recovered items include cassava griddle shards, proving that the Lucayans in Abaco cultivated manioc and produced cassava bread. Nevertheless, Craton and Saunders still contend that manioc could not have been grown in Abaco and Grand Bahama. See Craton and Saunders, p. 19.

[8] Mr. David Gale of Hope Town, Abaco, told the author about stone carvings found, and later destroyed, at Bridges Cay. Mr. Val Jones, formerly of Hope Town, reported seeing an unusual round rock with carvings near Carter's Cay. Mr. Alton Lowe of New Plymouth had acquired various Lucayan artifacts, including arrowheads and axe-heads excavated from a site near Cedar Harbour on Little Abaco Island, from the estate of a former headmaster of the school at New Plymouth.

[9] "Skeleton found in Abaco believed to be Lucayan's" *The Tribune* (Nassau), 26 July 1990, pp. 1A, 7A.

[10] Millikin University provided a summer grant for Steve Dodge in 1989 which enabled him to participate in survey work with Ian Lothian. In 1991 and 1992 Joel Wynne of Wynne Building Corporation, Port St. Lucie, Florida, provided funds for digs undertaken by George Anthony Aarons, Archaeological Consultant at the Bahamas National Archives. A preliminary report of this work is available. See George A. Aarons, et al., *Prehistoric and Historic Archaeological Field Research in Abaco, Bahamas: 1988-1991, Report Number One* (Decatur, IL: White Sound Press, 1992).

[11] S. F. Cook and W. Borah, "The Aboriginal Population of Hispaniola," in *Essays in Population History: Mexico and the Caribbean*, Volume I (Berkely: University of California Press, 1971), cited in Keegan, p. 220.

[12] Amerigo Vespucci, Letter from Seville, 1500, in Frederick J. Pohl, *Amerigo Vespucci, Pilot Major* (New York: Octagon, 1966), p. 87, cited in Keegan, p. 212.

[13] Arne Molander believes Ponce de Leon found the old Lucayan woman on Walker's Cay or Grand Cay in Abaco. See Arne B. Molander, "Ponce de Leon Belongs to the Bahamas," *Journal of the Bahamas Historical Society* 6, 1 (October, 1984), 40-47.

[14] Craton and Saunders say it is possible that Lucayans fled to the north (p. 54). Machu Pichu is a mountaintop site in Peru discovered in 1911. It is believed that remnants of the Inca Indian empire fled to Machu Pichu after the conquest of Peru by Pizarro, and that they lived in Machu Pichu for many years without discovery by the Spaniards.

[15] Comments by Jane Rose regarding incidence of cerion shells (a very small land crab) with broken tips. She contended that domesticated hutia consumed the cerion. Panel discussion "The Natural Environment of the Lucayan Indians," Bahamas 1492: Its People and Environment, Freeport, Bahamas, 16 November 1987.

[16] Keegan, pp. 38, 126, 147.

[17] Another explanation is that Bahama is a derivative of Lucayan morphemes (small meaningful units of language) and meant large upper midland. See Julian Granberry, "Lucayan Toponyms," *Journal of the Bahamas Historical Society* 13, 1 (October, 1991), 3-12.

[18] Julian Granberry, "Lucayan Toponyms," *Journal of the Bahamas Historical Society* 13, 1 (October 1991), 3-12.

[19] In the first edition of this history of Abaco Steve Dodge proposed that *habacoa* might have been derived from the Spanish term *haba de cacao* which, literally, means coffee beans. The term also has two special geologic meanings; it is used to describe a rock comprised of smaller particles (resembling, in cross section, an accumulation of coffee beans). It is also used to describe rocks which have many nodules or lumps on their outer surface. Either meaning might have been the justification for naming a northern Bahamian island *habacoa*. The eroded limestone outcroppings which form a significant portion of the coastline of Abaco and Grand Bahama are craggy and could have been called *haba de cacao* by early explorers. If the Spaniards broke some of the limestone they might well have described its granular composition by calling it *haba de cacao*. The Granberry explanation is almost certainly a better one.

[20] Michael Craton, *A History of the Bahamas* (Waterloo, Canada: San Salvador Press, 1986), p. 45.

[21] George Aarons has suggested that some ruins discovered by Ian Lothian and David Bethel in southeastern Abaco could be from an early French colony. See George A. Aarons, "The Settlement of the Bahamas Between 1492 and 1648: Fact or Fiction," *Journal of the Bahamas Historical Society* 14, 1 (October 1992), 9-20.

[22] Craton and Saunders, p. 110.

[23] Woodes Rogers, Letter, New Providence, 31 October - 1 November, 1718, CO 23/1 (part 1)/14. All citations to materials found in the British Colonial Office (CO) Archives will provide the number of the file, the number of the volume, and the number of the folio, in this order. If a volume is divided into parts, the part number will appear in parentheses after the volume number. All materials read by the author were read in Nassau at the Bahamian National Archives, which has a microfilm copy of CO file 23.

[24] "Wrecking" is the Bahamian term used to describe salvaging the cargo and parts of ships which have been wrecked on the reefs or shoals of the Bahamas. It does not necessarily imply any purposeful attempt on the part of Bahamians to lure ships to the reefs or shoals. For many years, wrecking was a major sector of the Abaconian and Bahamian economies. For a statement regarding pre-loyalist inhabitants of Abaco, see Paul Albury, *The Story of the Bahamas* (London: Macmillan, 1975), p. 259. Also, Paul Albury, Interview with the author, Nassau, 2 March 1979.

[25] Woodes Rogers, CO 23/1(part 1)/14.

[26] Minutes of the Council, 26 May 1719, CO 23/1(part1)/86.

[27] George Phenney, Letter, New Providence, 10 February 1721, CO 23/1(part 2)/103.

[28] Description of Bahama Islands enclosed with Captain Penney's letter of 2 March 1723, CO 23/1(part3)/16.

[29] Woodes Rogers, CO 23/1(part1)/14.

[30] Description of Bahama Islands enclosed with T. Shirley to Hillsborough, Nassau, 9 December 1768, CO 23/18/18.

[31] Claraco to Unzaga, New Providence, 19 May 1783, in Joseph B. Lockey, *East Florida 1783-1785: A File of Documents Assembled, and Many of them Translated* (Berkeley, University of California Press, 1949), p. 112.

Chapter Three-

The Colonization of Abaco

The American Revolution was a civil war as well as an international conflict. Although estimates vary widely, most historians believe that only 35-50% of the population of the thirteen North American colonies were patriots—that is, supporters of the revolt. About 30-35% probably did not care one way or the other, and between 15-35% were opposed to the Revolution. Some of these were simply loyal to George III, others disapproved of the republican system of government, and some opposed democracy and feared that social revolution would accompany political revolution. Some probably opposed the revolution because they disliked its leaders, or because crops were stolen from their farms by the Continental Army, or for other nonpolitical reasons. All who opposed the Revolution were called loyalists, and once a man tilted toward loyalty to the British Crown, his inclination was probably reinforced by community action. Loyalists were sought out by patriots; they were tarred and feathered and run out of town. Their possessions were expropriated and their lands taken over. They were denied the protection of the laws. Loyalists had to flee to parts of the United States under British control, and some joined British militia forces. They went to places such as Florida, which did not join the thirteen other colonies in rebellion, and New York City, which was held by the British from August 1776, when George Washington's new army lost the Battle of Long island, until the end of the war. Charleston and Savannah were also under British control during part of the Revolution, and many southern loyalists found safety in those cities.

The British defeat at Yorktown in October 1781 was not a militarily decisive end to the war—Britain could have sent another army to America. But the British decided to concede and grant the colonies their independence. They evacuated Charleston in December 1782—9000 soldiers, loyalists, and slaves left for Florida, New York, Jamaica, Nova Scotia, St. Lucia, and England. A few months later, in February 1783, the British signed the Treaty of Paris, which called for the evacuation of New York and, much to the surprise of loyalists who had established farms and plantations in East Florida,* a companion treaty signed with Spain called for the return of East Florida to Spain. During the war Spain had fought on the side of the United States, and therefore shared in the spoils. The Peace of Paris required that loyalists would have access to state courts in order to regain confiscated properties, but the states, for the most part, later refused to honor this provision. The government of the United States under the Articles of Confederation lacked a judiciary and was unable to compel compliance by the states. Many loyalists anticipated this end result, and flocked from New York to areas still ruled by Britain rather than returning to their homes in the now independent United States. Some went to England or Canada, others went to the Bahamas and the British Caribbean. Loyalists in Florida hoped the British government would reverse itself and retain the colony. They delayed as long as they could and then reluctantly left Florida for the Bahamas, Jamaica, Nova Scotia, or England.

Few loyalists welcomed the opportunity to move again. Many had been forced to flee from their homes and farms early in the war; they had lived as refugees in New York and in East Florida; at the end of the war they were refugees again, and on the move again. Possessions which had been retained through the ravages of the war now had to be disposed of, and fields which had been cleared and houses which had been built had to be sold at deflated prices. The legislature of East Florida explained their plight in a letter to the king:

> At a juncture when we must soon expect to be deprived of those most inestimable of all blessings during our stay here that of protection in our lives, libertys and propertys under the mild and lenient Administration of a British Government at a juncture when the inhabitants must soon determine either to live for a time under a Government in the hands of the natural enemies of their Country or abandon their Territorial possessions, improvements and houses many of them just finished and purchased with the small wreck of their effects saved at the evacuations of Carolina and Georgia to seek another Assylum.[1]

Lord North, in a letter to the Governor of East Florida, admitted the embarrassment of the British government in regard to the plight of the East Floridians, and recommended that they seek refuge, with the assistance of the British government, in the Bahamas.[2]

* East Florida included most of the present-day state of Florida. It was controlled by Spain from the time it was first settled until 1819, when the United States purchased it, except for the period 1763 to 1783, when Britain controlled it. West Florida was controlled by Spain and stretched along the Gulf Coast from East Florida to New Orleans, including the coast of the present day states of Alabama, Mississippi, and part of Louisiana.

Not all East Floridians accepted this advice. One petitioned Charles III of Spain for territory between the St. Johns and St. Marys Rivers, to be governed internally as a loyalist enclave in Spanish Florida. His petition provides further insight into the desperate situation of the Florida Loyalists:

> Abandoned by that Sovereign for whose cause we have sacrificed everything that is dear in life and deserted by that country for which we fought and many of us freely bled, and may it please your Majesty we are all Soldiers—thus left to our fate bereft of our slaves by our Inveterate Countrymen. We may it please your Majesty are reduced to the dreadful alternative of returning to our home, to receive insult worse than death to Men of Spirit, or to run the hazard of being murdered in cold blood, to go to the inhospitable regions of Nova Scotia or to take refuge on the barren rocks of the Bahamas where poverty and wretchedness stares us in the face or do what our Spirit can not brook (pardon Sire the freedom) renounce our Country, Drug the religion of our Fathers and become your Subjects.[3]

Loyalists in New York were also preparing to move; the city was to be turned over to the government of the state of New York in November 1783.

On 21 June 1783, an announcement regarding Abaco appeared in the *Royal Gazette*, a New York City newspaper. It announced that all those who wished to settle Albico [sic] in the Bahama Islands should meet at seven o'clock that evening. Four days later, on 25 June five loyalists sent a letter to Sir Guy Carleton, the British commanding officer in New York, requesting assistance for the colonization of Abaco. They asked for a small military force and a few cannons, and also for horses, horned cattle, saws, black smith tools, and "some coals." They described Abaco as a fertile place, made specific mention of the availability of ship building woods,

Loyalists living in New York City had to depart before November 1783, when the city was to be turned over to New York State in accordance with the terms of the Treaty of Paris, unless they wanted to stay and live under the control of the patriot government. This notice appeared in the *Royal Gazette* (New York) on 21 June 1783.

To all those who may be desirous of going to the Bahama Islands, to settle the Island of Albico,

AS a number of Loyalists have got permission to emigrate to that place, from his Excellency Sir GUY CARLETON, on the same terms that his Majesty's loyal subjects are going to the North ward: Those who choose to embrace this opportunity, are desired to give in their names and places of abode, at Mr. John Davis's, lower end of Little Queen-Street, near the North River, where the subscription List is open.

N. B. The Subscribers are all requested to meet this Evening, at Seven o'Clock, as the List will be closed.

New-York, June 21st, 1783.

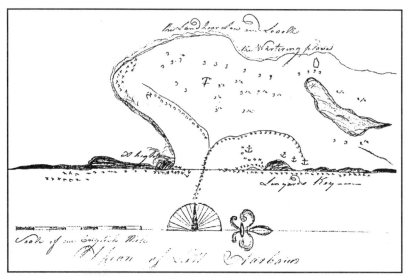

Sketch chart of Little Harbour which accompanied letter from loyalists to Sir Guy Carleton, British Commander in New York City, requesting assistance for the colonization of Abaco. British Headquarters Papers 8227, New York Public Library.

and stressed the strategic importance of Abaco's location adjacent to the major north-south shipping routes. Their letter included a rough hand drawn sketch chart of the Little Harbour area, which is where they hoped to settle.[4]

A few days later, on 28 June, the same newspaper published a description of Abaco for prospective emigrants:

> The Island of Albico (to which a number of Loyalists are now pre-paring to resort and form settlements) is among the most fruitful in produce, and the most important to the British Government, and wants only inhabitants, and a small degree of cultivation, to render it as flour-ishing as any of the West India Islands. . . .
>
> The above island is blessed with a good harbour, and well featured by nature, with eighteen feet on the Bar, and within the harbour 24 feet of water.
>
> The island abounds with Timber,. . .
>
> Vast quantities of delicious TURTLE are caught on the Banks, and within even an hundred yards of the island. Great Number of Whales are taken. There were 14 sail of vessels about three weeks ago; success-fully employed in the Whale Fishery; they cut up the Blubber on the island.[5]

Although parts of this description are correct (Abaco did have timber and turtles), the description exaggerates the suitability of Abaco for farming, implies that agricultural activities had already been successful, claims that Abaco, which had been ignored and neglected by Britain for over one hundred years, was very important to Britain, and probably exaggerates the productivity of whaling in the Bahamas. Some questioned the truthfulness of this and similar descriptions, and the British military government ordered Lt. John Wilson, an engineer in the British army, to go to Abaco to find out if it were true that Abaco had a better harbour than New Providence, and also if its soil were more fertile.[6] Wilson did not arrive in Nassau until November 1783, and did not get to Abaco until after February 1784. His report, therefore, was not written until long after the loyalist groups had departed for Abaco, and had no effect on their decision. He wrote that Abaco ". . . is by no means found equal to the descriptions that have been given of it by several persons . . . ," and that it lacked a good harbour and fertile soil. "One fifth part of the face of the country is nothing but rock," he reported, and he explained that the soil which did exist was only found in shallow pockets in the rock. He tempered his generally pessimistic report by describing three types of soil, some suited for cotton cultivation, some for vegetables, and some for guineacorn, and he predicted that skillful farmers from North America would produce more from the soil than the indolent Bahamians.[7]

The absence of this more realistic assessment of Abaco's resources allowed the more glowing descriptions to stand unchallenged, and by August 1783, the British commissary-general in New York, Brook Watson, reported that "near a thousand souls" were ready to leave for Abaco.[8] These departing loyalists were ignorant regarding the difficulties they would soon confront—they believed they were journeying to a promised land, a place where they hoped their loyalty would be rewarded with easy living, and that they

The first group of loyalists to leave New York for Abaco did so in August 1783. This advertisement for the sailing of the Hope, which carried a second or third group of immigrants to Abaco, appeared in the Royal Gazette (New York) on October 24, 1783.

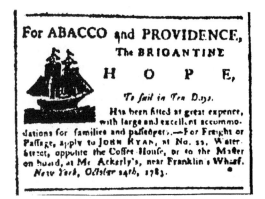

For ABACCO and PROVIDENCE,
The BRIGANTINE

H   O   P   E,

To sail in Ten Days.

Has been fitted at great expence, with large and excellent accommodations for families and passengers.—For Freight or Passage, apply to JOHN RYAN, at No. 33, Water street, opposite the Coffee House, or to the Master on board, at Mr. Ackerly's, near Franklin's Wharf.
New York, October 24th, 1783.

would be joined by 1500 loyalists from East Florida who would help them build the new colony.[9] The first contingent sailed in late August or early September 1783.[10] Some reports indicate that they first sailed to Florida,[11] but this is unlikely because Florida was already crowded with refugees and such an intermediate stop would have served no practical purpose. Additional groups of refugees left for Abaco in October and November, one of which included 509 settlers. The British commissary-general reported that a total of 1458 loyalists left New York for Abaco prior to the British surrender of the city to the United States.[12]

The loyalists from New York who settled in Abaco were reportedly the poorer loyalists.[13] Those who had greater means went to more developed areas, some to Britain itself. Many of the migrants had served in British militia units during the war, but they were not professional soldiers and were probably a fairly representative cross-section of the colonies in regard to vocational skills. Farmers, merchants, smiths, carpenters, and mechanics were most likely among them. Although some sailed on commercial transports, most were provided with free transportation by the British government, which also provided provisions for at least six months and offered forty acres of free land for each family head, plus twenty acres for each dependent or slave. They believed that the economy of the thirteen United States would languish without the protection of Britain, and without the privileged access to the British market which colonial status provided. They believed they could establish a thriving agricultural/mercantile/commercial colony in Abaco and transplant the commerce of Boston, New York and Philadelphia to Abaco. Britain would trade with Abaco rather than with the United States.

A substantial number of those who looked forward to a new life in Abaco were black. The British had encouraged black slaves to leave their patriot masters during the war and come over to freedom on the British side. Many did so. But the peace treaty signed at Paris prohibited the departing British from "carrying away any Negros, or other Property of the American Inhabitants." Sir Guy Carleton, the British commander in New York, decided to allow emigration of blacks from New York, but to keep a record of the names of all blacks so that citizens of the United States could be compensated later if they had legitimate claims to blacks who were allowed to emigrate. The record was called the "Book of Negroes," and although the information provided is sparse, we do know more about the blacks who migrated to Abaco than we do about the whites. The book includes the names of thirty-five persons who sailed for Abaco on the *Nautilus* on 21 August 1783, and forty-five who sailed on the *William* on 22 August 1783. The status of each was recorded: Joe Grant was nineteen years old and had been born free at Bristol in Barbadoes; Flora Bush was twenty-six and was formerly the property of Patrick Simons at Cherry Point, Virginia, having left him in 1781; Venus Jordon was sixty-four years old and had left her owner, Captain Wenyfield of Boston, in 1776; and Daphae Rivers, twenty-two, was formerly the property of Samuel Fulton of Charleston, whom she left in 1779. In all twenty-two claimed to be free by virtue of birth, governor's certificate, manumission or purchase, and forty-four said they had left their owners during the American Revolution and were therefore free by virtue of the British proclamations. Each of the blacks—even if they were listed as free—was also assigned to a white who was migrating to Abaco. So Joe Grant, who was born free in Barbadoes, was "in the possession of" John Shoemaker, and Daphae Rivers, who had left Samuel Fulton of Charleston four years earlier, was in the possession of Elias Davis. This was apparently some form of temporary indenture, but we have no specific information regarding it. Sandra Riley says it is puzzling that Sir Guy Carleton indentured blacks going to Abaco, but sent other blacks to Nova Scotia as free men. She also points out that sixty-six of the eighty blacks were legally free but yet "in the possession of" somebody—and that this may well have been one of the causes of the black revolt in Abaco in 1788.[14]

It probably took a couple of weeks to sail from New York, where fall was beginning, to Abaco, where the long summer had two months remaining. A landfall was probably made somewhere in northern Abaco, and the vessels entered into Abaco Sound, sailing southeastward along the coast of Abaco, looking for a suitable location for a settlement. The coast of Great Abaco is forbidding in this area; it is comprised of straight, low, limestone cliffs for over twenty-five miles, with scrub growth behind. The refugees must have been disappointed. A few small beaches offer some relief, but there are no harbours. Finally they rounded a small point with land over thirty-five feet high bounded by a shallow salt water creek to the south which provided a safe anchorage for small boats. Southeast of the creek lay a small, low cay with a beautiful crescent-shaped pink coral sand beach which curved to the southeast, east, and then northeast. The beach, combined with some small cays which are about four miles offshore, provided what they believed would be adequate protection for an anchorage for large vessels; the water was two and one-half fathoms deep (15 feet). At some point they had given up the plan to settle at Little Harbour (it is possible that they just never found Little Harbour), and they decided to build their town on the northern bank of the creek. They named it Carleton, in honor of Sir Guy Carleton, the British commander for North America stationed in New York City. Carleton was located near the north end of the present Treasure Cay beach.[15]

Though John Wilson reported that they chose the "very worst part of Abaco,"[16] his statement was an exaggeration. The settlement was on high ground and ground water was available. The land surrounding the town offered some adequate farmland and a pine forest, not too far distant, provided lumber. One of the principal disadvantages of the site was its lack of a fully protected harbour for large ships. Its creek was suitable for small boats only, and the sector of Abaco Sound which they at first believed was a harbour sheltered by off-lying cays, is actually far too exposed to be a harbour. It is subject to rather large ocean swells during certain weather conditions. Also, the soil was not as productive as the refugees had at first thought it would be.

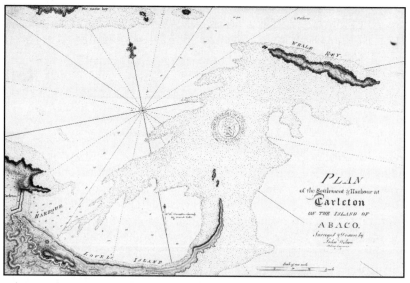

Plan of Carleton drawn by John Wilson, Acting Engineer, who accompanied Brig. Gen. McArthur on his visit to Abaco in 1784 (Public Records Office, WO 78/807 M1156, London). Used with the permission of the Public Records Office.

Clearing of land and construction of houses undoubtedly commenced even before the transport vessels weighed anchor. Although the British government had promised land grants, the land in the Bahamas had not yet been purchased from the proprietors,[17] and, as far as can be determined, no surveyor was present and no grants were officially made until two years later, in October 1785. There were probably some difficulties concerning land ownership and boundaries, but the incident which sparked real dissension in the new community was seemingly more trivial—eight of the residents refused to work in the cooperative provisions store. Captain Stephens of the Pennsylvania loyalists, who had been chosen as head of the militia by Sir Guy Carleton before the group departed from New York, ordered a court of enquiry:

> . . . three of the absentees made apologies which were admitted, two refused to appear and three of them treating the Court with Insolence and contempt, irritated the Officers so far they sentenced them and the two who refused to appear to depart the island in fifty-two hours.[18]

The majority of the residents of Carleton were shocked with the severity of the sentences. Indeed, it is unclear whether a safe conveyance was available (Nassau was over one hundred miles away, half of that over the open sea), and it is curious that the court chose the time limit of fifty-two hours. The residents formed an association to support the five men, and created a three-man

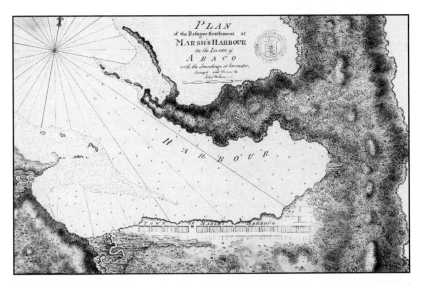

Plan of Marsh Harbour drawn by John Wilson, Acting Engineer, who accompanied Brig. Gen. McArthur on his visit to Abaco in 1784 (Public Records Office, WO 78/807 M1156, London). Used with the permission of the Public Records Office.

Board of Police to supersede the militia and assume responsibility for the governance of the town. Captain Stephens armed his servants and negroes and took, as hostages, two of the reputable inhabitants of the town to guarantee his own safety. The matter was temporarily resolved when the militia officers serving under Stephens became his sureties, guaranteeing "that he should not go out of his Town lot till released by proper authority." Stephens was detained in this manner from 13 November 1783, until released by Brigadier General Archibald McArthur on 9 February 1784. The residents had received word that McArthur, appointed by Carleton as Commandant of the Bahamas, and military reinforcements were on the way and, fearing they would support Stephens' position, "quit the settlement and retired to Marsh's Harbour six leagues South East of Carleton, where they have laid out a Town, and are well employed in clearing land and erecting habitations." General McArthur reported that the soil and water at Marsh's Harbour were better than at Carleton, ". . . and the harbour safer though not so deep." The total number of inhabitants of the two towns was 658, with two-thirds of them located at Marsh's Harbour.[19]

By 1785 there were over 1000 refugees in Abaco. Two-thirds of them had come from New York and one-third from Florida.[20] These persons were distributed in five or six towns. Carleton disappeared within a few years; of some 175 land grants made in Abaco during the late 1780s, only five were in the vicinity of Carleton.[21] Some settlers from Carleton moved north to Coco Plum Creek, where they apparently found better soil. Maxwell Town was established as a sister village to Marsh's Harbour, perhaps by the second or third group of loyalists to arrive from New York. It disappeared within a few years. There were two settlements in southern Abaco whose residents had come from East Florida. These towns were founded later than Carleton and Marsh's Harbour because Florida's final transfer from Britain to Spain

A military button recovered at the site of Carleton was identified as one which was worn by the third loyalist regiment of South Carolina.

did not occur until July 1785. They were called Spencer's Bight and Eight Mile Bay and their combined population was about 350 persons. Spencer's Bight was settled by Captain Smith of the King's Rangers, some discharged soldiers and two or three families with a few slaves. Only seven land grants were made at Spencer's Bight during the 1780s, and the small settlement there was later known as Sweeting's Village. Others settled in the same general area. These included Martin Weatherford, who was granted 200 acres in the Little Harbour area and also was granted Bridges Cay. He brought six whites and twenty-five slaves with him from East Florida. John Cornish, who brought no family members with him, had five black slaves.[22] Cornish was granted Wheeler's Cay (now Cornish Cay) as well as some land on the mainland. Eight Mile Bay, described as a small "reef harbour" nine miles south of Little Harbour by the author of the 1784 survey report, was settled by "the negroes of Lt. Col. Thomas Brown of the King's Rangers." Brown planned to establish a large cotton plantation; he acquired twenty-three parcels of land in the area totaling 2980 acres and moved 170 slaves to the Bahamas. He was the only recipient of land grants in the region near Eight Mile Bay, but he gave up his plans for development of the area within a year or two.

Most historians have concluded that the exact number of loyalists who emigrated to the Bahamas is impossible to determine, and have estimated that from 5000 to 8000 were involved. This influx of people more than doubled the population of the Bahamas within three years and trebled it within six years.[23] One thousand of these immigrants were in Abaco in March 1784, and more arrived after that date. Although it is impossible to know exactly how many persons moved to Abaco, it is probably safe to conclude that about 2000 immigrants arrived in Abaco during the 1780s.

ORIGINAL LOYALIST SETTLEMENTS IN ABACO

CARLETON

MARSH HARBOUR AND MAXWELL

SPENCER'S BIGHT

EIGHT MILE BAY

They knew they would need boats and ships to build a commercial hub in Abaco which would grow to rival New York and Boston. They believed the shipping industry of the United States would die without the protection and privileges offered by the British Empire. Abaco could simply take over the business formerly enjoyed by the North American coloinies. They brought ships carpenters with them to fashion the timbers of Abaco into vessels which would carry their goods to ports throughout the world.

The carpenters built several large ships during Carleton's early years. *Huaibras*, a sloop of twenty-one tons, was launched in 1785. The *Fair Abaconian*, seventy-four tons, and the *Recovery*, one hundred fifty-five tons, were launched in 1786. The following year a schooner of one hundred nineteen tons, the *Ulysees*, was built. The rapid rise of this shipbuilding industry in Abaco must have been particularly galling to New Englanders, who suffered greatly during the first years of the independence of the United States. Because Britain denied ships from the United States access to Bahamian and other British West Indian ports, there was a surplus of ships anchored in harbours throughout the northeastern United States, and there was no work for shipbuilders. It seemed that the loyalist scheme of transplanting the economy of New England to the Bahamas might be working. Shortly after the new constitution provided the government of the United States with increased powers in 1789, that government tried to stimulate the United States' shipbuilding and shipping industries by providing discounts on duties for goods imported in ships built in the United States. But by this time it was clear that Abaco was no threat to Massachusetts.

By 1788 the vessels built at Carleton were involved in international trade to and from Nassau. During July, August, and September 1788, five of the thirty-five vessels which entered the port of Nassau from foreign ports were built in Abaco. They arrived from Jamaica carrying rum, sails, anchors, cables and coffee: from Charleston with corn, tobacco, lumber, and rice: and from New York with sheep, potatoes and poultry. The largest of the five, the *Recovery*, arrived from London on 14 July and left for New York with 2000 bushels of salt and 20 of wreck coffee on 1 August. The port records do not indicate even a single passage to or from Abaco.[24]

The dream of establishing an integrated commercial-agricultural-maritime colony in Abaco was defunct by the late 1780s—not because Abaco lacked ships—but because there were no cargoes produced in Abaco. It was the failure of agriculture to produce exports which caused the demise of the grandiose scheme for a new British Empire centered in Abaco. The ships were built in Abaco but had no commercial reason to return there once they left.

Agriculture failed because the soil was rocky and clearing the land proved to be much more difficult than had been anticipated. Although the climate was salubrious throughout most of the year, the dry season from January to May thwarted agricultural pursuits during these months. Also, the soil was thin and lacked the reserve nutrients necessary for sustained cultivation. After the six months' provisions provided by the British government were exhausted, many settlers had little to eat. Disputes among the inhabitants undoubtedly helped to discourage some settlers, and a severe hurricane which hit Eleuthera and Abaco on September 22, 1785, probably disenchanted others. Many decided to leave and moved on to Nassau or elsewhere.

Mistakes made by the settlers also contributed to the failure of their plans. Rather than establishing a single commercial and agricultural center with farms surrounding it, such as Carleton was intended to be, the settlements were atomized, very small, and inefficient. Many of the farms were completely isolated. Parcels were granted on Pensacola, Manjack, Powell's, and Cotnary's (Scotland) Cay. These cays could only be reached by boat from the settlements on the "mainland" of Abaco, and the trip required several hours. According to the terms of the land grants, the grantee was to clear and plant two acres out of every twenty within the first three years. Many failed to meet this requirement and the land reverted to the Crown. Some grantees never even reached Abaco. They applied for land because they did not want to miss out on the largesse of the British Crown, and perhaps hoped to sell it at a profit, or to develop it if all other alternatives failed. Some applied for a grant, sent their slaves and agricultural implements to Abaco, and hoped for the best.[25]

Abaco did not become a center for the production of cotton as some of the refugees from East Florida had hoped. Most of the large cotton plantations in the Bahamas were located on islands south of Eleuthera. It is very likely that small amounts of cotton were grown at Abaco by loyalists from East Florida who brought slaves with them, but most of these efforts were short-lived and some did not progress beyond the planning stage. Thomas Brown, who had planned to build a plantation at Eight Mile Bay, moved his slaves to a plantation on Caicos Island and involved himself in business activities in Nassau. Jonathan Belton, who had moved ten slaves to Abaco, sold his land and seven slaves to John Ferguson on November 14, 1785.[26] Abaco did not play an important role in the cotton boom of the late 1780s, when harvests of close to one million pounds of cotton per year were made in the Bahamas. When the chenille bug and depleted soil caused production to decline sharply in the 1790s, Abaco did not suffer as greatly as other areas. Many plantations were abandoned during this period. Those few which did survive were dealt the final blow by the abolition of slavery in the Bahamas in 1838. Despite the failure of Abaco to become a major center for cotton production or general commerce, the fledgling communities survived.

The most successful of the initial settlements in Abaco, it seems, was Marsh's Harbour. By 1785 about 44% of the population of Abaco lived in Marsh's Harbour with another 21% in neighboring Maxwell; 25% still resided in Carleton, and about 10% were at Spencer's Bight.[27] Marsh's Harbour had a well protected anchorage, fresh water was available, and some good soil could be found in the vicinity. In spite of Marsh's Harbour's preeminence, life was extremely difficult and the loyalists who lived there were incredibly poor. Philip Dumaresq, former captain of a loyalist privateer and son of a prominent Boston loyalist, owned almost all the land on the north and east sides of Marsh's Harbour. In a letter to his father-in-law he described his experiences:

> the Climate is delightful, but am sorry to say that the soil is not equal to our wishes, being so very shallow, that in a dry season the force of the Sun communicating to the Rock burns up all kinds of vegetables, however I do not think we have had a good chance as there has been an uncommon drought almost since our arrival - Guinea Corn Potatoes Yams, Turnips Cabbages Bean Pease - Oranges Limes Plantains grow very well and the lettoes seem to thrive - we have an abundance of wild grapes which convinces me that good Wines might be made, and it is said that indigo would do very well - but we are all poor and have not strength to do much, we have fine water - I have a spring in the Center of my Garden, where I dug through the rock about nine feet deep, of as good water as was ever drank, and in the greater plenty - I have seen no fresh meat except Pork since I have been on the island, that you may imagine our manner of living cannot be very agreeable. Poultry may be raised in plenty - the hens are continually laying or setting - as to myself and family I cannot say that we have any encouraging prospects - we live a retired life although any society - the people being of the lowest kind. Becky has not been out of her house except to the Garden since our arrival, nor is there a female that she can form any society with. I have five children. Three boys and two Girls. . . . the only thing the Governor could do was to make me a magistrate to keep me from being insulted by the Abaco Blackguards.[28]

To His Honor James Edward Powell Esq.r Lieutenant
Governor and Commander in Chief in and over the Bahama
Islands, Chancellor, Vice Admiral and Ordinary of the
same &c. &c. &c.

The Petition of Cornelius Blanchard
in behalf of the poor Inhabitants settled at Carleton upon the
Island of Abaco —

Humbly Sheweth

That in consequence of a Commission from His Excelly
Sir Guy Carleton then Commander in Chief of His Majesty's Forces in North
America, appointing him Captain of a Company of Loyal Refugees destined to
form a Settlement upon the Island aforesaid, your Petitioner accordingly left
New York on the 21st of September 1783, and arrived at Carleton the place of his
destination.

That on their arrival, not finding the Country so fertile
as had been expected, certain commotions arose, which prevented even those who were
desirous of making such trial as they wished — That so soon as these troubles
subsided the new Residents made every effort to gain themselves support: but
no sooner did they begin to reap the fruits of their Industry, than a Number
of Negroes had taken the Wood, and have so robbed the Places, that they have
now no support left —

Therefore prays your Honor will be pleased to take
their Situation into Consideration and grant such supply as to your
Honor shall seem necessary —

And your Petitioner as in duty
bound will pray —

Cornls Blanchard.

Bahama Islands, New Providence
April 6th 1785.

Cornelius Blanchard, who settled at Carleton, wrote to the Governor of the Bahamas seeking relief because the soil was not "so fertile as had been expected," commotions had interfered with production, and the settlement had been robbed. Reproduced with the permission of the Albert Lowe Museum, New Plymouth.

Within a couple of years Dumaresq left Abaco and moved to Nassau, where he held several different positions in the government. Others left Abaco also; the population declined.

In spite of the apparent failure of the attempt to establish a burgeoning new empire in Abaco, some persons, mostly those who resided in Nassau, remained optimistic. Lt. Governor James Powell wanted to develop the whale fishery of the Bahamas, and Governor Dunmore, whose tenure lasted from 1787 to 1796, wrote that "there is no island in the world better adapted for the catching of that Animal [whales] than it [Abaco] is." He sent a vessel to Nantucket Island in an attempt to encourage migration to Abaco; the effort failed.[29] Governor Dunmore contended that the soil of Abaco was "perfectly well adapted for raising provisions of every kind," mentioned wild grapes, and urged that a few French Protestant families be encouraged to migrate to Abaco to establish a wine industry.[30] As far as can be determined, grape culture and wine making have never been attempted in Abaco. The wild grapes both Dumaresq and Dunmore wrote about were probably sea grapes or wine grapes. Sea grapes are the fruit of a hardy broad-leaved tree which is often found just behind the ocean dunes. The plant is well adapted to seaside locations because it can withstand salt spray and drought. Its fruit is edible, but it does not produce good wine. Wine grapes are the size of pearls and, despite their name, apparently have never been used to make wine.

Dunmore's optimism was overblown—perhaps he wanted to inflate the importance of his own post by exaggerating Abaco's economic potential. Dunmore had been Governor of Virginia during the early 1770s when his ineptness had helped to bring on the American Revolution. He was unemployed during the war years, and his tenure as Governor of the Bahamas was marked by numerous disputes, nepotism, and the construction of grandiose forts which were never used for combat. It is fair to say that he was not a credible witness regarding Abaco's economic potential.

Governor Dunmore also became concerned about civil disorder and race relations in Abaco. He was informed that some of the blacks in Abaco had absented themselves from their owners or employers, and were plundering the island. They acquired muskets, fixed bayonets to them, and raided the white settlements. Some of the blacks believed they were entitled to be free under British law, which provided freedom for any slave who had pledged loyalty to Britain during the American Revolution. They believed they had been illegally kidnapped in New York or Florida by the loyalists. Other blacks probably had been abandoned in Abaco and had no source of food other than from the white settlements and no way to acquire it except by stealing it. The whites organized to protect themselves and their property. They rounded up the blacks. Some blacks were killed and some wounded in the resulting confrontations. Three prisoners were "immediately executed."[31] With bands of black outlaws and white vigilantes roaming the countryside of Abaco, the situation was obviously out of control. Governor Dunmore decided to visit Abaco, where he advertised amnesty and a fair hearing to determine the status of all runaway blacks. He reported:

> Upon our arrival at Abaco all the outlaying Negroes came in except five or six who are supposed to have got off the island. Those that were entitled to their freedom were declared so, and the others returned peaceably to their owners, and the utmost harmony now subsists upon the island,. . .[32]

The inhabitants of Spencer's Bight confirmed Dunmore's own assessment of his effectiveness and thanked Dunmore for his intervention which, they claimed, had resulted in the "quiet and peaceful restoration" of most of the blacks to their "lawful owners."[33] We have no evidence regarding whether or not the blacks believed Dunmore's intervention brought real justice or simply an end to their rebellion.

Though governors in Nassau remained optimistic in regard to the loyalist settlements in Abaco and tried to help them, the governors did not get along well with many of the loyalists who settled in Nassau. The loyalists in Nassau were, according to Governor Maxwell (Governor from 1780 to 1782, and 1784-1785), of a very different kind than the more humble loyalists who had settled in Abaco and other Out Islands. The Nassau loyalists were ambitious men who demanded more and more from the government, and were not content with the efforts of Governor Maxwell. They demonstrated against his government and apparently hoped that Governor Tonyn, formerly of East Florida, would be named to replace Maxwell. The movement was headed by James Hepburn, a loyalist who resided in Nassau, owned a plantation on Cat Island, and became the President of the American Board of Loyalists. Governor Maxwell opposed the efforts of this group strenuously and, at first, he won the full support of the British government in London. An early attempt on the part of the Nassau loyalists to gain support from Abaco failed when Thomas Willot, a magistrate at Maxwell Town, refused to allow the appointment of a deputy to meet with the board of loyalists in Nassau. Willott went to Nassau himself and, after meeting with the loyalist leaders, condemned their activities in a letter to Governor Maxwell:

> I am amazed to see those very persons Who Call themselves a committee representing the Loyalists. . . Committing every species of Disloyalty, Anarchy, and riot. . . . [34]

The election for a new twenty-five member General Assembly in 1785 returned eight loyalist candidates, but the loyalists were not content because six more of their candidates, who had gained more votes than the candidates of the old inhabitants, were ruled defeated. They challenged these seats and when the members concerned refused to withdraw so the challenges could be heard, the loyalist representatives from Cat, Abaco, Exuma, and Andros Islands withdrew.[35]

At this point Governor Maxwell was recalled to London and replaced, temporarily, by Lt. Gov. James Edward Powell. The American Board of Loyalists hoped, of course, that Maxwell would not be sent back to the Bahamas, and this time they were joined by fifty-three "loyal inhabitants" of the town of Maxwell in Abaco, who disavowed Governor Maxwell in a letter to the Bahamas Gazette.[36] Maxwell was not returned to the Bahamas. The rump assembly continued to meet, despite the objections of the loyalists, during most of the term of Governor Dunmore (1787-1796). A statement of protest from "the Planters and other inhabitants of the island of Abaco" claimed that the loyalists, who had sacrificed greatly on the king's behalf during the American Revolution, and who had, by their "uncommon exertion in Planting and Commerce . . . rescued the Bahamas from insignificance," were not represented in the General Assembly. The protest stated that they "feel themselves subject to Laws they have no Share in making," and urged dissolution of the assembly. The document was signed by some who were probably residents of Nassau rather than Abaco, such as Thomas Brown, owner of a defunct plantation at Eight Mile Bay, Abaco, but it was also signed by some who lived in Abaco such as Martin Weatherford and John Cornish.[37] Dunmore did not dissolve the assembly. Some of the loyalists in Nassau, including James Hepburn and James Cruden, planned a revolt against Dunmore's government. They sought support in Abaco.[38] The revolution did not materialize. The loyalists gained small victories by winning some by-elections during the next few years, and they gradually increased their role in the government of the Bahamas, but the extremists such as Hepburn had been defeated.

By 1788 the flurry of activity in Abaco was over. Most of the loyalists had come and gone, leaving a remnant of about 400[39] whites and blacks living at Spencer's Bight, Marsh's Harbour, Maxwell Town, Carleton, and Coco Plum Creek. Most of those who had political influence or reserve wealth or investments elsewhere were gone. The emigration from Abaco was as rapid and dramatic as the immigration to Abaco had been; of fifty-three residents of Maxwell Town who signed a letter published in the *Bahama Gazette* in 1785, only two or three surnames are common in Abaco or the Bahamas in the twentieth century. Many of those who remained were poor. Some probably had no alternative but to remain where the British vessels had deposited them. According to Thelma Peters, Abaco reached its low ebb in about 1790, and then began to grow slowly as migrants from Harbour Island and Spanish Wells, Eleuthera, joined the loyalists who remained in Abaco.[40]

Paul Albury has said that the migration of the Harbour Island men was in part due to the pretty girls of Abaco, but that it was also the result of overcrowding on Harbour Island—a small cay with limited space.* Enterprising young men must have eagerly accepted the challenge of developing the almost limitless fishing, agricultural, and wrecking opportunities of Abaco. These newcomers to Abaco were not, of course, newcomers to the Bahamas. Their ancestors had settled Harbour Island over 100 years before the loyalists had arrived at Abaco. They brought a knowledge of fishing and boat building which may well have been of vital importance to the loyalists remaining in Abaco. They helped the loyalists to learn to exploit the sea surrounding Abaco rather than rely primarily on the land mass of the main island, and helped to found new settlements at good harbours on the cays lying to the east and northeast of Great Abaco which were closer to the best fishing grounds on the outlying reefs. The family names of many of those who came to Abaco from Eleuthera are still common in Abaco in the late twentieth century—Russell, Bethel, Sands, Sawyer, Roberts, Pinder, and Albury. Harbour Island-born historian Paul Albury contended that there is hardly a white Abaconian who cannot claim a Harbour Island ancestor.[41]

---

* Harbour Island lies just off the northern coast of Eleuthera, about thirty miles southeast of Hole-in-the-Wall, Abaco.

Agriculture became a secondary activity; boat building, fishing, and wrecking became the primary activities. As fishermen and small farmers these people lived, at first, on a near subsistence basis— only the products of wrecking were exported from Abaco and involved the settlers in a market economy. Later, boat building in some communities and agriculture in others became economic mainstays. Towns located on the cays rather than on Great Abaco Island became the principal settlements. These included New Plymouth, on Green Turtle Cay, and Hope Town, on Elbow Cay.

Marsh's Harbour continued to survive and apparently absorbed the remnants of Maxwell Town. It was an integrated settlement, including free blacks as well as whites. Hope Town was white, founded, in part, by Wyannie Malone, a widow from South Carolina with four children. In 1902 Hope Town had only twelve blacks, and in 1980 the settlement was still primarily white, with just a few blacks living there. Some other settlements made on the outlying cays were white, as was the very small settlement on Man-0-War Cay, but New Plymouth, on Green Turtle Cay, was a mixture of blacks and whites. It is impossible to determine whether the black residents of New Plymouth and of Hope Town were free blacks who arrived with the loyalists, blacks who were freed by the British Navy in the Bahamas after the British government outlawed the international slave trade in 1807, or whether they were slaves who remained within or moved to those communities after the emancipation of all Bahamian slaves in 1838. Generally, it seems that settlements in which agriculture played an important role became integrated communities (New Plymouth and Marsh's Harbour), whereas settlements which were primarily seafaring communities such as Hope Town remained almost exclusively white.

The population grew slowly to about 900 in 1840, roughly double what it had been in 1790. By 1849, however, it had doubled again and grown to almost 2,000, and by the 1890s it was as high as 3,686.[42] The principal reason for this spurt of growth was the economic success of the new settlements on the outer cays, especially New Plymouth on Green Turtle Cay. There were 193 persons in New Plymouth in 1815; by 1856 there were about 1,000 persons and New Plymouth was a busy place; it was the home port for forty fishing smacks and twenty wrecking schooners.[43] New Plymouth built its success around fishing, fruit growing, lumbering, and wrecking. Evidence of each of these activities can be found on a list of exports from Abaco in the year 1834:

cedar 2400 ft. , Madeira wood 3000 ft. , timbers, 1880, pitch pine 1720, bananas 422 bus. , bark 450, Braziletto 23/4 tons, box wood 1 1/ 2 tons, Conch shells 1500, Copper 1045 lbs. , Coco Nuts 100, . . . Limes and oranges 23625 doz. , Pine Apples 1270, Salt . . . Shells 6 Bbls 50 boxes, sponge 1000, Turtle 4295, Turtle Shell 536, Wax 49.[44]

New Plymouth had apparently found the combination of activities which worked best during the early nineteenth century. Much of the fruit growing was done on land located on Great Abaco Island, but land on Green Turtle Cay and Manjack Cay was also cultivated. Abaco Sound is rather narrow in the vicinity of Green Turtle Cay, making the mainland of Abaco more accessible than it is from other outlying cays, such as Great Guana, Man-0-War, and Elbow Cay. This was far more important during the early nineteenth century than it is today, because the farmers had to sail to their farms in small dinghies.

The export of lumber provided a reasonably good income while also producing new cleared land for citrus. Copper was consistently exported from Abaco during most of the nineteenth century. The uninitiated researcher would reach the conclusion, quite logically, though incorrectly, that somewhere on Abaco a copper mine existed. Some of the other items exported during the nineteenth century would lead one to believe that Abaco was a reasonably well developed, small but highly diversified, manufacturing center. This, of course, was not true—the variety of manufactured goods came from vessels wrecked on the reefs of Abaco. The consistent presence of copper on the export lists is due to the fact that almost all ships were sheathed with copper, which resisted the growth of barnacles and other marine organisms on the hull. The copper plates were salvaged from wrecked vessels and exported.

The other communities of Abaco, though not as populous or prosperous as New Plymouth, were better off than they had been during the hard times of the 1790s. Boat building developed rapidly. Abaco became the most important boat building center in the Bahamas, producing almost half of all boats built in the colony between 1855 and 1864. Most of this early boat building was done at Hope Town, Cherokee, and Marsh's Harbour. These towns also engaged in fruit and vegetable growing, but their products were mostly for local consumption, whereas New Plymouth grew fruit for shipment to Nassau.

The settlement of Man-0-War was founded sometime during the 1820s and remained very small throughout the nineteenth century. Benjamin Archer, a loyalist who lived in Marsh's Harbour, purchased sixty acres of farm land on Man-0-War Cay. Benjamin's daughter, Eleanor, accompanied him to Man-0-War when he sailed over to work in the fields. According to Norman Albury, a retired sail maker and patriarch of the community at Man-0-War in 1973, Eleanor was a well developed thirteen year old. On one trip to Man-0-War she met Benjamin Albury, a sixteen year old boy from Harbour Island who had come ashore at Man-0-War after his boat was wrecked on the reef. Benjamin and Eleanor fell in love, stayed on the cay, were married, and had thirteen children. They are known to local residents as Pappy Ben and Mammy Nellie, and in 1977, 230 of the 235 Bahamian residents of Man-0-War Cay were descendants of Ben and Nellie Albury.[45]

Fishing and farming were the principal activities at Man-0-War, and boat building commenced sometime around mid-century. Man-0-War was not to become a prominent center for boat building until after 1900. Another small settlement was established on Great Guana Cay at about the same time, and Cherokee Sound was probably founded by people from the East Florida settlements at Eight Mile Bay and Spencer's Bight, who were, perhaps, joined by migrants from Harbour Island. No other white settlements were founded in Abaco; the next group of new towns were founded by blacks after the emancipation of the slaves in 1838.

There were never large numbers of slaves in Abaco. The failure of cotton cultivation was, in part, the reason for this. Also, more northern than southern loyalists settled in Abaco. They were poorer and lacked slave property. Whereas the population of the Bahamas was about two-thirds black in 1786, the population of Abaco was about half white and half black. When emancipation was forced on the Bahamas by action of the British government in London, there were 499 whites, 61 free blacks, and 361 black slaves in Abaco.[46] Once freed, many of the former slaves moved away from the white settlements and established new towns. It is not possible to provide details regarding the founding of the black settlements, but some, including Bluff Point, Cornish Town, and Old Place on Great Abaco Island, may well have been founded shortly after emancipation. Crossing Rocks and Sandy Point, on the southern part of Great Abaco, may have been founded in similar fashion, as well as the two settlements on Mores Island—Hard Bargain and the Bight. There was a small settlement on Cave Cay, located just south of the western tip of Little Abaco Island, but the town was moved, by the government, to Little Abaco after it suffered extensive hurricane damage during the 1930s. The new town was, appropriately enough, called Crown Haven. All were exclusively black settlements except Sandy Point, which included some mulattoes. These towns combined agriculture with exploitation of the sea, but were generally not as successful as the white settlements on the outer cays. Purposely isolating themselves from the whites, they also cut themselves off from what little access there was to markets outside of Abaco from ports such as Hope Town, New Plymouth, and Marsh's Harbour. They lived outside the market economy for all of the nineteenth and much of the twentieth centuries, and most of their inhabitants were subsistence fishermen and farmers.

END NOTES

[1] East Florida Legislature to George III, 30 April 1783, in Joseph B. Lockey, *East Florida 1783-1785, a File of Documents Assembled and Many of Them Translated* (Berkeley: University of California Press, 1949), pp. 104-105.

[2] Lord North to Governor Patrick Tonyn, London, 4 December 1783, in Lockey, *Documents*, pp. 178-180.

[3] John Cruden to Charles III, October 1784, in Lockey, *Documents*, pp. 301-302.

[4] Thomas Stephens, John Davis, Henry Smith, John Pintard, and Thomas Victor to Sir Guy Carleton, New York, 25 June 1783, British Headquarters Papers (BHP) 8227.

[5] *Royal Gazette* (New York), 28 June 1783, p. 3.

[6] Lt. Col. Robert Morse, Letter to Lt. John Wilson, New York, 14 July 1783. Copy in Harcourt Malcolm Collection, Nassau Public Library.

[7] John Wilson, Report on the Bahama Islands, 1784. Boston Public Library, MS. U. 1.6. Another pessimistic assessment was made earlier by a former resident of Georgia who chartered a boat in New Providence and visited Abaco sometime before July 1783. His report apparently did not become public information. He wrote that what the Bahamians called good soil was "poor Sandy Soil, such as most of our Sea Islands," and that Bahamians were ignorant in regard to agriculture and soil quality. He lamented the fact that he might have to move to the Bahamas upon the evacuation of Florida. See extracts of a letter from Lewis Johnson to Lt. Gov. Graham, New Providence, July 1783, CO 23/26/26.

[8] Wilbur H. Siebert, *The Legacy of the American Revolution to the British West Indies and Bahamas: A Chapter out of the History of the American Loyalists* (Columbus: Ohio State University Press, 1913), p. 21, and Thelma Peters, *The American Loyalists and the Plantation period in the Bahama Islands*, Ph. D. dissertation, University of Florida, 1960, p. 45.

[9] *Royal Gazette*, 5 July 1783, p. 5.

[10] Siebert contends the first group left before 22 August (p. 21). Cornelius Blanchard, a resident of Carleton, in a petition written in 1785, indicates that he departed from New York on 21 September 1783. Brigadier-General Archibald McArthur, in a report to Lord Sidney written on 1 March 1784, claims the residents of Carleton left New York in September. Also, according to the *Royal Gazette*, the brigantine *Charlotte* was scheduled to depart for Abaco and Providence on 30 September 1783 (Royal Gazette, 13 September 1783, p. 2).

[11] "The Abaco Experience," *Bahamas Handbook*, 1975-76 (Nassau: Etienne Dupuch, 1975), 61-70.

[12] Siebert, p. 21. Also see *Royal Gazette*, 4 October 1783, p. 2, 25 October 1783, p. 3, and 5 November 1783, p. 2.

[13] Peters, p. 45. Also, at least one of the Abaco settlers was of questionable character. Dennis Flynn, who received a land grant near Carleton in 1786, was reported to be a prisoner in New York in 1783 for forging and passing bad bills (*Royal Gazette*, 6 August 1783).

[14] Sandra Riley, *Homeward Bound: A History of the Bahama Islands to 1850* (Miami: Island Research, 1983), p. 141.

[15] See Steve Dodge, *The First Loyalist Settlements in Abaco: Carleton and Marsh's Harbour* (Hope Town, Bahamas: Wyannie Malone Historical Museum, 1979).

[16] John Wilson, Report, 1784.

[17] The proprietors had surrendered the right to govern the Bahamas to the crown in 1717, but retained title to all unowned land. The British government purchased the land in 1787.

[18] Brigadier-General Archibald McArthur to Lord Sidney, Nassau, 1 March, 1784, CO 23/25/75.

[19] *Ibid.*

[20] Survey Report, 1784, copy at Wyannie Malone Museum, Hope Town, Abaco, Bahamas. The Unknown author of this report accompanied General McArthur and Lt. Wilson on their visit to Abaco in February 1784. This ratio of New York to Florida loyalists is confirmed by the distribution of tools and implements by the Governor of the Bahamas. Two-thirds went to the "New York faction" and one-third to the "Florida faction." See Return. . . and Distribution. . . ," New Providence, 15 June, 1784, CO 23/25/146.

[21] All information regarding land grants made during the 1780s was acquired from Book B, Department of Lands and Surveys, Nassau.

[22] See Return of Loyalists who have arrived in the Bahamas Islands from North America, CO 23/25/138.

[23] The population in 1783 was 4058; In 1786 it was 8957; In 1789 it was 11,300 (Michael Craton, *The History of the Bahamas* [London: Collins, 1968], p. 166).

[24] List of all ships and vessels which have entered in the port of Nassau Bahama Islands between 1 July and 30 September 1788 with the quantity of quality of lading, enclosed with Dunmore to Sydney, Nassau, 28 January 1789, CO 23/29/69.

[25] See Patrick Kennedy to Evans Nepean, 8 September 1786, CO 23/15/234.

[26] Thelma Peters, pp. 60-61

[27] After a severe hurricane in 1785, flour was distributed to the various settlements on the basis of these percentages. See Council Minutes, 1 October 1785, CO 23/25/386.

[28] Philip Dumaresq to Sylvester Gardiner, 6 March 1785, in The Gardiner, Whipple, and Allen Letters, Vol II, 49, in the Library of Massachusetts Historical Society, Boston, copy in the Wyannie Malone Museum, Hope Town, Abaco, Bahamas.

[29] James Powell to Sydney, New Providence, 19 March 1785, CO 23/25/312, and Observations by Lord Dunmore on Such of the Islands as he Visited, Sept. , 1790, Dunmore MSS., Nassau Public Library, in Zoe C. Durrell, *The Innocent Island: Abaco in the Bahamas* (Brattleboro, Vermont: Durrell, 1972), p. 48.

[30] Dunmore, Dispatch to the Public Records Office, 13 December 1793, 2350 #40 CO23/83, in Durrell, p. 49.

[31] Dunmore to Sydney, Nassau, 20 November 1787, CO 23/27/75.

[32] Dunmore to Sydney, Nassau, 18 July 1788, CO 23/27/164

[33] Inhabitants of Spencer's Bight to Dunmore, Spencer's Bight, 28 May 1788, CO 23/27/168.

[34] Thomas Willott to Maxwell, New Providence, 15 September 1784, CO 23/25/228.

[35] Members from Abaco were James Ridley and Hugh Dean (Craton, p. 169).

[36] *Bahamas Gazette*, 9 April 1785, in Peters, p. 92.

[37] The Planters and other inhabitants of the Island of Abaco to Dunmore, no date, CO 23/27/119. Another protestation regarding the same subject is from the Planters and other inhabitants of Abaco, to William Pitt, Chancellor of the Exchequer, no date, CO 23/27/170. A letter of support for Dunmore and disapproval of the protests is Richard Pearer to Dunmore, Abaco, 13 May 1788. CO 23/27/173.

[38] Deposition of William Augustus Bowles made before John Miller, New Providence, 9 April 1788, CO 23/27/158.

[39] Lydia A. Parrish, "Records of Some Southern Loyalists, being a collection of manuscripts about some eighty families, most of whom immigrated to the Bahamas during and after the American Revolution," Manuscript in Widener Library, Harvard University, p. 35.

[40] Peters, p. 62.

[41] Peters, p. 64, and Albury, p. 250.

42 Population statistics were derived from annual reports titled *Colony of the Bahamas* and popularly called Blue Books.

[43] Paul Albury, "Abaco," Address to Nassau East Rotary Club, Nassau, 11 October 1974, tape recording at Bahamian Archives, Nassau, Bahamas.

[44] *Colony of the Bahamas*, 1834 (Blue Book), p. 153.

[45] Haziel Albury, *Man-O-War: My Island Home* (Hockessin, Delaware: Holly, 1977), p. 5.

[46] *Colony of the Bahamas*, 1834 (Blue Book), p. 118.

Chapter Four-

From About 1850 to About 1900

The population of Abaco grew slowly during most of the last half of the nineteenth century, increasing from about 2000 in 1850 to about 3600 by 1890, but decreasing to about 3300 by the turn of the century. The economy was anything but stable; during some years products from Abaco were sold in Nassau or the United States at good profits, but more often poverty affected all of the settlements. Most of the economic pursuits of this period were, like the cultivation of cotton during the late eighteenth century, transitory endeavors. For one reason or another, most of them blossomed and provided a living for many Abaconians for a period of years, and then declined in importance, forcing the people to adjust their lives accordingly. When harvests were poor or when markets disappeared for some products, they tried to produce others which were more easily obtained or more saleable. But the extreme isolation of Abaco, even from Nassau, which was no great metropolis, made it almost impossible for Abaconians to understand market conditions. They were often doing the right thing at the wrong time, and their economic well-being was frequently at the mercy of many factors far beyond their control. They were dependent, as any farmer is, on the weather, and during some years droughts burned up their crops. Hurricanes sometimes destroyed a year's work in a matter of hours. Fishermen and spongers were subject to the usual streaks of good or bad luck. But the factor which made economic planning impossible was the rather wide fluctuations of the prices their products fetched in Nassau or in United States' markets. The Abaconian farmer or sponger did not find out if his labour had resulted in a profit or a loss until long after his energy and capital had been expended. It is no wonder that entrepreneurs were discouraged after discovering that a season's effort had produced little or nothing for reasons which were beyond their knowledge and understanding.

For two-thirds of the nineteenth century Abaco had no government mail service, and had to rely on privately owned and operated vessels to carry communications as well as commodities between Abaco and Nassau. In 1867 the House of Assembly passed a bill to provide for postal communication[1] between Nassau, Eleuthera, Harbour Island, and Abaco on a fortnightly basis. The "mailboat" was still to be privately owned and operated, but a government contract to carry mail encouraged regularity and dependability. The mailboat carried much more than mail—it transported "exports" from Abaco to Nassau, some of which were trans-shipped to the United States or England, and carried almost all items imported to Abaco on the return run. The mailboat also carried passengers. It was Abaco's principal means of contact with the outside world and was Abaco's main link with Nassau, but it was frequently unreliable. Farmers who wished to ship perishable produce to Nassau often found that their cargo had rotted on the dock at Marsh Harbour or elsewhere because the mailboat had been delayed or had omitted a regular stop. From time to time the schedule was altered. In 1897 the Resident Justice at Green Turtle Cay complained that the monthly sailing service between Green Turtle Cay and Nassau was inadequate because vegetables rotted before they could be shipped to market. A particularly vivid description of Abaco's dependence on the mailboat is found in a report from Cherokee Sound, which explained that the

> . . . starving condition of people was not caused by the hurricane, but by the mail being detained in Nassau on account of the stormy weather and the smack fishermen not sending home supplies for their families, and the shopkeepers here being out of everything eatable, I was out of food for four days, . . . I heard no complaint from the people until a few days before the mail arrived from Nassau, saying some were starving . . . and if the weather continued and the mail had to pass on her way over they must all starve.[2]

Goods exported directly from Abaco to the United States were usually carried in small cargo schooners owned and operated by Abaco men. These vessels sailed to United States' ports on an irregular basis, and only during the harvest season, so it was impossible for them to bring market information back to Abaco in time for it to be useful. It was impossible to predict accurately how long the passage of these vessels would take, what the condition of perishable fruit would be upon arrival, and the price which would be paid. The isolation of Abaco prevented substantial economic growth during this period.

WRECKING

By the middle of the nineteenth century wrecking had become one of Abaco's most important industries. The island group was ideally suited for this enterprise. Its barrier reef stretches for over one hundred miles in a northwest-southeast direction and lies several miles to the northeast of the low-lying cays. Strong northeasterly winds, common after the passage of cold fronts during the winter months, made this reef a treacherous and, at night, invisible, lee shore. Most ships bound from North American ports such as New York, Boston, and Baltimore for points south of Florida in the American hemisphere laid a course to the east of Abaco because they did not attempt to sail, or power, against the four knot northward flowing current of the Gulf Stream in the Florida Straits. Thus, one of the principal shipping lanes of the world lay just east of Abaco's barrier reef. Also, ships from Europe bound for ports in the Gulf of Mexico usually made a landfall at Hole-in-the-Wall, Abaco, before proceeding through the Bahamas by way of the Northeast and Northwest New Providence channels, which separate Great Bahama Bank from Little Bahama Bank.[3] Early in the nineteenth century there were no aids to navigation—no buoys and no lighthouses. These conditions provided Abaco with a seemingly inexhaustible supply of wrecked ships from which many of her men salvaged a living.

The wrecking industry was well developed, and was carefully regulated by the government—wreckers had to be licensed, and all salvaged goods had to be carried to Nassau where they were sold at auction. The government received 15% as import duty; warehousemen, commission agents and laborers got about 15%; the wrecker received 40-60%; and the ship owner was given the 10-30% which was left. The small percentage received by the ship owner has been part of the basis for the charge that wrecking was immoral. The wrecker, however, accepted considerable risks to his boat and his person while off-loading cargo from a hull which was in the process of breaking up on a reef. Without the wrecker, all the cargo would have been lost.

Another aspect of the charge that wrecking was immoral was that wreckers allegedly lured ships to their destruction by deceiving captains with substitute aids to navigation, such as false lights, which directed them toward rather than away from shallow areas. The desire for a wrecked ship may well have tempted the wreck-

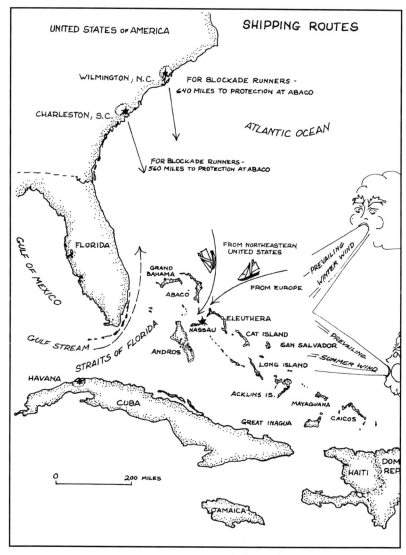

Abaco was an excellent place for wrecking because ships bound southward from the northeastern United States usually went east of Abaco to avoid the adverse current of the Gulf Stream. Ships from Europe frequently made a landfall at Hole-in-the-Wall at the Southern tip of Abaco before proceeding to Nassau or beyond to Havana or ports in the Gulf of Mexico. During the United States Civil War, Abaco was well located to accommodate Ships going to or coming from Charleston or Wilmington.

ers to do this, but for a variety of reasons it is doubtful that this was a frequent practice at Abaco. First, Abaco was so well endowed by nature with dangers to shipping that treachery was almost unnecessary. Second, prior to the construction of the lighthouses the sighting of any land light (real or false) would have influenced the captain of any ship to stand further offshore to the east rather than to head for the reef. Third, after the construction of the lighthouses, a false light would have had the same effect.[4] A technique which was workable was to put the light out. This was tried on more than one occasion. For the most part, however, lack of opportunity complemented the natural tendency of Abaco people toward honesty, and it is doubtful that many ships were purposely lured to their destruction on the reefs of Abaco.

Finally, in defense of the morality of wrecking it must be said that wreckers saved the lives of many shipwrecked sailors who otherwise would have drowned. They provided a service analogous to that provided during recent years by the Coast Guard in the United States and by Bahamas Air-Sea Rescue Association (BASRA) in the Bahamas. The fact that their primary motivation was not altruistic mattered little to the men who were rescued. In 1853 Captain Robert Sands of Abaco was cited by the Queen for saving lives of seamen at the site of a wreck, and in 1860, a United States report included the following statement regarding some wrecks near Abaco:

> Of the loss of life we have no account but this is believed to be small owing to the exertion of the wreckers, who are always on the look out for their prey, and have, I understand, frequently saved life at the risk of their own.[5]

Wrecking was clearly a very important aspect of the lives of many Abaconians. Some men pursued wrecking as a regular vocation, sailing back and forth along the reefs in search of recent wrecks, but most simply took up the trade whenever word of a nearby wreck reached their community. In 1856, half of the able-bodied men in the Bahamas held wrecking licenses.[6] Wrecking played an important role in the economy because it provided an inexpensive source of imported items, and produced some goods for export to the United States and England. Also, household items such as furniture and cookware, which were salvaged but were not part of a ship's cargo, were probably retained by the wrecker rather than sent to Nassau. This enabled many Abaconians to acquire goods they could not afford to purchase. No history of Abaco would be complete without the famous story of the minister at Hope Town whose pulpit faced toward the sea. One Sunday morning, while delivering his sermon, he saw a ship ground on the reef. Instead of informing his congregation, he reportedly brought his sermon to a quick conclusion and asked the worshippers to bow their heads in silent prayer. The congregation later realized that the minister had slipped out of the church in order to be the first wrecker to arrive at the wreck. The configuration of the church was eventually changed so that the parishioners faced the sea and the minister had his back to the reef. This new arrangement has stood the test of time, and was continued when the present Saint James Methodist Church was built in Hope Town in c. 1989.

During the 1860s two separate developments damaged the wrecking industry in Abaco. The first was the Civil War in the United States which stifled the external commerce of the southern

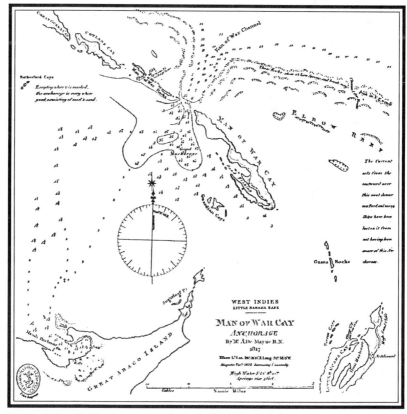

Chart of Man-O-War anchorage drawn in 1817 by A. DeMayne and reproduced by the British government in 1875. Hope Town Harbour is designated as Boat Harbour, the harbour at Man-O-War is reported as a good place to fish, and wells are shown in Marsh Harbour.

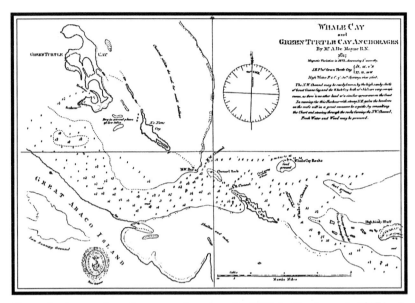

Chart of entrances from the sea north and south of Whale Cay drawn in 1817 by A. DeMayne and reproduced by the British government in 1875. New Plymouth is designated simply as "settlement."

states because the North blockaded the Confederacy. This decline was temporary, and the industry revived during the postwar years. The best year for the wreckers was 1870, when goods valued at £154,000 were salvaged throughout the Bahamas. After 1870 the value of salvaged goods steadily declined, and by 1900 the industry was dead. This deterioration was the result of the British government's decision to build lighthouses throughout the Bahamas. The first in Abaco was built at Hole-in-the-Wall in 1836. Almost three decades later a decision to build a second lighthouse at Hope Town to mark Elbow Reef was opposed by the inhabitants of the town, who sabotaged the construction and denied fresh water to the labourers. The British Imperial Lighthouse Service prevailed, however, and by 1863 the lighthouse was functioning. It is interesting to note that the light is still in place and in operation each night, still employing a kerosene mantle light with a large revolving Fresnel lens turned by a weight and cable mechanism which has to be wound several times each night. In 1979 some residents of Hope Town were alarmed by a rumor that the government intended to automate the light, and expressed their hope that the light be maintained by a keeper as it had been for 116 years. The light, which was viewed as detrimental to the economy of the town when it was under construction in the 1860s, had become an asset for tourism.

Twenty years after the construction of the Elbow Reef lighthouse, the British Admiralty decided to conduct surveys and produce accurate charts of the Bahama Islands. Earlier efforts had been spotty, and the charts which were published included some inaccuracies. Charts of the "Man-0-War Anchorage" and the "Whale Cay and Green Turtle Cay Anchorages" in Abaco had been issued in 1817 and reprinted in 1875 (see reproductions on pages 61 and 62). During the 1880s the new charts were issued. These were more accurate than any issued previously, and reprints are still available, with some minor changes, from the governments of Great Britain and the United States. No complete resurvey has been done for almost one hundred years, though privately-financed efforts have produced large scale charts for use by cruising yachtsmen. The more accurate charts, coupled with the lighthouses as well as the use of more modern vessels and navigation equipment, destroyed the wrecking industry by the turn of the century.

THE CIVIL WAR

Although the Civil War in the United States temporarily depressed the wrecking industry in the Bahamas, the war was a boon for the islands. As a colony of Great Britain, the Bahamas were neutral. This theoretically entitled them to trade non-contraband goods with both sides. Goods from Great Britain destined for the North were sent directly to northern ports because the Confederacy lacked an effective navy and could not prevent this trade, but goods from Britain destined for the Confederacy were subject to capture by the United States Navy, which tried to enforce President Lincoln's blockade of southern ports. Although trade in non-contraband goods was supposed to be legal, the United States and Great Britain disagreed concerning what constituted non-contraband goods. As a practical matter, any ship attempting to enter or leave a Confederate port was liable to possible seizure. In order to avoid capture by Union vessels, goods were carried from Britain to Nassau in ocean steamers, then transferred to lightweight, fast, steel steamers painted gray or light blue-gray (for camouflage at dawn and dusk), which attempted to run the union blockade. The profits were phenomenal because imports were very scarce in the Confederacy, and southern cotton was in short supply in Britain. Three successful voyages might well repay a ship owner for his investment, and the new wealth showed itself all over Nassau. Bay Street was widened, a new dock was built, and the public debt was paid. Abaco's location made it important to the blockade runners. Ships leaving Nassau for Charleston or Wilmington sometimes laid a course to the east of Abaco so as to approach those ports from offshore in order to avoid early detection by Union vessels. They passed through the cordon of Union ships and entered the ports under the protection of darkness. After taking on a cargo of cotton, they left port at night. If they made it through the first line of ships without detection, they were usually sighted after dawn and pursued by a ship in the second line. The blockade runner then poured on the steam and headed for Abaco, where they could gain protection on the banks. Bahamian pilots were capable of finding the deep water and avoiding the shoals; Union naval vessels avoided the banks. These chases from the Confederacy to the bank often lasted for two days, with the blockade runner jettisoning bales of cotton from her decks to lighten the vessel, if necessary.

Some blockade runners used New Plymouth as a port of entry, and then trans-shipped goods to Nassau. This undoubtedly brought excitement to the town, but Abaco did not profit directly

The *U.S.S. Ossippee,* shown here, was a sister ship to the *U.S.S. Adirondack,* the remains of which can still be seen on the reef near Man-O-War Cay. Photograph provided courtesy of the Naval Historical Foundation, Collection of W. Beverly Mason, Jr.

The *U.S.S. San Jacinto* sank on the reef between No Name Cay and Green Turtle Cay on 1 January 1865. Drawing courtesy of New Plymouth Library, Green Turtle Cay.

because the goods and the profits eventually went to Nassau. Some Abaconians probably acquired jobs as pilots or moved to Nassau during these years to participate in the boom.

The war brought the wrecks of two Union warships to Abaco. The first was the steam sloop *Adirondack*. She was less than six months old and was en route to Nassau to join other Union cruisers in the area to watch for the infamous Confederate raider, the *Alabama*. A strong westward setting current or a navigational error placed the ship on the reef off Man-O-War Cay during the early morning hours of 23 August 1862. Captain Gansevoort attempted to set a kedge anchor astern to pull the vessel off, but it did not hold. He lightened the sloop by dumping the large guns as well as coal overboard, but the vessel did not float free. He attempted to hire a wrecking schooner, many of which were on the scene, to set out one of his bow anchors, but the wreckers refused. He finally agreed to purchase a wrecking schooner "at an exorbitant price" to accomplish the task. This effort also failed to dislodge the *Adirondack*, and the ship subsequently broke up and sank. All the men were saved by the wreckers, and Captain Gansevoort signed an agreement concerning salvage of items he was not able to save himself. The remains of the *Adirondack*, including several large cannons, are still visible to snorkelers at the reef off Man-O-War Cay. The gunboat *San Jacinto* struck the reef between Green Turtle Cay and No Name Cay on 1 January 1865. She was in pursuit of a blockade runner and mistook a shore light for the ship she was chasing. The remains of the *San Jacinto* are also visible to snorkelers and divers.[7]

The prosperity the Civil War brought to the Bahamas was, of course, temporary, and boom was followed by bust. Nassau's value as a trans-shipment center ended with the war, and the new street lamps which had been installed along Bay Street were not always lit during the postwar years. In Abaco the war had brought little or no prosperity, and the postwar depression didn't cause very much change either. Abaco was too isolated to benefit from, or suffer as a result of, events elsewhere in the world.

PINEAPPLES AND SPONGES

The most prosperous settlement during 1850-1890 was unquestionably New Plymouth at Green Turtle Cay. Its population had increased from 193 in 1815 to over 1000 by 1856, when forty fishing vessels and twenty wrecking schooners were based there.[8] By 1885 the population reached 1500, and multistory buildings lined the narrow streets. The principal source of the prosperity of New Plymouth during this period was the cultivation of the pineapple.

The pineapple grows on a low plant with sword-shaped, spreading, blue-green leaves which have serrated edges. The plant requires a warm climate and good drainage; it grows to maturity and produces one fruit on a short stalk when it is eighteen to twenty months old. The pineapple had been grown in the Bahamas as early as 1723, when Governor Phenney reported that the Bahamian pineapples were "of the best kind in America."[9] Small quantities of the fruit were exported to England and the United States during the early nineteenth century, and by the late nineteenth century the Bahamas, especially Eleuthera, were probably the best known source of pineapples in the United States. The most profitable year was 1892, when 665,332 dozen pineapples were exported, producing an income of £56,061. The market was glutted eight years later when the Bahamas exported over 7,000,000 dozen pineapples, and low prices discouraged producers. The industry was also harmed by the acquisition of Hawaii by the United States in 1898, which provided free access to the United States for Mr. Sanford Dole's Hawaiian pineapples. Bahamian producers paid a duty of $7.00 per thousand.[10] The industry in Abaco reached its peak about ten years

Harvesting and shipping of pineapples.

before it peaked in the Bahamas as a whole, and its decline was the result of factors other than the glut and the acquisition of Hawaii by the United States, which killed it in Eleuthera, Cat Island, and Long Island.

As early as the 1830s small quantities of pineapples were exported from Abaco. Exports increased during the next forty years, and by the 1880s the pineapple was Abaco's principal export item. In 1885 the Resident Justice at Green Turtle Cay reported that the largest proportion of the male inhabitants in his district was engaged in the cultivation of pineapples, but ten years later the industry was in the midst of rapid decline. In 1897 a very small number of pineapples (3500 dozen) were produced in the Green Turtle Cay district; the Resident Justice reported that this was the remnant of an industry which had produced 125,000 - 130,000 dozen pineapples annually several years before. He explained that losses in three successive years had discouraged the planters.[11] Pineapple production in the Hope Town district paralleled that of Green Turtle.[12]

Some of the difficulties of growing and marketing pineapples in Abaco were similar to problems faced by the industry in the rest of the Bahamas, and probably caused the decline of pineapple cultivation in Abaco. Perhaps the most significant factor was the difficulty of getting the fruit to markets in the United States in good condition. Often the fresh fruit was simply piled in the hold of a cargo schooner. Contrary winds might well delay the vessel, and, in any case, the pineapples at the bottom of the hold were inevitably damaged. Also, after several years of intensive cultivation, the thin soils were nearly exhausted, providing lower yields and lower profits for growers. Thus, although pineapple cultivation produced significant returns for Abaco during the 1870s and 1880s, and had important linkage effects because fruit-carrying schooners had to be built and operated, the industry was unimportant by the turn of the century.

Throughout the pineapple producing years, citrus remained a staple crop in Abaco and considerable quantities were exported. In 1854, 322,800 fruits and oranges were exported from Abaco. Production increased more gradually than pineapple production, and 480,000 oranges were sold in 1897. Although these numbers appear to be rather large, an average of three million oranges were sent from the Bahamas to United States markets annually from 1870 to 1900.[13] In 1897 Abaco produced less than one-sixth of the total exported. During the 1890s most of the citrus grown in Abaco was grown in the Hope Town district, a fact which is indica-

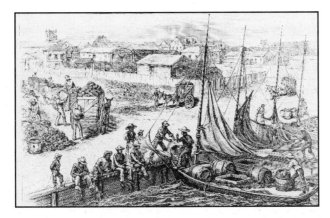

These drawings were made during the 1870s to depict sponging near New Providence. They were published in *Frank Leslie's Illustrated Newspaper* on 20 July 1878. They show the hooking of sponges, the cleaning of sponges in a kraal, and the unloading of sponges at the wharf on Bay Street in Nassau.

tive of the agricultural decline of Green Turtle Cay.[14] The cultivation and export of citrus fruits suffered from many of the same maladies as the pineapple industry—exhausted soil, fruit spoiled in shipping, and fluctuations in market prices, but citrus was a staple export for Abaco and the Bahamas until the large scale development of Florida as the principal supplier for the United States. Other products which were consistently exported from Abaco during the last half of the nineteenth century included sponge, turtle, turtle shells, and boats. Items which appeared occasionally on some lists of exports included shells, sugar, and salt.

Sponge fishing was an important activity in all of the Abaco settlements during this entire period. Sponges were sent to Nassau during the 1830s and 1840s, and during the 1890s sponges replaced pineapples as the highest valued item on Abaco's export lists. This, of course, served to cushion the economic impact of the decline in income from pineapples, but sponge harvests and prices varied so much from year to year that the economic well being of the Abaconians was far from secure.[15] Sponges are animals—not plants—which filter seawater for nutrition and anchor themselves to the bottom of the sea. They are found in the Mediterranean Sea and in the tropical western Atlantic. They grew prolifically on "the mud" of Great Bahama Bank west of Andros Island, and also on Little Bahama Bank west of Abaco. These sponges were in shallow water and were much more accessible than deep-water Mediterranean sponges or most other Atlantic sponges. In spite of this, sponging in the Bahamas was hard work.[16]

No sponging took place from August through mid-October because of the possibility of getting caught out in a hurricane. The vessels were moored in port or careened for repair work and repainting during these months, and preparations were made for the commencement of the next season.

When the men were not working on the boats, they spent some time in the fields, which were tended by the women and children when the men were out sponging. By the middle of October the sponge schooners and sloops were ready to depart and were being provisioned for their first journey to "the mud." The scene was similar in each of the communities—barrels of salt beef and sacks of flour, sugar, and vegetables were loaded on the sponge vessels as the families of the communities were made ready to do without husbands and fathers again. The sponge sloop or schooner served as a mother ship for dinghies which were used to hunt for and collect the sponges. A fifty-foot schooner carried a total crew of about seventeen men, consisting of a captain, a mate, a cook, and dinghy boat crews of two men each. These crews owned and maintained their own dinghies and equipment. "The mud," located west of Andros, was the best sponging area in the Bahamas; it was about 200 miles from Marsh Harbour, and the passage was frequently stormy. After arriving at the mud, the sponging began at sunrise.

The dinghy boats were manned by a sculler aft and a hooker forward. The sculler moved the dinghy across the banks by twisting, pushing and pulling a single oar at the stern of the boat as the hooker searched the bottom for sponges through his glass-bottomed bucket (called a water glass). The best sponges were sheep's wool sponges, known as "checkerboards" by the hookers because of their black and white spotted appearance. The second most valuable sponges were velvet sponges; other species tore too easily and were not as valuable. The hooker had to be able to identify a good quality sponge through his water glass, give precise instructions to the sculler, snag it with "L" shaped hooks fastened to a long pole, tear the sponge away from the bottom, and bring it to the surface. The day's haul was brought back to the schooner to be spread on the deck and dried, a process which must have made the vessel almost intolerable for anyone with a sense of smell. The sponges were then deposited in kralls, fenced in areas in shallow water, to soak in the sea. After several days the sponges were beaten "to get the black gurry out," rinsed, and dried. After several weeks the entire catch was bagged and taken to Nassau to be sold.

Each hooker-sculler team competed with the others, and sometimes the catch of each was kept separate and sold, with each crewman paying a portion of the bill for provisions and paying 25% to the sponging vessel. This was divided between the owner, the captain, and the mate. Another system was to pool the catch and sell it, pay for the provisions, and then divide the receipts into shares, with the owner of the vessel receiving two or three shares, the captain and mate several shares, each hooker one and one half shares, the owner of each dinghy one-half a share, and scullers one share each. Whichever system was utilized, it was a hard way to make a living—Haziel Albury of Man-0-War Cay reported that one share was usually $25-30 for a six week trip.

Several six to eight week voyages were made to the mud each year, and one or two shorter trips to the Bight of Abaco. By late

July the season was over. Sometimes the profits were good, on rare occasions they were very good, but more often sponging produced only a subsistence wage. In spite of this, sponging was an important part of the economy of Abaco because it sustained the economy for such a long period of time (c. 1850-1920) and was the leading "export" sector during a shorter period around the turn of the century. Also, it provided greater impetus for the growing boat building industry of Abaco than did pineapple or citrus cultivation. Although cargo schooners were built to transport the fruit grown during the 1880s, the burgeoning sponge industry of 1890-1910 created greater demand for a greater number of boats and dinghies, which provided work for the boat builders of Abaco and spread the money earned throughout the communities. Sponging peaked in the Bahamas in 1905, when almost 1½ million pounds of sponges were exported. The industry declined gradually during the two decades following World War I.

The period during which pineapple cultivation declined and sponging increased is the same period during which New Plymouth experienced a gradual decline and Hope Town rose to greater significance, though Hope Town's rise was based on more than just sponging. In 1887 pineapples still headed the list of commodities shipped from the Hope Town district; they accounted for 74% of all exports. In contrast, sponges accounted for only 21%, with oranges, bananas, sugar, syrup, shells and coral making up the balance of 5%. Hope Town had three large vessels engaged in trade with the United States—carrying fruit and shells to Jacksonville, Florida, and returning with lumber and provisions. The following year Hope Town was made a port of entry for the Bahamas, making it much more convenient for local people to engage in direct trade with the United States. Nine years later, in 1897, sponges accounted for 69% of exports, pineapples 4%, oranges 9%, sisal 15%, and turtle shell 2%, and the carpenters were busy during that year building four small schooners for sponging. Though Hope Town still had its ups and downs, the population of the district increased to almost 1200 by 1895 and its economy was fairly well diversified. The peak years were probably reached between 1910 and 1920, when the population of the town itself was about 700. Sponging was the single most important industry during most of these years. In 1912 Hope Town had 32 vessels engaged in sponging, and they realized between £19,000 and £20,000, but sponging was not a panacea, and in 1916 it produced only £5,000, a 70% decline from the production in 1912. Sponging was supplemented by sisal, the growing of cane sugar and the production of syrup, as well as by boat building, shipping and the timber industry.[17]

SISAL

Some countries discover a plant or a mineral resource which becomes their economic salvation—Virginia found tobacco, the forty-niners in California found gold. Pineapples, citrus fruit, and sponges provided sustenance for Abaconians during the late nineteenth century, but certainly did not offer economic salvation. Most Abaconians continued to live at or near the poverty line. During the late 1880s Governor Ambrose Shea became convinced that he had found a crop which would alter the economy of the Bahamas. It was sisal, and it turned out to be a flash in the pan.

Governor Shea was excited by sisal because the plant was very hardy and grew like a weed even in the thin soil and harsh environment of the Bahamas. The mature plant is about six feet in diameter and is hemispherical. Its long, sharply pointed leaves extend from a central core, and the plant resembles a pin cushion with the points sticking out rather than in. Beginning in the plant's fourth year, and continuing for a decade, the long leaves could be cut every six months. A soaking and beating process was used to separate the leaves' long fibre from the pulp. The dried sisal fibres could then be twisted into twine, and the twine could be made into rope. Although some rope was made in the Bahamas for local use, almost all Bahamian sisal was exported as raw fibre in bales. Sisal plants had been first introduced to the Bahamas in the 1840s. Sisal was grown for local use, not for export. During the 1880s rope and twine manufacturers in the United States imported fibres from Mexico (Yucatan) and the Philippine Islands. The United States had no domestic supply and no import duty for sisal. Governor Shea decided that a Bahamian sisal industry which could capture a sizeable portion of the United States market could provide a good living for many Bahamians. The industry would not be affected by the transportation problems which had plagued the export of perishable commodities such as citrus fruits and pineapples, and income from it would not be as subject to the vagaries of nature as income from sponging. Sisal grew in the Bahamas with little care. He believed that sisal was a "magic plant which would completely transform the Bahamian economy."[18] In 1889 legislation sponsored by Shea was passed which placed a 20% duty on sisal imports, provided a temporary one cent per pound bounty for domestic sisal production, and made land available on a special basis to Bahamians as well as foreign investors for cultivation of sisal.[19]

Large investments to clear land and to build sisal processing mills were made throughout the Bahamas. It was believed that the sale of the first years' cuttings (five years after the initial investment) would repay all of the investment, and that the sale of subsequent cuttings would be 100% profit. The optimism regarding sisal soon spread from Nassau to Abaco. Many field labourers residing in the Green Turtle Cay district found employment, and the people were said to be hopeful regarding the future. The Resident Justice at Cherokee reported that the land near Sweeting's Village and Crossing Rocks was "well adapted in every way to the growth of sisal," and that many plants were being developed in nurseries. The Resident Justice for Hope Town reported that the cultivation of sisal "has been largely engaged in" and that a foreign-owned company was establishing a sisal operation several miles south of Marsh Harbour.[20] Mills for processing sisal were eventually established at Marsh Harbour, Hope Town, Great Guana Cay, Cocoa Plum Creek, Little Abaco Island, and perhaps at Sandy Point. It was possible for small growers to clean the sisal by hand, but it was very time-consuming and usually yielded an inferior product. The largest investments in Abaco were made on Little Abaco Island, where the Munroe Fibre Company, the Sisal Fibre Company, and the Bahamas Fibre Company all had large operations. A short

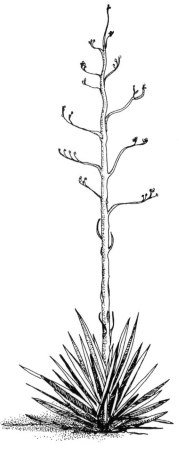

Sisal plant

railroad was built to transport the sisal, but by the middle 1890s some of the sisal operations had shut down because of low demand, low prices, low quality, and low or nonexistent profits.[21] In 1898 the market for sisal suddenly improved because the Spanish-American War prevented the United States from importing sisal from the Spanish-owned Philippines. Most Bahamian mills were reopened, and sisal production became the single most important industry in the Green Turtle Cay district in 1899. For once the Bahamas was doing the right thing at the right time. Production increased in the Hope Town district also, and Abaco provided almost half of the Bahamas' production of 400 tons.[22]

The acquisition of the Philippine Islands by the United States at the conclusion of the Spanish-American War gave the Philippine sisal industry privileged access to the United States market. Bahamian sisal was no longer in great demand; the mills again shut down and the sisal grew wild. Hand cleaning continued to provide a way for the poor to supplement their meager incomes, but the low quality of most of the fibre produced in this way further depreciated the reputation of Bahamian fibre in the United States market. This, of course, was not understood by the Abaconians, who were simply looking for a way to survive. In 1907 the Resident Justice at Green Turtle Cay explained that he continued to encourage sisal production in spite of its drawbacks because it was the most reliable form of income for a poor man. The Resident Justice from Cherokee lamented the fact that there was no small machine in his district to service the poor man. During the period before World War I the price fluctuated from one to two cents per pound. Few bothered to clean sisal when the price was down, but when the price went up the Commissioner at Hope Town reported that the town gained "quite a busy appearance."[23] The Bahamian sisal industry had a few good years during World War I, when internal disorders in Mexico interfered with production there. The price of sisal jumped as high as fourteen cents per pound, but during the 1920s the old pattern emerged again. By the 1930s sisal brought as little as one cent per pound, and the industry was finished.24

The nineteenth century way of life ended slowly in Abaco and lingered well into the twentieth century. Abaco had tried to change, but had not. Pineapples, sisal and sponges all failed to transform the economy and bring affluence to Abaco. In each case the reason for failure was beyond the control of Abaconians. While a significant portion of North America and Europe modernized and industrialized, Abaco stayed about the same.

END NOTES

[1] See Rawson W. Rawson, *Report on the Bahamas for the Year 1864*)London, 1866), p. 75, and An Act to Provide for Postal Communication between Nassau, Eleuthera, Harbour Island and Abaco, 30 Vic. c 18 (13 May 1867).

[2] Annual Colonial Report, 1898, in *Annual Colonial Reports, 1861-1907*, p. 256.

[3] See Rawson W. Rawson, *Report on the Bahamas for the Year 1864* (London, 1866), and Charles Ives, *The Isles of Summer* (New Haven, Conn.: 1880), pp. 33-35.

[4] This is true in regard to the Elbow Reef light, but a false Hole-in-the-Wall light could have caused a southbound ship to turn west too soon and hit the reef or Great Abaco Island.

[5] Quoted in Paul Albury, *The Story of the Bahamas*, p. 250.

[6] *Ibid.*, p. 135.

[7] For detailed discussions of the circumstances which led to the wreck of the *Adirondack*, see Haziel Albury, *Man-O-War: My Island Home* (Hockessin, Delaware: Holly, 1977), pp. 138-141, and *Official Records of the Union and Confederate Navies in the War of the Rebellion: Operations of the Cruisers*, Jan. 19, 1861 - Dec. 31, 1862, Series I, Vol. I. For information regarding the wreck of the *San Jacinto*, see Iris Lowe, "New Plymouth," *The Tribune* (Nassau), 17 February 1975, p. 5.

[8] Paul Albury, *The Story of the Bahamas*, p. 250.

[9] Governor Phenney, Description of Bahama Islands enclosed with letter of 2 March 1723, CO23/1 (Part 3)/16.

[10] Michael Craton, *A History of the Bahamas* (London: Collins, 1968), p. 248.

[11] Report of Resident Justice, Green Turtle Cay, 1897.

[12] In 1887 Hope Town district produced 51,000 dozen pineapples, valued at £5287, but in 1895 the crop yielded only £1022 and in 1912 only £35 (Reports of Resident Justices and Commissioner, Hope Town, 1887, 1895, 1912).

[13] Paul Albury, *The Story of the Bahamas*, p. 161.

[14] Eighty-five percent were produced by the Hope Town district. See Reports of Resident Justices, Hope Town and Green Turtle Cay, 1897.

1885- £860.10 Prosperity has not been better because sponging throughout season has almost proved a failure.

1886- sponging has not paid well

1887- £1518 sponging was better—18 schooners and slooops were involved in the industry.

1888- £1203.10

1895- £2005.4; increase over previous year

1896- £2507.5.6

1897- £3214.12

1908- sponging is main activity in district

1912- between £19,000 and £20,000; 32 vessels

1916- £5700

1918- more attention has been paid to soil as sponging and turtling have not been of much value in 1918; 25 vessels

1919- 24 vessels, good catches and good prices, but after deduction for the outfit I am afraid the figures did not look very handsome to the sponger.

1924- a few vessels in Marsh Harbour, but sponging is a thing of the past, inhabitants look upon it with scornful face, although whenengaged in it, district was more prosperous.

[15] The Resident Justices and Commissioners stationed at Hope Town assessed the sponge industry as follows in their reports written for the years indicated:

[16] For descriptions of sponging in Abaco and in the Bahamas see: Haziel L. Albury, *Man-O-War: My Island Home*, pp. 65-68; Sonny Cook, "The Abaco Scene in the Days of Yore," *Abaco Account*, III, 3 (April, 1966), 25-26; Paul Albury, *The Story of the Bahamas*, pp. 158-160; Michael Craton, *A History of the Bahamas*, pp. 252-255; and A. G. Esfakis, "We Had Sponges," in *Third World Group: Bahamas Independence Issue, 1973* (Nassau, 1973), 130-131.

[17] Reports of Resident Justices and Commissioners, Hope Town, 1887, 1897, 1912, 1916, 1918.

[18] Paul Albury, *The Story of the Bahamas*, p. 164.

[19] Michael Craton, p. 251, and Paul Albury, p. 164.

[20] Reports of Resident Justices at Green Turtle Cay, Cherokee, and Hope Town, 1889.

[21] The Resident Justice at Green Turtle Cay reported that two of the operations on Little Abaco Island appeared to be closed and the Resident Justice at Cherokee reported that there was no demand for sisal (Reports of Resident Justices at Green Turtle Cay and Cherokee, 1897 and 1895 respectively).

[22] The Green Turtle Cay district produced 160 tons, and the Hope Town district produced 38 tons. Bahamian production was 400 tons. See Reports of Resident Justices, Green Turtle Cay and Hope Town, 1899, and Craton, p. 251.

[23] Report of Resident Justice, Green Turtle Cay, 1907, Report of Commissioner, Cherokee, 1912, Report of Commissioner, Hope Town, 1912.

[24] Haziel Albury, *Man-O-War: My Island Home*, p. 70.

Chapter Five -

The Twentieth Century

There was one place in Abaco where the twentieth century came on time. It was not Hope Town or New Plymouth or Cooperstown or Marsh's Harbour—it was Wilson City. Named after Governor Sir William Grey-Wilson, Wilson City was on Spencer's Point not far from the old settlement of Sweeting's Village. Wilson City was a company lumber town built by the Bahamas Timber Company, a United States corporation which had acquired a 100-year timber license to cut the pine forests of Abaco, Andros, and Grand Bahama Islands.

Wilson City was a marvel in its time. Its heart was a modern saw mill operation and a huge steam derrick and a railroad to load and carry felled timber to the mill. Most of the lumber was shipped to Cuba, although some went to Nassau and some to the United States. Next to the saw mill the Bahamas Timber Company built a town to provide housing for workers and managers. All houses were supplied with electricity, and an ice plant produced as much as 1200 25-pound blocks of ice per day. Wilson City, Abaco, had electricity in 1908, the same year electrical service was initiated in Nassau. The company also built a store, and supplied it with an amazing array of goods from the United States unobtainable anywhere else in the Out Islands of the Bahamas. And Abaco's first tennis court was built in Wilson City. It must have seemed a miracle to Abaconians—a modern industry from the United States was building a state-of-the-art facility and community in their previously isolated corner of the world. They were to become part of the successful United States industrial revolution, be paid regular wages for regular work, receive some fringe benefits, and, in general, become part of the modern world.

Workers were attracted to Wilson City from all over Abaco. A Commissioner in Hope Town expressed concern that his district would be depopulated because of migration to Wilson City, and men from as far away as New Plymouth took jobs there. Some moved their families; others went to Wilson City alone and travelled home to visit every few months.[1] Wages paid at Wilson City were higher than those paid for similar work elsewhere in Abaco in order to attract workers. A white worker was paid 4s. per day (about $1. 00) compared to 2s. 6d. , which was the rate the colonial government paid those who worked on road repairs in Hope Town. This was a 60% premium. Black labourers made about 2s. per day. There were fringe benefits as well. Housing was provided at low rental cost, and the company employed a medical doctor whose services were provided for all company employees, apparently paid for through a payroll deduction plan, though medicine and special services were extra and had to be paid for with cash. Probably most important overall was the fact that Wilson City offered the first security of a regular job with regular wages. It was an attractive alternative to the unreliability of incomes gained by pineapple cultivation or sponging, which, as one man put it, was based on luck. Security and a regular income from a giant company which also provided electricity and ice was an attractive alternative to the old "conch" life-style, and convinced many Abaconians to move to Wilson City and the twentieth century.

Most Abaconians who had lived there had fond memories of it in the 1980s. Grisilda Bethel of Hope Town lived there when she was a girl, and still remembered it with delight seventy years later: "It was just like a city . . . had beautiful street lights . . . you could

The saw mill at Wilson City was built by the Bahamas Timber Company of St. Paul, Minnesota, and was in operation from 1908 to 1916. Photograph used with the permission of the Wyannie Malone Historical Museum.

The planing mill at Wilson City. Photograph provided by Gray Russell, former resident of Wilson City.

This locomotive, photographed on Grand Bahama Island, is very similar to those used at Wilson City, Abaco. Photograph provided by Gray Russell.

The pier at Wilson City with Lynyard Cay in the background. The boat in the foreground made regular trips to Cuba. Photograph provided by Gray Russell.

get all the ice you wanted . . . a great big piece for threepence." She also remembered that cloth was sold at the company store for 8d. per yard.[2] Reggie Malone remembered counting his father's weekly wages by stacking it in six stacks of 4s. each, and Alvard Bethel said his father, who was employed as a skilled carpenter, made 8s. per day (about $2.00). Alvard himself was employed in the drying kiln when he was eight years old; he was paid 2s. per day.[3] They all had positive memories of Wilson City; all believed it was the beginning of real modernization for Abaco.

The town was designed and built by the Bahamas Timber Company of St. Paul, Minnesota. It was not uncommon for United States corporations to build model communities during the late nineteenth and early twentieth centuries. Corporations believed they could extend their success to the communities around them. In a sense the model communities they built were devised to show that capitalism, which had led to the miraculous growth of the United States economy, could provide for its workers in a humane and beneficial way. They were capitalistic responses to the utopian socialist communities of the middle nineteenth century. They were built to reform and restructure society. In the case of Wilson City, construction of a new community was a necessity rather than just a social experiment; there was no other way to get workers to the mill. But the same paternalistic, capitalistic philosophy which led to Pullman, Illinois, inspired Wilson City, Abaco. The results were generally beneficial for Abaconians who enjoyed good wages and modern conveniences, but there were some disadvantages as well.

Working hours were long—ten hours per day—and there were six days in the work week. Children were employed. Some accused the company of neglecting safety—the Commissioner at Cherokee Sound reported thirty-one deaths versus thirteen births in his district in 1912 and said that "there would be a lessening of suffering" from accidents on the railroad if the men operating the locomotive knew how to bandage wounds. He also contended that nothing much had been accomplished at the Wilson City School. Because so many families in the community stayed there for such a short time—usually only a few months—the teacher could do little more than keep the children "out of harm's way."[4] In addition to these, there were other, more subtle, disadvantages of receiving modernization from one United States corporation.

The company sometimes demonstrated a very harsh and arrogant paternalism. Elijah Hallenbach was one of the principals in

Housing at Wilson City. The best housing was for foreigners and was located on the hill near the water tower (top). Housing for Bahamian whites was further down the hill and is shown on the left side of the same photo. The dormitory building in the middle photo was sometimes called the bachelor's quarters and was for men who came to Wilson City to work without their families. It provided meals as well as sleeping accomodations. Below is a photo of Jericho, the separate walled community for blacks. Photographs provided by Gray Russell.

the Bahamas Timber Company, and he made an exploratory tour of Abaco before Wilson City was built. He had a bad leg and had to be carried ashore to make his explorations. He told the Abaconian who carried him ". . . here I am hopping around on one leg just to keep you poor bitches from starving."[5]

The town was designed and built to reflect this industrialist's view of a proper social hierarchy. The foreigners, who consisted mostly of United States citizens from the Jacksonville, Florida, area, lived in rather large houses built on a hill with a commanding view of Spencer's Bight, the Sea of Abaco, and the Atlantic Ocean beyond Lynyard Cay. Their homes were reached via a wooden boardwalk. Each house had a porch with a railing and a separate kitchen structure on the other side of the boardwalk which was serviced, at its back, by an extension of the railroad from the general store and a small electric car which could be used to transport groceries and other goods. A few Bahamians lived in these homes—the captain of the tug boat lived in the first house along the boardwalk—but most were occupied by the foreign managers. White skilled and semiskilled workers lived along a street near the base of the hill called Rocky Road. The twelve to sixteen houses were smaller than those on the hill and apparently did not have detached kitchens. The road was made of crushed rock. Black workers outnumbered the whites. They lived in a segregated area out on the point near the dock. It was called Jericho, apparently because it was surrounded by a wall. The houses were arranged in three to four rows and were smaller. The streets were simply sand or dirt. "In other words, there were the foreigners, the coloureds, the whites—that was the separation," explained Alvard Bethel.[6] Wilson City was a segregated hierarchy of these three groups, with limited and controlled mixing of the groups. White children did not play with black children at Wilson City.

The idea of racial superiority was not brought to Abaco by the Bahamas Timber Company, but the company did come as the harbinger of modernization, yet its social impact reinforced the white Abaconian's prejudice against blacks. The whites certainly must have been pleased to discover that the great company from the United States supported their views. The company which modernized Abaco exploited children as well as blacks, and reinforced socially regressive concepts as well as providing ice and electricity. Its impact on Abaco was mixed.

The saw mill produced from fifteen to eighteen million board feet of lumber each year. By 1912 the average daily employment was 540 persons (about 12% of the population of Abaco), and the company paid £21,000 annually in wages to Bahamians. There were indirect benefits to the economy of Abaco as well. Because wage labourers at Wilson City did not have time to fish and farm as most Abaconians did, a significantly large market for food was created there. Other Abaconians supplied Wilson City with food and boats and other commodities, and the new money therefore found its way into many of the old communities.[7]

At the time most thought that Wilson City would last forever and the modernization would continue. But the mill, which was designed to produce about 30 million board feet of lumber per year, produced only 9 million board feet in 1916. Ice production was only 20 percent of the 1908 figure, and average daily employment was down to 375 from 540 in 1912. The company suffered a "disastrous" year in 1916 with "constant breaking down of machinery and locomotives, and failure of [the] water pipe which was laid down in September."[8] Reggie Malone was probably not far off the mark when he said that the entire scheme of the Bahamas Timber Company was "miscalculated—the timber wasn't there to cut for any length of time."[9] The railroad had to be constantly extended to bring timber greater distances to the mill. This, and the deterioration of the original machinery, raised costs and caused production declines. The Commissioner at Cherokee feared that a shutdown would be a "hard knock" for Abaco and all the Bahamas. In addition to the loss of the jobs and salaries which the company had provided, he lamented the loss of a source of low-priced lumber. He believed many Bahamians had been able to build homes which would have been beyond their means were it not for the Bahamas Timber Company. As he feared, the mill did close at the end of 1916, but the lumber industry in Abaco was not dead.

Within a couple of years another lumber camp called Norman's Castle was built. It was located on the west side of Abaco opposite Cocoa Plum Creek. By 1925 twelve million board feet of lumber were exported, and the commissioner at Green Turtle Cay reported that the majority of the male population in his district—400 men—worked at Norman's Castle. The company built 250 houses, a railroad to move timber to the mill, and employed a doctor who was "kept busy most of the time, as accidents occur frequently." In 1926 two men died because of crushed legs in railroad accidents. Fish were sold at Norman's Castle at exorbitant prices, and Cedar Harbour and Cooperstown profitably supplied the settlement with sweet potatoes. About 75% of the crime in the Green Turtle Cay district occurred at Norman's Castle—not too shocking a statistic for a boom town which employed more than half the men in the district. Like Wilson City, Norman's Castle was a passing phenomenon. When the best timber in the immediate area was exhausted, the Abaco Lumber Company[10] moved the operation and utilized portable saw mills. In 1936 only 3. 2 million board feet of lumber were produced because the mill was moved during the year. During the early 1940s lumber was shipped from Cornwall and Cross Harbour, both of which were located southwest of the site of Wilson City. In 1944 the company moved all its operations from Abaco to Pine Ridge on Grand Bahama Island. Two years later that operation was purchased by Wallace Groves, formerly guilty of mail fraud in the United States. and future developer of Freeport on Grand Bahama Island. Lumber operations were the first economic pursuit in Abaco which involved large investments of foreign capital and which operated for a significant period of time. In many ways they were the harbinger of the future, though by the late 1940s they were regarded as part of the past in Abaco.

World War I occurred during Wilson City's waning years, and it came as a shock to Abaconians. Britain had not been involved in a major European war for ninety-nine years. Though the war and the reasons it was fought had little direct relevance for Abaconians, they rose to the occasion and loyally supported the British effort. Perhaps the most significant effect of the war, in Abaco, was that the scarcity of shipping caused a dramatic increase in freight rates, which encouraged the construction of large lumber-carrying schooners. The *Abaco* (266 tons) was launched in 1917, and the *Abaco, Bahamas* (484 tons) was launched in 1922. The price of

PRINCIPAL LUMBER CAMPS IN ABACO

NORMAN'S CASTLE

WILSON CITY

CORNWALL

CROSS HARBOUR

sponges and sisal also went up during the war years, though the cause of the increase for sisal was an internal revolution in Mexico rather than the World War. When the conflict was over the Commissioner at New Plymouth patriotically rejoiced:

> In conclusion I cannot refrain from saying that the people of this district rejoice that Peace is once again settling down over the World and we all feel proud that the Union Jack still floats proudly in the breeze in every clime—untarnished despite the machinations of its enemies and may it always stand in the future as it has done in the past especially in the titanic struggle of the past four years a shield for the weak and defenseless against any mighty and arrogant oppressor. God save the King. [11]

The end of the war brought a reduction in shipping rates which made some of the recently built lumber schooners uneconomic, and sponge and sisal prices returned to their low prewar levels. The tomato became the boom crop of the 1920s. It grew reasonably well in the sandy Bahamian soil, and, though shipping to market was still a problem, small steam or diesel freighters could and sometimes did get tomatoes to New York in good condition. In 1923 tomatoes ranked second on the list of Bahamian exports behind sponges, which were still number one. In Abaco tomato cultivation got off to a slow start and experienced an early death. It was "attempted" at Hope Town, Man-0-War, and Great Guana in 1925, and a "very small shipment" was sent to Nassau. In 1926 tomatoes were reportedly doing well, but then were "swept away" by a hurricane. In 1929 the United States government placed a duty of 1½ cents per pound on imported tomatoes to protect farmers in Florida, and tomato cultivation for export in the Bahamas died the same way that pineapple cultivation had. [12]

Nassau prospered during the 1920s by exporting a product which did not have to be grown, caught, or mined—liquor. While prohibition was in effect in the United States (1920-1933) liquor was brought to Nassau in large quantities and then illegally "run" into the United States. Some Abaco men were probably involved in this lucrative trade, but most of the profits stayed in Nassau. A. I. Bethel of Hope Town was a young man then and had experience at sea, but he turned down an offer of a job on a bootlegging voyage. Perhaps he did so because he preferred a quiet, law-abiding life in Hope Town to the excitement of rum-running from Nassau to the United States. He said, "I might be one of the unlucky ones, and be shot or arrested." [13]

Despite Wilson City and Norman's Castle and railroads and electricity, Abaco had not really entered the world of the twentieth century even by 1920. The lumber camps were anomalies. They were foreign and they were temporary. They did not permanently alter life in Abaco. The isolation of Abaco was still extreme. There was virtually no direct contact with any place outside of Abaco except for Nassau, Jacksonville (Florida), and a couple of ports in Cuba. All of these shipping routes were serviced by sailing vessels. The mailboat, which was the principal contact with Nassau, was the *Albertine Adoue*, a sixty-foot schooner. In 1922 a Hope Town Commissioner complained about the service:

> It is impossible in these progressive days to expect a mail service to be satisfactorily performed by a sailing vessel. Apart from speed there is no comfort nor privacy to be obtained for passengers, and it is to be hoped in the near future that something more modern and serviceable will take the place of this wind jammer. [14]

In 1923 the hopes of the Commissioner were fulfilled when the *Priscilla*, a 100-foot steel-hulled converted sailing vessel powered by a 115 horsepower Fairbanks Morse diesel was placed on the Abaco route. Some said she was an old America's Cup defender. [15]

The advent of power mail service between Abaco and Nassau was of great importance. It significantly reduced the degree of Abaco's isolation and made commerce more feasible. During the same year or during the following year, wireless telegraph service was initiated between Hope Town and Nassau. The Commissioner called it the "greatest boon bestowed on Hope Town and its nearby settlements."[16] Two way communication with Nassau which in 1920 required at least two weeks if the wind and seas were favorable, could be accomplished in a matter of minutes by 1925. It was also possible for Hope Towners to listen to telegraphic news broadcasts and to learn of developments throughout the world on the same day they occurred, rather than getting the information two weeks to two months after the events. People residing at Marsh Harbour or Man-0-War or Great Guana could sail to Hope Town and gain contact with the entire world.

The introduction of the wireless and the initiation of diesel mail and freight service were dramatic changes for Abaco. Combined with the advent of an export lumber industry, they seemed to signal the arrival of Abaco into what the rest of the world called the twentieth century. Real change, however, did not occur. Life went on much as it had been before. Abaconians lived by sponging,

Abaco's early twentieth-century mailboats: The *Albertine Adoue* (top), the *Priscilla* (middle), and the *Stede Bonnet* (bottom). Photographs used with the permission of the Albert Lowe Museum (for the *Albertine Adoue*) and the Wyannie Malone Historical Museum.

fishing, or boat building, or by growing citrus or sisal or subsistence crops. Life was simple and most people were poor. There was no electricity, no refrigeration, and there were no power boats except for the *Priscilla*, which, it was soon discovered, was no panacea. In 1926 the *Priscilla* omitted stopping at East Marsh Harbour when it was behind schedule and fruit was left on the dock there to rot.[17] Abaco had made some gains and some changes had occurred, but neither the economy nor the life-style was radically transformed. In 1930 Abaco was much more similar to the Abaco of 1880 than it was to the Abaco which would exist in 1980. The big changes for Abaconians still lay in the future.

Though few realized it at the time, foreigners and tourism were to play an important part in the future of Abaco. The construction of vacation homes by people from the United States, Canada, and Britain, and the involvement of foreigners in agricultural schemes, began during the 1920s. A retired doctor from the United States purchased a tract of land near the entrance to Marsh Harbour and built a house on it in 1925. During the same year several cays and some acreage on Great Abaco Island were sold to foreigners. One migrant from the United States started a small farm on which he raised poultry and grew citrus and bananas. The Commissioner at Hope Town rejoiced in all of this, and predicted growth for tourism as he extolled the virtues of Abaco's harbours, fishing and wild boar hunting. His description of Hope Town's assets reads like an advertisement written for the 1990s:

> To those in search of health and others anxious for quiet, will find both at HOPE TOWN under the shade of waving coconut palms, which flank the eastern side of the Island facing the Atlantic Ocean, only to be disturbed by the waves as they burst against the rocks or roll up along the beaches of 'Pink Sand' which offer opportunities for delightful and refreshing bathing throughout the year."[18]

The isolation of Abaco caused it to be by-passed by economic modernization, but its isolation also insulated it from the worldwide depression of the 1930s. Abaconians were, for the most part, outside the market economy, and it was the market economy that was adversely affected by the depression. Abaconians had no jobs to lose and owned no securities which became worthless. In Abaco life went on as before—almost everyone was still poor. In some societies the 1930s were dominated by depression, new deals, or by the rise of fascist groups to power; in Abaco the most important events of the decade were the end of sponging, the advent of crawfishing, and one of the worst hurricanes of the twentieth century.

There was no easy money to be made by sponging, but it still provided a living for many Abaconians during the 1930s. Good years became more scarce because overfishing and hurricane damage had depleted some of the best sponge beds of the Bahamas. Cultivation of sponges, accomplished by cutting a mature specimen into several pieces and tying each one to a rock, was initiated. Abaconians were hopeful this effort would be successful, but then, in 1938 and 1939, a fungus of unknown origin spread throughout all the sponge beds of the entire western Atlantic Ocean and killed 90% of all the sponges. The sponge population gradually recovered to a level adequate to support commercial exploitation again by the 1960s, but the modern sponge fisherman had to compete with less expensive plastic (cellulose) sponges, which depressed demand and prices for natural sponges. Only the poorest people in the poorest settlements were still engaged in sponging during the 1970s. The industry, which had been the bread and butter for many Bahamians for many years, was gone.

The crawfish, or spiny lobster, had been part of the Bahamian diet for a long time, but it wasn't until the middle 1930s that anyone tried to export them to the United States. Captain Eddie Sawyer of Marsh Harbour was the first. He bought crawfish from fishermen in Abaco and carried them to Florida in a fifty-foot boat with a live well. There he sold them for about three cents apiece. The Abaconians from whom he bought crawfish caught them in the traditional manner with a dinghy, a water glass, a tickler, and a bully net. Crawfish were more plentiful "down the cays" than they were in the areas near Elbow Cay or Green Turtle Cay, so fishermen from Hope Town and New Plymouth camped on cays such as Allans and Grand during the fall and winter crawfishing season. They lived in thatched roof huts and kept their crawfish in ice boxes until they were picked up by a large boat and taken to Florida. The men were paid about two cents for each crawfish. In 1936 the development of the crawfishing industry was described as "phenomenal"—in the Green Turtle Cay district alone 200 men were involved in it and there were five local boats engaged in transporting the crawfish to the United States.[19] The beginning of commercial crawfishing helped to offset the losses suffered as a result of the end of commercial sponging.

Hurricanes have been as much a part of Bahamian life as sponges and crawfish. They are circular storms which are usually several hundred miles in diameter. No one knows exactly how hurricanes

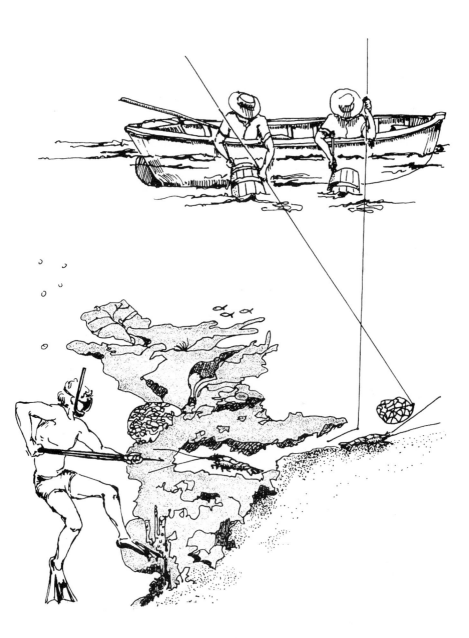

Until recently Bahamians caught crawfish from a dinghy using water glasses, a tickler, and a bully net. The modern technique is to use a mask, fins, a snorkle, and a Hawaiiian sling.

are formed; each storm is unique and the birth process varies from one storm to another. Two factors seem to be essential—the temperature of the sea water must be 79 degrees Fahrenheit or warmer, and there must be some form of atmospheric disturbance to begin the process. The disturbance which spawns the hurricane is sometimes an unstable trough of low pressure air embedded in the normal easterly trade wind flow, or it can be an area of low pressure spun off from the intertropical convergence zone where the prevailing winds of the northern and southern hemispheres meet (sometimes called the doldrums). A third possible nucleus around which a hurricane can form is a low pressure area consisting of the remnants of a polar trough which fractured as it moved southward into the tropics. If various other criteria are fulfilled, cyclonic flow (counter clockwise in the northern hemisphere) develops around the low pressure area, and warm, moist air from the surface of the sea rises, shedding its moisture as it is cooled by rising. The air spirals upward around the center, or "eye, " the edge of which serves as a chimney for updrafts. This causes even more intense low pressure in the eye and therefore more intense

A hurricane

cyclonic flow around the eye. It is called a tropical storm until the wind speed reaches seventy-five miles per hour, when it becomes a hurricane. The storm is sustained by a continual supply of warm moist air which is cooled when it is spiraled upward. When the hurricane moves over land or cooler water this supply is cut off. The cooler air cannot rise as rapidly or as high around the eye. This causes the cyclonic action to slow down and the hurricane dies.

Hurricanes normally form in the tropical zone during August, September, and October, and they move in a northwesterly direction toward North America. The Bahamas frequently lie in their path. On 21 October 1926, a very devastating hurricane hit Abaco. The three-masted schooner *Abaco, Bahamas* broke loose from her mooring in Marsh Harbour and was stranded on one of the small cays in the harbour. She was never refloated. Another three-masted lumber schooner, the *Abaco,* was blown ashore at Hope Town. In a delightful example of innocent double entendre, the Hope Town Commissioner wrote:

> The Marsh Harbour library has had a set back on account of the Public Building where it is kept having been swept from Its foundation and carried to a distance of 600 feet at back of settlement where it still rests In the swamp. [20]

In 1932 another hurricane struck Abaco. At Man-O-War Cay houses were blown from their ground pins and roofs were blown from houses. The government, as was usual after a hurricane, sent medical aid and also assisted the residents in the reconstruction of their homes.[21] Some of the black settlements on Abaco had also suffered extreme damage, and the government also provided assistance, but the assistance did not include provision for rebuilding the towns. Instead the government decided to resettle the residents of several of these communities on the outskirts of Marsh Harbour. Residents of Cornish Town and Old Place were offered five acre tracts and assistance in building homes at a new settlement which was laid out just to the west of Marsh Harbour. It was called Dundas Town in honour of C. C. Dundas, Governor of the Bahamas from 1937 to 1940. When this resettlement scheme was judged a success, a second settlement, Murphy Town, was established northwest of Dundas Town. Stone houses were built there for the former residents of Bluff Point. The new town was named for Sir William Murphy, Governor of the Bahamas from 1945 to 1950. One of the original settlers of Dundas Town explained the

Hope Town shortly after the 1932 hurricane. Photograph taken by Hartley Key and provided courtesy of Iris Lowe and the Wyannie Malone Historical Museum.

origin of Murphy Town: "Our chances were running good, so they decided to come too."[22]

The resettlement schemes were successes. The government provided a nursery staffed by an agricultural officer to promote the development of farming. Many of the homesteaders were able to grow most of their own food, and surplus products could be sold easily in nearby Marsh Harbour. Some of the new migrants were absorbed into the Marsh Harbour labour market. The schemes effectively helped those who had lost their homes as a result of the hurricane and also were beneficial for Abaco. They consolidated the population, making public administration easier, and they increased the size and viability of the economic unit at Marsh Harbour. By 1958 the population of the Marsh Harbour area was just over 600 people, with 55% living in Dundas Town and Murphy Town.

The decade of the 1940s was one of striking contrasts in Abaco. Some local boys went off to help fight the war. This broadened their horizons, as well as those of many other Abaconians, who took pride in the fact that Abaco was playing a role, however small, in world affairs. New technology was introduced. The first radios were brought to Man-O-War Cay during World War II, and the first refrigerator, a kerosene burner, arrived there in 1949.[23] Ba-

Bahamas Airways Catalina in Hope Town harbour. Photo courtesy of Dave Gale.

hamas Airways Limited initiated the first scheduled air service between Abaco and Nassau in 1947. Seaplanes landed at Marsh Harbour, Hope Town, Man-0-War, Great Guana, and Cherokee Sound. The service commenced with four and eight place planes, but soon utilized a Catalina with twenty-one seats. Despite these advances, Abaco still did not change very much. Abaco dinghies were still the basic mode of transportation, there were no automobiles, and although Abaco had power mailboat service, Captain Sherwin Archer of Marsh Harbour supplemented the regular service beginning in 1940 with his sponging sloop, the *Arena*. When he stopped at settlements in Abaco he took orders "for anyone who wanted anything from a thimble to a sewing machine, a pound of nails to an anchor, . . . a pair of sunglasses to a wedding ring!"[24] Captain Archer purchased the items in Nassau, and delivered them when he returned to Abaco. He provided a service similar to that provided by Sears and Roebuck in rural parts of the United States during the 1920s. After several years the *Arena* acquired an auxiliary engine, and in 1950 she was replaced with the *M. V. Tropical Trader*. This marked the end of regular freight service between Abaco and Nassau under sail.

During the 1950s Abaco was reasonably prosperous. Larger numbers of foreigners visited Abaco and an increasing number of

Captain Sherwin Archer's converted sponge sloop Arena was the last vessel which made regular commercial runs to Nassau under sail. She was replaced in about 1950. Photograph used with permission of Ruth Rodriguez, © 1978, all rights reserved.

them built vacation homes there, providing employment for carpenters and caretakers. Crawfishing continued to be very lucrative, and many who were engaged in other activities during the spring and summer dropped everything to go crawfishing when the season opened in August. There were some important agricultural developments. J. B. Crockett, a retired industrialist from the United States who had built a house in Marsh Harbour, started a farm of several hundred acres which he called Heveatex Plantation. A wide variety of crops were grown, including strawberries, paw paws, bananas, cucumbers, cantaloupes, Irish potatoes, pineapples, and citrus fruits. Most of the produce was shipped to Nassau. Despite this operation, the Commissioner at Hope Town reported that agriculture was the weak link in the economy and that the diet of Abaconians was a monotonous combination of rice or other starch foods and fish.

Fishing was most important and most profitable at Cherokee, where fifty-six men worked seven smacks. In 1957 they caught fish valued at £20, 000. This was almost double the estimated value of the crawfish catch for the entire Hope Town district, which involved 185 men. There were over sixty ship's carpenters in the Hope Town district in 1957. They built dinghies for the local market, and occasionally built a smack boat. Some of the boatbuilders were increasingly involved in building small yachts for purchase by people from the United States. The improvements in the economy were modest, but almost everyone in Abaco felt their impact.

The population of Abaco during the late 1950s was about 3600—the same as it was during the 1880s. There had been significant fluctuations during that seventy-year period, despite the fact that the beginning and ending numbers are equal. The population reached a peak of about 4500 in 1912-1913, when Wilson City was in full operation. After 1916, when Wilson City shut down and it was more difficult to make a living in Abaco than it had been, people moved to Nassau or to Miami or Key West where there were jobs available. The end result was that the population fell to what it had been before Wilson City and stayed at that level through the 1950s. During the 1960s dramatic changes took place in Abaco and new economic opportunities caused migration to Abaco. Some who had left now returned, and some came from elsewhere in the Bahamas. The developments which caused this change were the growth of tourism, perhaps best represented by the construction of a large new resort hotel complex at Sand Banks Cay, and a large new timber operation run by the Owens-Illinois Corporation. By 1970 the population of Abaco had almost doubled; there were 6,507 people living in Abaco.

The first tourist hotels in Abaco opened during the middle 1950s. They were typically quite small and were developed by foreigners, who, because they understood the United States market, were first to realize the potential of Abaco as a tourist resort. The New Hope Lodge near Hope Town opened in 1954, and by 1960 there were several other hotels in operation, including the Great Abaco Club (Marsh Harbour), the Bluff House (Green Turtle Cay), the Great Guana Resort, the New Plymouth Inn, and the Hope Town Harbour Lodge. These hotels provided a new source of employment for Abaconians, and the increased flow of tourists opened up new opportunities for everyone from fishing guides and taxi drivers to storekeepers and outboard motor mechanics. The development of subdivisions for sale of lots to foreigners provided additional employment in the construction trades. The advent of tourism clearly diversified the economy of Abaco.

The largest single development catering to tourists involved the construction of a resort hotel complex at Sand Banks Cay about twenty miles north of Marsh Harbour and very close to the site of the original loyalist settlement of Carleton. Development of this area was Leonard Thompson's idea. He was from Hope Town. He had flown for the Royal Canadian Air Force during World War II and he flew for Bahamas Airways after the war. During the late 1950s Thompson acquired a conditional purchase lease on a substantial amount of land on Sand Banks Cay. The area is one of great natural beauty. A sand bank stretches from the mainland of Abaco about two miles to Whale Cay, providing brilliant color variations as the sunlight penetrates the shallow water. A crescent-shaped beach borders the north side of Sand Banks Cay—it is probably one of the most beautiful beaches in the Bahamas. Because he lacked the investment capital required to develop the land, he joined with R. E. Dumas Milner, a real estate developer from Jackson, Mississippi. Channels were dredged, roads and docks were built, and a hotel building was completed in late 1961. Just before the hotel was to open, it burned to the ground. Rebuilt on the same site, a new hotel operated in 1963. During the remainder of the 1960s villas were built near the hotel for sale to private owners, a marina was opened, and an eighteen-hole golf course was built, no mean task in an environment which does not favor the cultivation of grass. Tennis courts, a small shopping center, a church, and a library were eventually added. Lots were sold for the construction of private homes. The small airport the government had built to service Green Turtle Cay was enlarged. The name of the entire area was changed, unfortunately, to "Treasure Cay" in order to appeal to consumers and tourists from the United States. The beautiful and geographically descriptive name of Sand Banks Cay passed from use.

The second development which changed Abaco during the 1960s was the pulpwood timber operation of the Owens-Illinois Corporation. Owens-Illinois gained access to the pine forests of Abaco by acquiring National Container Corporation during the middle 1950s. National Container held the 100-year timber license which had been originally granted to the Bahamas Timber Company shortly after the turn of the century and had later been transferred to the Abaco Lumber Company. Owens-Illinois is in the container and packaging business and was interested in Abaco's pine forests not for lumber, but for pulpwood. The task of cutting timber from all over Great Abaco Island and transporting it to Jacksonville, Florida, was a massive one. Owens-Illinois rose to the challenge by investing huge sums of money in Abaco beginning in 1959. A channel was dredged and a shipping terminal built at Snake Cay, about six miles south of Marsh Harbour. The old Hudson River side-wheeler, the *Robert Fulton*, was moved to Snake Cay to house administrative offices, a clinic, a school, and some of the employees. Worker housing was later built at Snake Cay and an airport was built just south of Marsh Harbour. Land-based air transport soon replaced the seaplanes of Bahamas Airways. The government of the Bahamas moved the Commissioner's seat from Hope Town to Marsh Harbour in order to provide easier access to government services for Owens-Illinois. Hope Town resented the move, but so did Marsh Harbour, which "naturally resented any possible yoke on its former independence."[25]

Owens-Illinois built the first major highway on Great Abaco Island to allow transportation of logs to Snake Cay for export. The highway linked the various communities of Great Abaco by land for the first time, and therefore opened Abaco to the automobile age. There were only two licensed automobiles in Abaco in 1959; thirteen years later in 1972 there were over 2000.[26] No society has ever adjusted to the automobile without pain. Abaco was no exception, and probably suffered more than most because the automobile was introduced so rapidly to people who previously had so little contact with it. Many Abaconians, who were more used to boats and wide expanses of water than to cars and narrow roads, apparently had difficulty adjusting to traffic regulations. In 1960 the Commissioner at Marsh Harbour complained that Abaconians viewed the motor car as a new toy, that accidents were never reported as was required by law, and that some people simply parked their cars in the middle of the road. He also reported that:

> One young man last year obtained pleasure by driving down the narrow front road at 40 m. p. h. firing a pistol above his head from sheer joie de vivre.[27]

Owens-Illinois transformed Abaco in other ways as well. At the peak of their activity they employed over 1000 people in Abaco. Half of their employees were Bahamians.[28] Many moved to Abaco from other islands in search of employment, and Marsh Harbour became a veritable boom town, with Barclay's Bank, the Canadian

Imperial Bank of Commerce, and Chase Manhattan Bank all open-
ing up branches in the town within a couple of blocks of each
other. Supermarkets replaced small grocery stores. The pulpwood
operation provided jobs for those who wanted them, and the increased flow of people and money provided markets for crops and
fish as well as other goods and services. The principal problem
with the operation as far as Abaco was concerned was that it was
not permanent. Cutting was scheduled to last about ten years,
until 1969, when it was expected that the usable trees would be
gone. The company left five prime seed bearing trees on each acre
so the forest could replenish itself, but recognized that commercial exploitation would not be possible again until sometime after
the year 2000. As the end of the pulpwood cutting operation approached, Owens-Illinois looked for other ways to utilize its investment in roads, buildings, and labour in Abaco.

After substantial research and evaluation by independent professional consultants, Owens-Illinois decided to build a sugar plantation in Abaco. The company was aware of the fact that the soil of
Abaco was thin and lacked the nutrients necessary for intensive
agriculture, but it planned to add the required nutrients to the soil
by fertilizing. Abaco was only to provide space, sunshine, and fifty
inches of rainfall each year. One group of experts reported that
tests with sugar cane produced results ". . . beyond their wildest
expectations."[29] The political climate in the Caribbean area and its
economic results may well have influenced Owens-Illinois' decision as much as the guaranteed
sunshine and rainfall in Abaco.
Fidel Castro had gained control
of Cuba in 1959, and in 1960 the
United States discontinued purchases of Cuban sugar because of
Castro's expropriation of petro-
leum refineries owned by United
States' companies. This provided
opportunities for other sugar
growers to fill the gap created by
the United States' boycott of Cuban sugar. Also, the sugar quota
system used by the government
of the United States to regulate
sugar imports could guarantee a
market to any country or com-

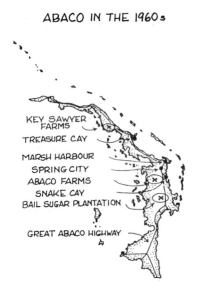

ABACO IN THE 1960s

KEY SAWYER
FARMS
TREASURE CAY
MARSH HARBOUR
SPRING CITY
ABACO FARMS
SNAKE CAY
BAIL SUGAR PLANTATION

GREAT ABACO HIGHWAY

pany which could gain a quota. Owens-Illinois sought and received an initial 10,000 ton sugar quota from the government of the United States. The company looked forward to continued utilization of its investments in Abaco and supplying a guaranteed market in the United States. The prospects for Owens-Illinois and for Abaco looked very good.

Owens-Illinois exchanged the 100-year timber license for title to 50,000 acres of crown land located inland from Snake Cay. This grant of crown land was supplemented by smaller private acquisitions. A subsidiary of Owens-Illinois called Bahamas Agricultural Industries Limited (BAIL) was established to run the sugar operation. Heavy equipment was moved in to level the land and pulverize some of the limestone in order to make the land more suitable for the growing of cane. The plantation which was built soon became the largest agricultural development in the Bahamas—the fields were two to three miles wide and seventeen miles long. A permanent town for workers was built at Spring City, about halfway between Marsh Harbour and Snake Cay. It had schools, a fresh water system, an electric generating plant, and a sewage treatment facility. Housing for executives was built at Casuarina Point, several miles south of Snake Cay. A sugar refinery with a capacity of 50,000 tons per year was built near Snake Cay, and Bahamian workers were sent to Louisiana and Guyana for training. BAIL's investment was large, but so were the hopes for the future of sugar production in Abaco.

Cane was first harvested and sugar exported in 1969 and 1970, but the yield per acre was substantially lower than what had been anticipated. Only 15,000 tons were produced in 1969 and only 19,000 tons in 1970. In November 1970, Owens-Illinois announced that it had sustained losses of over ten million dollars during the first two years of operation, and that although continuing improvements in productivity were anticipated, it could not afford to continue the enterprise. The 1971 crop was not to be harvested, but the fields and the facilities were to be maintained while a buyer was sought. The entire operation, including the plantation, the mill, the port facilities, and the worker communities, was offered for sale.

Some other efforts to develop agriculture in Abaco have met with greater success than those of Owens-Illinois. The experimental Heveatex Plantation established by J. B. Crockett in the 1950s led to larger operations by 1960 run by Abaco Farms Limited (also known as Scott and Mattson Farms). Abaco Farms produced tomatoes and cucumbers, but normally had difficulty competing in the United States market because of import duty levied in order to protect farmers in Florida from foreign competition. During years when Florida suffered from severe winters with hard frosts, however, the inflated prices resulting from the scarcity of produce such as cucumbers and tomatoes made it easy for crops grown in Abaco to be very competitive and even to capture a good share of the United States' market. In 1962 Abaco Farms had a very good year because a harsh winter caused widespread damage to the cucumber crop in the United States. The Commissioner at Marsh Harbour proudly reported that at one point during the year Abaco and Andros supplied 90% of all the cucumbers sold in the United States.[30] Many of the tomatoes grown on the farm were canned in Abaco for export to Canada and Great Britain.

These agricultural developments, as well as the timbering operation of Owens-Illinois, relied heavily on imported labour for both supervisors and manual labourers. Supervisory personnel came primarily from the United States. Manual labourers came from the Turks and Caicos Islands or from Haiti. Owens-Illinois employed a substantial number of Turks Islanders as labourers in its pulpwood operation. Many of these people worked for Owens-Illinois on Grand Bahama Island before moving to Abaco, and moved on to Andros Island after the Abaco forests were exhausted. The Turks and Caicos Islands lie to the southeast of the Bahamas and were separated from the Bahamas in 1848. They are a colony of Great Britain whose principal industries, salt production and fishing, cannot support the population. Most of the agricultural labourers in Abaco came from Haiti. They migrated to the Bahamas to find jobs and to escape from the extreme poverty and political repression which has plagued Haiti for many years. The per capita income in Haiti was only $58 per year in 1961. The nation was controlled by the Duvalier family for twenty-five years and no political opposition was permitted. Jean Claude Duvalier inherited the position of President for life from his father, Papa Doc, in 1971. Haitians were attracted to agricultural jobs in Abaco because the pay was much more than they could earn in Haiti. These jobs, which involved heavy manual labour in the fields, were shunned by both white and black Bahamians, who favored other kinds of work. Some Haitians brought their families with them; others sent money home to support them. Most entered the Bahamas illegally and most were exploited in one way or another.

Haitians came to Abaco in a variety of ways. Some passed through Nassau and rode the mailboat to Abaco; others came direct from Haiti. The total distance from Port-au-Prince, Haiti, to Marsh Harbour is about 625 miles. Often the vessels which carried them were overloaded, and the conditions on board were uncomfortable as well as unsafe. The Commissioner at Marsh Harbour in 1960 referred to the traffic as a minor form of slavetrading and reported that seventy Haitians brought to Abaco on the *M. V. Doris Davis* had been deprived of food for four days.[31] Most Haitians avoided proper immigration procedures, but some employers deducted £10 ($28.) from each new Haitian's salary to pay the Bahamian entry fee. In many cases the employer did not forward the fee and the papers to the immigration authorities, so the Haitians were still illegal immigrants, though £10 poorer.[32] The salaries earned by Haitians in Abaco, though much better than what they could earn in Haiti, were only about $33. per week in 1960. They lived in company housing. During the early 1960s there were about 1000 Haitians in Abaco, comprising up to 20% of the population. Occasionally there were strikes. In 1964 there were two strikes at Owens-Illinois. The Commissioner described them as "illegal" and "unfortunate."[33] In 1965 there was another illegal strike, and eleven Owens-Illinois workers were sentenced to six months hard labour as a result. The grievances of the Haitians who struck Scott and Mattson Farms during the same year speak for themselves in regard to the wretchedness of the living and working conditions of the Haitians. The workers complained of the fact that no first aid station existed, and the company responded that the first aid station which had existed was abused because large numbers of workers reported sick each day. The company had solved this problem by eliminating the first aid station and therefore the availability of medical care for its Haitian employees. The Haitians also complained of the lack of toilet facilities at the farm settlement, which had only one toilet for every 200 residents. The company refused to meet with the Haitian committee, but agreed to build more toilets and to provide transportation to Marsh Harbour once a week, a response to another Haitian grievance. The company refused to increase wages. The Commissioner at Marsh Harbour was sympathetic with the Haitians and reported that "Scott and Mattson Farms are not dealing with the problem intelligently." He described the owners and managers of Scott and Mattson Farms as men "steeped in the tradition of the southern states of America where there is unlimited evidence of the inability to adjust to the emancipation of the coloured people."[34] Despite these expressions of sympathy, little was done to alleviate the exploitation of the Haitians, who continued to be illegal, officially unwanted, but apparently necessary labourers.

Haitian workers, tourists, and Owens-Illinois were not the only new ingredients in the Abaco of the 1960s. The heightened prosperity of many Abaconians provided them with the means to import more manufactured items from the United States, and the improvements in communications provided them with the desire for the acquisition of the machinery and conveniences of modern industrial society. Electric washing machines, refrigerators, motor bikes, and other items appeared during the 1950s and 1960s, but no device changed the life style of the Abaconians as much as the outboard motor. In the United States the outboard motor industry services a primarily recreational market; in Abaco it revolutionized local transportation, and its impact, in some communities, has been greater than that of the automobile. During the 1950s sailing dinghies started to give way to dinghies equipped with small Stuart-Turner or Briggs and Stratton inboard engines, and by the end of the decade some dinghies were fitted with small outboard motors. Although these powered dinghies were not much faster than the sailing models, they could go directly to windward instead of tacking back and forth, and they were not impeded by calms. By the 1960s planing speedboats with larger outboard motors were in use. Some were imported from the United States, and some were built in Abaco. These fast boats made it possible to travel from Hope Town to Man-0-War in ten minutes. A trip from Green Turtle Cay to Marsh Harbour on a reasonably calm day could be made in a couple of hours instead of requiring a day or two. The outboard motor brought the insular communities of Abaco much closer together, and some Abaconians still marvel that journeys they used to regard as major expeditions are now accomplished with such great ease. The impact of this new mobility was very great—it directly affected the lives and the livelihoods of almost everyone in Abaco.

Owens-Illinois and Treasure Cay, the automobile and the outboard speedboat, and the influx of well-to-do foreigners who built vacation homes, as well as poor Haitian immigrants, all transformed Abaco during the decade of the 1960s, and it was never to be the same again. Though still small and quiet in 1970 and free from pollution and traffic and most of the other offensive by-products of industrial society, Abaco unquestionably had become a part of the modern world during the 1960s. By the end of the decade Marsh Harbour sported the only traffic light in the Bahama Out Islands and had daily air service to Nassau as well as to Florida. An Abaco Chamber of Commerce promoted economic development and 14,000 tourists visited Abaco in 1970. The growth and changes which Abaco had experienced still did not touch all aspects of life. Although outboard motors on Boston Whalers had replaced Abaco dinghies for many fishermen, some men still sailed to the reef. Two supermarkets in Marsh Harbour sold convenience foods and sliced bread imported from the United States, but delicious homemade-style hot bread was still available twice daily at Key's Bakery in Marsh Harbour.

A hundred fifty yards or so down the road from Key's Bakery in Marsh Harbour was a very small building called Sea View Clinic. It was, like Key's Bakery, something out of the past, and yet it also represented change and modernization in Abaco. It was part of the transition to the modern world. It was the clinic served by Evans Cottman, a medical practitioner who had once taught biology at the high school in Madison, Indiana.

Medical care had always been a problem in the Out Islands of the Bahamas. During the nineteenth century it was nonexistent, except for bush medicine. Sometime before the early twentieth century the colonial government of the Bahamas had endeavored to alleviate the problem by authorizing "Unqualified Licensed Practitioners" to serve the medical needs of people in the Out Islands. These persons were required to have a scientific educational background and were permitted to engage in general medical practice, though they were barred from performing major surgery. As early as 1916 Hope Town had two Unqualified Licensed Practitioners. Their services received mixed reviews, and disputes between supporters and detractors resulted in several "outrages," described as fights involving stone throwing, during the Christmas holiday in 1916.[35] The system obviously had disadvantages and probably many medical errors were accidentally committed, but the system also provided a certain amount of skilled medical care in places where none would otherwise have been available.

Dr. Robert Stratton, who first arrived in Abaco in 1911, came as a missionary and then served Marsh Harbour as well as other towns in the Bahamas as an Unqualified Licensed Practitioner. During the late 1940s he happened to meet a middle-aged high school

Evans Cottman was an unqualified licensed medical practicioner in Marsh Harbour during the 1950s and 1960s. He is shown here sculling out to the *Green Cross* in Marsh Harbour, a boat he sailed throughout Abaco and The Bahamas to provide needed medical services in the Out Islands. After a photograph in Evans W. Cottman, *Out Island Doctor* (London: Hodder and Stoughton, 1963).

biology teacher from the United States who was preparing for early retirement on Crooked Island.[36] Evans Cottman had come to Abaco to arrange to have a boat built. In Marsh Harbour he met Viola Sawyer, who was soon to be his bride, and Dr. Stratton, who convinced him that a master's degree in biochemistry was adequate preparation to practice medicine in the Out Islands. Within a couple of years Evans Cottman was in general practice in Marsh Harbour and sailing from there to settlements throughout Abaco in his thirty-one foot ketch *Green Cross*. He had the boat built in Marsh Harbour and learned to sail it well. He satisfied his wanderlust by sailing as far as Grand Bahama and Exuma, rendering medical treatment wherever he stopped. The arrival of *Green Cross* was usually heralded with the repeated cry "de doctah done reach," and Evans Cottman learned very early in his experience that even burn or ingrown toenail victims believed they had to be "sounded" in order for medical treatment to be considered adequate. The stethoscope had to be used to determine if the blood were "runnin good, " and a doctor's reputation depended on his use of it. Evans Cottman later built Sea View Clinic in Marsh Harbour, where he served the medical needs of many of the people of Abaco until his death in 1976. The last years of his practice overlapped with those of Dr. Ejnar Gottlieb, a bona fide medical doctor who had come to Marsh Harbour with Owens-Illinois. Dr. Evans Cottman, the *Green Cross*, and the Sea View Clinic were part of the transition period in Abaco—they represented the continuation of an older and simpler life, but they were also a harbinger of the future.

END NOTES

[1] Reports of Commissioners, Hope Town, 1908, and New Plymouth, 1907.

[2] Grisilda Bethel, Interview with the author, Hope Town, 6 August 1983.

[3] Reggie Malone, Interview with the author, White Sound, Elbow Cay, 29 November 1985, and Alvard I. Bethel, Interview with the author, Hope Town, Abaco, 28 November 1985.

[4] Report of Commissioner, Cherokee Sound, 1912. In contrast to the Commissioner's statement, Alvard Bethel, Grisilda Bethel, and Reggie Malone did not remember an unusually high number of accidents at Wilson City.

[5] Alvard I. Bethel, Interview with the author, Hope Town, 28 November 1985.

[6] Alvard I. Bethel, Interview.

[7] See Paul Albury, *The Story of the Bahamas* (London: Macmillan, 1975), p. 252, and Report of Commissioner, Cherokee Sound, 1912.

[8] Report of Commissioner, Cherokee Sound, 1916.

[9] Reggie Malone, Interview with the author, White Sound, Elbow Cay, 29 November 1985.

[10] The Abaco Lumber Company acquired the 100-year timber license from the Bahama Cuban Company which had acquired it from the Bahamas Timber Company.

[11] Report of Commissioner, Green Turtle Cay, 1918.

[12] Paul Albury, *Story of the Bahamas*, pp. 187-188.

[13] Alvard I. Bethel, Interview with the author, Hope Town, Abaco, 25 May 1979.

[14] Report of Commissioner, Hope Town, 1922.

[15] See Report of Commissioner, Hope Town, 1924; Haziel Albury, *Man-O-War: My Island Home* (Hockessin, Delaware: Holly, 1977), p. 89; and The *"Treasure Islands" of the Bahamas* (Nassau: Development Board, no date). If the *Priscilla* was a converted cup defender, the only one she could possibly have been was the *Mayflower* which defended the cup in 1886.

[16] Report of Commissioner, Hope Town, 1924.

[17] Report of Commissioner, Hope Town, 1926.

[18] Report of Commissioner, Hope Town, 1925.

[19] Report of Commissioner, New Plymouth, 1936. Information regarding early crawfishing was also gained from Dewitte Lowe, Interview with the author, Hope Town, 31 December 1980.

[20] Report of Commissioner, Hope Town, 1926.

[21] Haziel Albury, *Man-O-War*, pp. 121-122.

[22] David Cornish, Interview with the author, Dundas Town, 10 May 1979.

[23] Haziel Albury, *Man-O-War*, p. 97.

[24] *Ibid.* , pp. 90-91.

[25] Report of Commissioner, Marsh Harbour, 1960.

26 Zoe Durrel, *The Innocent Island: Abaco in the Bahamas* (Brattleboro, Vermont: Durrell, 1972), p. 55.

[27] Report of Commissioner, Marsh Harbour, 1960.

[28] Dan Toth, Telephone interview with the author, Toledo, Ohio, 25 January 1982.

[29] Report of Commissioner, Marsh Harbour, 1964.

[30] Report of Commissioner, Marsh Harbour, 1962.

[31] Report of Commissioner, Marsh Harbour, 1960.

[32] Report of Commissioner, Marsh Harbour, 1964.

[33] *Ibid.*

[34] Report of Commissioner, Marsh Harbour, 1965. The following note is handwritten in the margin of a copy of this report in the Bahamian National Archives: "It is our duty to step in. This is a job for the M of Labour Out Island Affairs and the Premier. Lets get going. RS"

[35] Report of Commissioner, Hope Town, 1916.

[36] For more information see Evans Cottman, *Out Island Doctor* (London: Hodder and Stoughton, 1963).

Chapter Six -

Independence and Separatism

The 1960s were very good years; Abaco was a reasonably prosperous place. The activities of Owens-Illinois buttressed the economy, the Treasure Cay Hotel attracted tourists from the United States, increasing numbers of yachtsmen cruised through the Abaco Cays, and crawfishing became more lucrative than ever before. As early as the 1950s significant numbers of tourists returned to purchase land and to build vacation homes in Abaco, and by the 1960s foreigners supported growing real estate, construction, and caretaking industries in Abaco. Imported goods and modern conveniences became more common, and almost everyone shared, in one way or another, in the new prosperity. In 1965 this generally happy trend was briefly interrupted by Betsy, a hurricane which stalled for three days over Abaco before striking Florida and Louisiana. The winds were well over 100 knots and the tides were six to seven feet above normal. Some houses and boats were lost, but despite the severity and duration of the storm , damage was relatively light. Though few Bahamians were aware of it at the time, a political storm was brewing during the middle 1960s which would result in far greater changes in the Bahamas than those wrought by Betsy.

The Progressive Liberal Party (PLP) was founded in 1953. It was the first political party to be formed in the Bahamas, and it was established for the specific purpose of challenging the white power structure. White Bahamians had always dominated the British colonial government. It was generally understood that the government was run by the "Bay Street Boys," a group of prominent merchants with businesses located along Nassau's main street. This group was so entrenched in power that there were no political parties; no one had seriously questioned or challenged their leadership. They took credit for the increased prosperity which tourism brought to the islands, and this seemed to confirm their assumed right to govern the colony. Their investments in promotion and advertising did bear fruit. During 1966 over 750,000 tourists visited the Bahamas, compared to only 32,000 in 1949.[1] The Bahamas was clearly experiencing a major economic boom, and it was longer lived and more deeply rooted than the temporary and superficial booms which occurred during the United States Civil War and prohibition eras. Though the owners of the hotels, restaurants, and stores benefited the most from this, the new wealth trickled down through the economy to taxi cab drivers, red caps, construction workers, fishermen, and shoe shine boys. The Bay Street Boys pointed with satisfaction to the economic growth over which they presided, and they ridiculed the little party which challenged them. Some of them called it a Negro communist party.

The PLP was not, and is not, a communist party. Though the party supported increased government intervention in the economy through programs such as social security and government ownership of some hotels, it has also demonstrated respect for both domestic and foreign private capital. It consistently aligned itself with the non-communist world. When the PLP formed the government, regular diplomatic relations were not conducted with the Soviet Union, and although there were regular relations with Cuba, they were not conducted at the ambassadorial level.

The PLP was, and is, a black nationalist party. It has consistently championed the black Bahamian majority. According to Lynden 0. Pindling, long-time leader of the PLP and former Prime Minister of the Bahamas, the early party's platform was modelled on Michael Manley's Peoples National Party (Jamaica), and its activist philosophy was based on that of the Southern Christian Leadership Conference (SCLC).[2] The platform of the PLP called for reapportionment and constitutional reform. The Bay Street Boys responded to the challenge of the PLP by establishing a political party of their own in 1958—the United Bahamian Party (UBP). The UBP and the Bay Street Boys it represented continued to win elections because the 80-85% of Bahamians who were black did not play an effective political role. The black population was apathetic. Politicizing them was a slow process made even slower by the existence of restrictions on the right to vote and gerrymandered districts which resulted in inequitable representation for areas heavily populated by blacks.[3]

Some of the obstacles to full black participation in the government of the colony were not purposeful contrivances of the UBP, but that party resisted attempts to alter the system through reform. For example, before 1930 the majority of Bahamians lived on the Out Islands. During the next thirty years there was significant migration to Nassau and New Providence, but the electoral districts for the House of Assembly were not changed. By 1960 the Out Island constituencies were generally over-represented in the House. Also, many of the Out Island districts regularly elected non-resident merchants from Nassau (Bay Street Boys) to the Assembly. This practice was a logical outgrowth of the difficulty of communication and transportation in the islands during the nineteenth and early twentieth centuries, when it would have been almost impossible for a man to reside in the Out Islands and also keep abreast of developments in Nassau. It was practical and convenient for Out Islanders to choose residents of Nassau as their representatives in the House of Assembly. Though powered vessels had replaced sailboats on most mailboat runs by the 1930s, and the advent of the wireless made communication significantly easier, this custom persisted in the 1960s. The result of this, as well as other traditions and regulations, was that the large black population of New Providence was grossly under-represented, certain Out Island constituencies such as Abaco were over-represented, and the Bay Street Boys dominated the House of Assembly. The UBP did not want this situation changed.

The people of Abaco generally accepted the system as it was; they saw no need to change it. Nassau had always been a distant place and government simply did not play a large role in people's lives. As long as the mailboat still ran and the post office was open and functioning, there was no reason to be concerned with government and politics. Most of the Abaconians had relatives and friends living in Nassau, and the entire country was small enough so that many of the white Abaconians were personally acquainted with the Bay Street Boys themselves. Leonard Thompson, who was born and raised in Hope Town, settled in Nassau after serving in the Royal Canadian Air Force during World War II. He started an airline which was eventually sold to the Bahamian government, and he made various other investments. His brothers also settled in Nassau. One of them opened a department store on Bay Street, and another went into the real estate business. They all shared in the general prosperity of the islands during the post-World War II years. By 1949 Leonard Thompson was elected to the House of Assembly as a representative for Abaco and he was one of the Bay Street Boys. Even those white Abaconians who did not have close friends or relatives in Nassau felt an affinity for the white business and political community which governed the colony. They had no reason not to—it was their government.

Since the Bay Street Boys have been out of power, it has become fashionable, especially amongst those in the PLP, to catalogue the abuses of the UBP government. Some of this is, of course, normal, and many of the charges are true. Stafford Sands was both the Minister of Tourism and the Minister of Finance during most of the 1950s and 1960s. He was a brilliant lawyer, but he was also arrogant and brusque; for many he epitomized, at the same time, the best and the worst of the UBP government. During his term in office he also served as a "consultant" to casino operators and reportedly "earned" more than a million dollars doing so.[4] Some other members of the government were also involved in questionable activities or conflicts of interest. In spite of the fact that there was some corruption, arrogance, and racism in the UBP government, it is also true that some of the charges made by the PLP have been self-serving, exaggerated, and false. For example, some use the term "Bay Street Boys" with pejorative connotations which imply that anyone associated with the UBP government was a racist or a crook. This, of course, is not true. Some have implied that the Abaconian whites were co-conspirators with Stafford Sands and others in order to enrich themselves and to repress blacks. The Abaconians did not condone the illegal activities of Sands and others, and the honesty of men such as Leonard Thompson has never been seriously questioned. To contend that white Abaconians purposely sought to repress blacks because of racism is to oversimplify the situation. The support that white Abaconians provided for the UBP government was much more innocent than that. While most of the Abaconian whites probably believed that whites were superior to blacks, they held this belief in a passive rather than an active sense. They had known no social system other than their own. They accepted what they understood and believed in it. To judge the Abaconian whites of the 1950s and 1960s by the post-civil rights movement standards of the 1970s and 1980s would be grossly unfair. They were as unaware of the injustices of the political system they supported as they were of the fact that it was about to disintegrate.

The fledgling PLP gained influence and legitimacy throughout the 1950s and the 1960s. In 1956 Sir Etienne Dupuch, editor of *The Tribune* (Nassau) and an independent member of the House of Assembly, sponsored an anti-discrimination resolution which prevented segregation in public places. It was approved by the House of Assembly. Black Bahamians were henceforth allowed access to hotels, restaurants, and theatres formerly closed to them and, according to white Bahamian historian Paul Albury, they "began to think of themselves, for the first time, as first class citizens."[5]

A second development occurred in 1958 when the government awarded an exclusive franchise to white-owned companies to transport passengers between the new international airport and downtown Nassau. The predominantly black taxi cab drivers' union went on strike and blocked the entrances to the airport. The action gained the support and backing of Randol Fawkes, the President of the Bahamas Federation of Labor, and also of Lynden Pindling, the leader of the PLP.[6] Hotel and construction workers joined the walkout, and the action soon became a "general strike" in which workers in many different vocations refused to work because of their sympathy for the taxi cab drivers and their opposition to the government. The strike forced the closing of major hotels in Nassau, bringing the tourist traffic—and therefore the economy—to an abrupt halt. The nineteen-day strike was resolved favorably for the taxi cab drivers, and blacks emerged from the experience with a new, and heightened, sense of their political power. An indirect result of the strike was a redistricting plan for the House of Assembly which was implemented on the basis of "compelling advice"[7] from the British Colonial Office. Four new House of Assembly seats, all of them on New Providence Island, were established. In a by-election[8] held in 1960, black PLP members won all four. The PLP had increased its representation in the House of Assembly from five (down one from the six won in the 1956 election) to nine seats. The new enlarged Assembly had a total of thirty-three seats; the PLP had become a significant opposition.

A third development involved the passage of an act to allow women's suffrage in 1961. This doubled the size of the black electorate, but it did not lead to black success in the 1962 general election. Although the PLP polled 44% of the vote nationwide, it won only eight of the thirty-three seats in the House of Assembly. The UBP won nineteen seats with 36% of the vote. It was clear that the composition of the House of Assembly did not reflect the wishes of the electorate, and the PLP continued to hammer away on its demands for reapportionment.[9] Another incident polarized the population and contributed significantly to the eventual electoral success of the PLP. In 1965, during debate in the House of

Assembly regarding a redistricting bill, PLP leader Lynden Pindling realized that the government did not intend to redistrict the nation in a fair and equitable manner. He said:

> This only shows they [the UBP government] mean to rule with an iron hand . . . if this is the intention of the Government, I can have no part of it.

Pindling then walked to the Speaker's table and took the 165 year old Mace, the symbol of the Speaker's authority, and threw it out the window, saying:

> This is the symbol of authority, and authority on this island belongs to the people, and the people are outside. Yes, the people are outside and the Mace belongs outside too.

Those who opposed Pindling and the PLP were shocked. They viewed Pindling's action as an act of childish vandalism. The response of the *Nassau Guardian*, a pro-UBP newspaper, was to ignore the intransigence of the UBP regarding redistricting and to sponsor a fund-raising campaign to replace the mace, which had been smashed on the pavement outside. For those who supported Pindling the act was a symbolic protest which sparked their drive to gain more equitable apportionment of the House of Assembly. More harmless than the Boston Tea Party, it nevertheless focused immediate attention on the issue of representation.[10]

Between 1962 and the next general election, held in 1967, changes in the structure of government were made. Beginning in January, 1964, the Bahamas gained self government except in the matters of foreign policy, defense, and internal security. Also, it was decided that the House of Assembly would be expanded to thirty-eight members at the time of the next general election, with sixteen to twenty from New Providence and eighteen to twenty-two from the Out Islands. This was not acceptable to the PLP, and Lynden Pindling told a special committee of the United Nations that poor areas of the Bahamas were under-represented by about 50% compared to the more affluent areas.[11] In spite of these inequities, the PLP won eighteen seats in the January 10, 1967, election. The UBP also won eighteen seats. Two independents held the balance of power. Randol Fawkes, leader of the Bahamas Federation of Labour, threw his support behind the PLP, and Lynden Pindling became the Prime Minister of the Bahamas. The Bay Street Boys had been beaten and the Bahamas had a black government.

Abaco had participated in the election, but did not participate in the victory of the PLP. A total of seven men had run for the three Abaco seats; all three UBP candidates were successful. Three of the losers were independents. The PLP had fielded only one nominee in Abaco, Mr. D. B. Archer, who won only 174 votes from 1908 registered voters in Abaco.[12] It is not surprising that all-white communities, such as Man-O-War Cay, provided no votes at all for Mr. Archer, and that Hope Town, which had only one black family, provided only one vote for the PLP. What is somewhat surprising is that the all-black settlement of Cooperstown provided only 76 votes for Archer, compared to 177 for Leonard Thompson. The five small black settlements on Little Abaco Island (Fox Town, Wood Cay, Crown Haven, Cedar Harbour, and Mount Hope) gave Archer only 32 votes and Leonard Thompson 119 votes. John Bethel, another white UBP winner in Abaco, led all the other candidates in Little Abaco by winning 143 votes there. It is clear that the PLP had made no important inroads in Abaco. The nation achieved majority black rule without help from the blacks of Abaco, who still voted for the Bay Street Boys.

Abaco's blacks were not politicized, and they as well as the whites, were surprised and shocked by the outcome of the election. Leonard Thompson, who was handily re-elected to his seat in the House, reflected on the election fourteen years later:

> I think everyone was a little concerned—the uncertainty—let's face it, he [Pindling] got in mostly along racial lines—there was a lot of racial feeling—most whites were concerned.[13]

There was heightened reason for concern after a new redistricting act was passed in 1967 and another general election was held in April 1968. The PLP won twenty-nine of the thirty-eight seats in the House of Assembly. It was obvious that black majority PLP rule in the Bahamas was not to be a passing fancy. A majority in Abaco continued to vote for opposition candidates, but the impact of Abaco's opposition was blunted because Abaco's three seat district in the House of Assembly had been changed to two separate single member constituencies, reducing Abaco's power in the House by 33%. The PLP won the Cooperstown constituency, forcing Leonard Thompson's retirement after nineteen years in the House of Assembly. The UBP won the Marsh Harbour constituency, but the total UBP opposition was reduced to less than 25% of the House. The PLP had firm control of the nation, and many Abaconians were not at all pleased.

Abaconians grumbled about the new government and its policies. They complained about increased expenditures for education. Most of the increased government support went to previously neglected black villages or neighborhoods. The Abaconians strongly opposed the Bahamianization program, which severely limited the role of foreign capital and labor in the Bahamas. The government was trying to make certain that Bahamians would benefit from the development of the Bahamas. The Abaconians contended that the government was killing the golden goose—that investors and skilled personnel from abroad were needed if growth and development were to proceed. Although the Abaconians strongly opposed the government in regard to these matters, these issues were over-shadowed by their chief concern, which was that the blacks would seek independence for the Bahamas. The fear with which white Abaconians viewed independence was exaggerated beyond its real importance. The whites believed they would be severed from their heritage. They feared permanent separation from the England which they, from a distance, loved, and subjection to the authority of a hostile, racist, and incompetent black government in Nassau. Without England, who would protect them? The issue soon emerged from the shadows into the open. In 1970 a group of Abaconians, anticipating future government initiatives, let it be known that if the Bahamas were to seek independence, Abaco would prefer separation from the Bahamas and continued colonial status. They formed an organization called the Greater Abaco Council. When Prime Minister Lynden Pindling announced, in the Speech from the Throne in 1971, that the Bahamas would seek independence "no later than 1973,"[14] the worst fears of the Abaconians were realized. During the years following Pindling's announcement, Abaconians tried several different methods of separating themselves from the Bahamas in order to avoid becoming part of an independent Bahamas governed by the PLP.

Both sides prepared for the confrontation they knew was coming. As early as March 1971, Prime Minister Lynden Pindling tabled (moved)[15] an act which provided for up to twenty years imprisonment for any persons who planned armed coercion against the Bahamian government. The Prime Minister explained that existing laws were not adequate to cope with conspiracies against the government. Abaco was not specifically mentioned. During the same month the new UBP leader, Errington Watkins, struck out against the Pindling government. Watkins charged that the PLP government "... came into power on one issue and one issue alone, race hatred,. . ." He charged the government with corruption, and in defense of the old UBP regime, he said: "I am not saying that every-thing about the old UBP was correct, but I'm saying they got fat and the country grew fat, today members of the government are growing fat and you are growing thin."[16] Watkins made a special bid for the support of Abaconian dissidents and announced that he would run for the Marsh Harbour constituency in the next general election. In July a petition with the signatures of about 75% of the adult population of Abaco was presented to the Governor, Lord Thurlow. The petition asked for separation of Abaco from the Bahamas if the government of the Bahamas sought "premature independence." It cited the loyalty of the ancestors of the Abaconians and asked that the Abaconians be allowed to continue to be loyal and to retain their British identity. The petition was sent on to London, but the British government ruled it could re-ceive petitions from no entity other than the government of the Bahamas. The signers of the petition were saddened and shocked— the Queen to whom they were loyal had deserted them in their hour of need.[17]

Before granting independence to the Bahamas, the govern-ment of Great Britain required that an election be held in order to gain the assent of the people. A separate election, or plebiscite, on the question of independence would have provided this, but it was decided that a general election in which a vote for the PLP would be understood as a vote for independence would suffice. Many white Bahamians believed this confused the issues and that it was unfair. Leonard Thompson claimed that a separate plebiscite never would have approved independence, and Paul Albury hints, with some bitterness, that Great Britain encouraged this procedure so as to rid itself of the Bahamas as soon as was possible.[18]

The general election was scheduled for September 19, 1972. The old UBP was discredited by its earlier history and could not hope to win many black votes, so opposition elements regrouped and formed the Free National Movement (FNM). This party did not oppose independence per se, but did contend that the Ba-hamas was not quite ready for it. The FNM was comprised of the old UBP and two small groups which had splintered from the PLP. The party was led by Cecil Wallace-Whitfield, who was formerly a member of the PLP and was a member of the House of Assembly for a New Providence constituency. Some of the party's strongest supporters were Abaconians.

The plan of the Abaconians was simple. If the FNM could win the two seats in Abaco and the two seats in Grand Bahama, they hoped the British government would split Little Bahama Bank (which includes only Abaco and Grand Bahama) from the rest of the Bahamas and retain it as a Crown Colony.[19] Leonard Thompson came out of political retirement to run for the Cooperstown constituency. He ran for Cooperstown rather than Marsh Harbour because of a party decision that Marsh Harbour was a "safe" constituency and that Thompson had a fairly good reputation among the island's blacks. Errington Watkins was the FNM's nominee for Marsh Harbour. Watkins was a former police officer from Nassau and a relative newcomer to politics.

The campaign was a vigorous one, and the election did not occur without difficulties. On 14 July 1972, when Prime Minister Pindling was in Marsh Harbour to advocate his independence program, several explosions occurred while Pindling was speaking. No one was injured. The Prime Minister paused and then finished his speech, and no one was arrested, but it was obvious that there were some people in Marsh Harbour who were willing to carry their protests beyond the voting booth.

The hard-fought election did not produce the results desired by the Abaconians. The FNM candidates for the two constituencies on Grand Bahama lost to their PLP rivals. Errington Watkins did win easily in the Marsh Harbour constituency, defeating the PLP's Gordon Hudson by winning 833 votes compared to Hudson's 283. Hudson received only 2 votes from Man-O-War Cay (compared to 132 for Watkins) and won only 4 votes in Hope Town. Hudson would have made a better, though still not victorious, showing if Dundas Town and Murphy Town, Marsh Harbour's black suburbs, had not been separated from the Marsh Harbour constituency and added to the Cooperstown constituency. This gerrymandering was done by the PLP to assure the election of at least one PLP candidate from Abaco. It was successful,[20] but the results were probably less resounding than the PLP had hoped for. In the Cooperstown constituency, Scherlin Bootle (PLP) defeated Leonard Thompson by only 4 votes (562 for Bootle and 558 for Thompson). Although Bootle carried all of the polling divisions which were primarily black, Thompson still won large numbers of votes in those same divisions. For example, Thompson won 108 votes in Dundas and Murphy Town compared to Bootle's 152, and he won 91 votes in Little Abaco Island's black communities compared to 118 for Bootle. Leonard Thompson believes he could have challenged the election results in court and that he would have been declared the winner, but he was discouraged from doing so by the poor showing of the FNM nationally and the failure of the plan to win all the Abaco and Grand Bahama constituencies, as well as by the cost of such a challenge. Also, he believed the PLP government would "crucify" Abaco if Abaco had two FNM representatives. He hoped for better treatment of Abaco if there were at least one successful PLP candidate.[21] He decided once more to retire from politics. The PLP had won the Cooperstown constituency again, but it was the result of blatant gerrymandering. The victory was too thin to be considered a mandate. Throughout Abaco 62% of all voters had voted for the FNM.

Outside of Abaco the PLP enjoyed success and received the desired mandate for independence. The party won twenty-nine of the thirty-eight seats in the House of Assembly. Prime Minister Pindling issued a White Paper on independence on October 18, 1972, and arranged to have an independence conference with the British government in London during early December. The FNM leadership decided that the election had provided a mandate for independence to the PLP and that they would cooperate with the government. Many Abaconians felt betrayed by the FNM, and Errington Watkins took a stand opposed to that of the party's leadership. He said: "I am one who believes in independence never; Abaco believes in independence never." He criticized the FNM: "No, we don't have a weak opposition, we have none at all. We have a junior branch of the Progressive Liberal Party."[22]

The next attempt by Abaco to separate was spearheaded by Leonard Thompson and the Greater Abaco Council. About a month after the election he was contacted by Sir Frederick Bennett, a member of the British Parliament. Thompson was advised to talk to a friend of Bennett's, a Mr. Ronald Bell, also a member of Parliament, who was known as one of the best constitutional lawyers in England. The Greater Abaco Council brought Mr. Bell to Abaco to meet with them. Bell told them that there was still a chance that Abaco could be separated because of the political climate in England, and said that there was already significant support in Parliament for Abaco. The Greater Abaco Council enlisted Mr. Bell as its attorney. Several months later Bell suggested that Thompson bring a multi-racial delegation of Abaconians to England for the independence conference. Thompson did so. At first they received encouragement, but then their support eroded. The minister they were supposed to present their case to was sympathetic, but two days before the presentation was to be made, he was transferred, and the man who replaced him was hostile to the Abaconians and their cause. Sir Frederick Bennett now sided with the PLP and refused to see Leonard Thompson, whom he had previously encouraged. Thompson and Bell were told that there was no chance that Britain would separate Abaco. Thompson described the position of the British Government:

> As a matter of fact this is what the chap told me—Lord Balniel was his name—he said, 'we just want to get rid of you; we'd like to get rid of the colonies.' I'll never forget that.[23]

Thompson again retired from politics, and the Greater Abaco Council disbanded. Others in Abaco were not dissuaded by this defeat, and hoped that they could win separation and Crown Colony status for Abaco in the House of Commons or the House of Lords. Errington Watkins was one of them; Chuck Hall was another. Though born and raised in Nassau, Hall's mother was from Abaco. He had been active in the UBP, and after the 1972 election he championed Abaco separatism. He made several trips to London seeking support there for Abaco. Bennett told him to forget it; Bell told him there was a slim chance of success. Hall and Watkins formed the Council for a Free Abaco to continue the quest, and Watkins became its chairman. The Council published a pamphlet in order to win support in Abaco and to gain financial assistance in the United States and elsewhere. The pamphlet explained:

> There is no freedom for the Abaconians in rule from New Providence and no possibility of fairness from a government that is dedicated to racism, committed to false economic policies, and so nationalistic as to threaten its future by inviting foreign experts to leave.[24]

Independence was scheduled for 10 July 1973. By late spring the situation was very tense. Errington Watkins and the Council for a Free Abaco prepared a new petition to go to the House of Commons and the House of Lords. The petition was signed by more than half of the registered voters of Abaco. Like its predecessors, the petition asked for continued Crown Colony status for Abaco and noted that the people of Abaco had been loyal to the Crown for almost two hundred years.[25]

This petition, like the others, had little effect in Britain. There was some debate in the House of Commons and the House of Lords regarding the Abaco issue when the Bahamas Independence Bill was presented for approval in May and June. The British government supported the bill and opposed separation of Abaco on the grounds that it was not desired by a majority of Abaconians, that no major Bahamian political party supported it, and that it would result in disastrous fragmentation. Some Conservative members of the House believed that Abaco should not be forced to become part of the independent Bahamas if it did not wish to do so. Mr. Ronald Bell introduced an amendment to exclude Abaco from independence, arguing that Abaconians would be "victimized" by the PLP government—a government he described as being representative of a "virulent black nationalism."[26] Prime Minister Lynden Pindling flew to London to counter these charges. Pindling contended that Abaco did not deserve self-determination simply because it was an island and said that universal application of that doctrine would be disastrous for the Bahamas. He said the Abaco matter was part of a massive land grab. He also said that there were no outward signs of revolt in Abaco and denied that arms were being shipped into Abaco: "Nothing is going to happen in Abaco, man. I am not getting hot and bothered over this."[27] Mr. Bell's amendment was defeated, and the Bahamas Independence Bill was passed on 22 May by a vote of 74:4. In spite of this resounding defeat, some of the Abaco separatists were still optimistic that they might win in the House of Lords. They contended that the vote in the Commons had been taken at 2:00 A.M., after many of their supporters had gone home. Lord Belhaven was the chief

During the months before independence there were rumors about a possible secessionist revolution in Abaco, as seen in the 17 May 1973 edition of *The Tribune* (Nassau). Used with the permission of The Tribune, Ltd.

proponent for Abaco in the House of Lords. Many of the same arguments were repeated. An amendment to separate Abaco failed by a vote of 50:1. The Bahamas Independence Bill then passed in the House of Lords on 12 June 1973.

While these events occurred in London, still another futile effort to separate Abaco had failed in Nassau. Errington Watkins, who had flown back to Nassau between the votes in the House of Commons and the House of Lords, initiated this effort by introducing a resolution in the House of Assembly which called for a United Nations' supervised referendum in Abaco to decide Abaco's future. The resolution had gained the support of three other FNM members: Cleophas Adderley, Michael Lightbourn, and former UBP Premier of the Bahamas, Sir Roland Symonette. The FNM leadership vehemently opposed the resolution, and claimed that if a referendum were permitted in Abaco, referendums would have to be held in all of the other islands as well. The resolution was, of course, defeated, and Watkins and the others who supported the resolution were expelled from the FNM for violating party discipline. Watkins said he was proud to have been expelled from the FNM because the FNM had sold out the people of Abaco, and he went to Abaco to explain the matter to his constituents.[28]

On Saturday, 16 June Watkins delivered speeches at Sandy Point, Crossing Rocks, Cherokee Sound, and Marsh Harbour. He told his audiences that no stone had been left un-turned, but that they had lost. He explained that some members of the House of Commons had castigated the people of Abaco and had tried to give the impression that those who supported Abaco separatism were racists. Watkins said:

> I said to myself. Why are we who have been so loyal for 200 years trying so hard to stay with them when they fight so hard to kick us out. . . . We have no other choice at this stage but to go along with an independent Bahamas. I don't mean we must join the PLP—God forbid—but we must do everything we can to make Abaco a success in an independent Bahamas.

He told the people not to interfere when the new Bahamian flag was raised: "The Union Jack is just as bad as the one they will come to put up." He said he would personally burn the British flag if he did not have such respect for the Queen and the Crown. He told the people: ". . . this is foolishness about violence—forget it." When he offered to resign because of his expulsion from the FNM the people refused to accept it. When he asked if they would be willing to help him form a new political party, he received enthusiastic support. He also expressed the hope that ". . . Pindling will grow up and administer this country fairly without fear or favor or malice or ill will towards anyone."[29]

Although the Council for a Free Abaco had decided not to pursue illegal means of separating Abaco from the Bahamas,[30] a relationship had been established with some persons in the United States and Britain who were not as reluctant to consider resorting to arms to achieve their goals. Chuck Hall, who with Watkins had founded the Council, had contacted a former employee of the United States Embassy in Havana who he knew had strong anti-communist convictions. Hall asked him about a possible military stand in Abaco and was given the names of two persons to contact—one of whom was Mitchell WerBell of Defense Systems International located in Powder Springs, Georgia. WerBell responded enthusiastically. He assisted the Council and both he and an Atlanta, Georgia, attorney named Edwin Marger were in London in May to help lobby for a separate Abaco. WerBell was the son of a cavalry officer in the Russian Imperial Army. He was a swashbuckling type, and boasted of his involvement in the anti-communist effort in the Dominican Republic in 1965. Defense Systems International was a second-hand arms supplier which also developed, manufactured, and marketed some new weapons designed by WerBell. The Council had also developed contact with Lt. Col. Colin "Mad Mitch" Mitchell, a Conservative member of the House of Commons who was sympathetic to Abaco's plight. Mad Mitch was a war hero; he had distinguished himself during World War II and in Palestine, Korea, Cyprus, and Aden. In 1970 he left the British army because of a dispute concerning his unorthodox practices. Watkins was, at first, not aware that these contacts had been made, and when he and the press discovered them, he became extremely upset. He asked Chuck Hall and Mitchell WerBell- "What are you guys trying to do?" He became nervous that he was being used as a front for a military operation he didn't know about.[31]

In May Errington Watkins was accused by the Prime Minister of being "more than accidently associated" with WerBell and a conspiracy against the government of the Bahamas. These charges were made in the House of Assembly.[32] Pindling said that he had met with the members of the Greater Abaco Council (Leonard Thompson's group). He said they no longer opposed independence. He said he believed that the Greater Abaco Council had been the effective and legitimate representative of the anti-independence movement in Abaco, and that they—and the people of Abaco—had now abandoned what they knew was a lost cause. He said that Watkins and the Council for a Free Abaco were involved in a conspiracy run by non-Bahamians who had criminal designs on the sovereignty of the Bahamas. He contended that these foreigners did not understand Bahamian politics and did not realize that half of the Abaconians were black and therefore not of English descent. He also said that they did not seem to understand that one of Abaco's representatives, Mr. Scherlin Bootle of Cooperstown, was a member of the PLP. Pindling cited some evidence which seemed to implicate Errington Watkins, Chuck Hall, and Albert Albury of Marsh Harbour in seeking a military solution to the Abaco problem. Watkins immediately replied: "I will not take part in, condone, or in any way, shape or form be involved in any violence against this country." Watkins said he had never said he would take up arms. In response to a question from the Prime Minister, he said he did not know if Mr. WerBell was recruiting mercenaries. He pledged that neither he nor the Council for a Free Abaco planned violence or illegal activity.[33]

These charges and responses were made in an environment which was rapidly heating up with rumors of impending military activity. Stories in the press reporting WerBell's connection with the Council for a Free Abaco had appeared as early as March and April. It was alleged that WerBell was hiring mercenaries. One story which originated in Georgia indicated that 300 former British paratroopers were ready to sign up for duty in Abaco. This claim was made by Bennett Bintliff, a partner in a firm headed by Mitchell WerBell called Zeta Company. Bintliff also claimed that several Abaconians were receiving advanced arms training. He said no move would be made until after independence so that Britain would not be involved.[34] Other reports indicated that Lt. Col. Colin "Mad Mitch" Mitchell was considering an appointment as Abaco's security advisor.[35]

In June, amidst heavy press coverage, Mad Mitch flew to Georgia where he met with WerBell, and then flew to Abaco accompanied by Chuck Hall. The Bahamian government allowed him to enter the Bahamas for three days only and on the condition that he not hold press conferences or public meetings. Mitchell stayed at the Union Jack Club in Marsh Harbour, where he met with local residents as well as with Errington Watkins. The purpose of Mitchell's visit was not clear. One source claimed he wanted to be

Abaco's "security advisor," but that he demanded too much money and was not hired by Mitchell WerBell.[36] Whether this is true or not, it does seem that Mad Mitch and Mitchell WerBell did not get along well. Another source contends that the purpose of his trip was simply to publicize the state of affairs in Abaco.[37] Whatever the goals were, the principal result was that the situation was temporarily defused because Mad Mitch down played the viability of a revolution in Abaco. When asked by newsmen about a possible revolt, he said that most of the residents of Abaco were over forty-five years of age, and when asked if the men of Abaco could be trained for a military operation, he replied: "The thought of it would give a military commander ulcers."[38] After his visit and his departure, it was clear that no military action was imminent and that Abaco would become part of an independent Bahamas on 10 July 1973.

Prime Minister Lynden Pindling spoke to the press regarding independence and Abaco on 9 July. When asked about the threats made by Abaconians, he claimed that there had never been ". . . a real threat by Abaconians." He said: "The people of Abaco had a feeling about independence and people from outside saw it as an opportunity to exploit the situation." He demonstrated patience and generosity regarding the role of the Abaconians in the Bahamian nation:

> I believe it will be a while before the white community will be . . . enthusiastic [about independence], however the place of Abaconians in history is somewhat different from the other white or black Bahamians. They felt that as loyalists they had a special niche and there were many of us that appreciated that, but what we didn't understand were those that tried to exploit this.[39]

Independence came to the Bahamas and to Abaco without major incident on 10 July 1973, but the separatist scheme was still alive and it had found new support. Beginning in June, Michael Oliver, a real estate sub-developer from Carson City, Nevada, with strong libertarian convictions, began to provide financial support for Abaco separation. Oliver had previously tried to establish a new nation on an atoll in the Pacific, but had been evicted by the government of Tonga. When he learned about the struggle of the Abaconians, he offered his assistance.[40] Oliver's goal was to create a sovereign state which would be organized on the basis of libertarian principles. He believed that investments and business would thrive in an atmosphere in which property and income would be free of government control and taxation, and he was able to raise money from others who also supported these goals. By this time, Errington Watkins had bailed out, but Chuck Hall, Mitchell WerBell, and a few others were still involved in Abaco separatism. They joined forces with Oliver to create the Friends of Abaco (FOA),[41] a fund-raising effort based in the United States, and the Abaco Independence Movement (AIM), a political party which was the chief beneficiary of the FOA. AIM was founded in August 1973, in Marsh Harbour, and Chuck Hall became its chairman. Rallies were sponsored and members were recruited in other Abaco settlements. Bumper stickers, T-shirts, and party platforms were printed. A one-page mimeographed newspaper called *The Abaco Independent* commenced publication in September 1973. The newspaper and the party consistently explained that their goals were to seek home rule and self-determination for Abaco by peaceful, constitutional means.[42] The newspaper was frequently clever in exposing the faults or alleged faults of the government. An article titled "AIM opposes Auto Test Plan" explained:

> The Abaco Independence Movement has declared its opposition to a plan to test the endurance of the Prime Minister's $40,000 Rolls-Royce on the Great Abaco Highway.
>
> Said an AIM spokesman, 'We have nothing personal against the PM or his Rolls. One would have to really hate the man to ask him to drive his new car on these roads . . . Abaco is the only major island without a black-topped main road.'[43]

The newspaper and the party advocated the creation of the Abaco National Land Trust. They contended that all Abaconian citizens had rights to the unsettled Crown land on Abaco, which was owned and controlled by the independent national government in Nassau after 1973. Each adult Abaconian was to receive a share in this Trust, and was to receive a portion of the proceeds from leasing the land. AIM contended that there would be rapid economic growth in an independent Abaco because of the lack of taxation and government intervention in the economy, and predicted that each Abaconian could receive an income of over $15,000 per year within three to five years from lease income. Each Abaconian was also to receive a one-acre house lot.[44]

A free trade zone was to be established in a sixty square mile area in southern Abaco. The Abaco National Land Trust would own two-thirds of the land in the zone, and the Atlas Corporation, a development company based in the Cayman Islands, would own the other third. A harbor was to be developed on the west side of the island, and resort hotels were to be built on the Atlantic side.

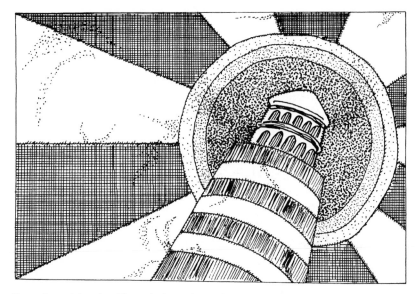

Flag adopted by the Abaco Independence Movement (AIM) to be the flag of an independent Abaco.

Very rapid growth was projected for this zone; it was to include an international airport with direct flights to New York and London, and heavy industry as well as offshore banking. The principal attraction would be an absolutely irrevocable pledge on the part of the government at Abaco not to tax or regulate the businesses in any way.[45]

The Abaco government envisioned by AIM was to be a very limited government, not only within the free trade zone, but also outside of it. Only those citizens who agreed in advance to contract for government services would receive them. These persons were to pay premiums set by the government to support the services. Import duties, which averaged 33% at the time, were to be progressively lowered to 5%. The government was specifically prohibited from engaging in ". . . any business enterprise . . . including roads, transportation or utility systems, and post offices or other communications systems."[46] These ideas represented the thinking of Michael Oliver and other libertarians who supported and assisted the movement rather than the thinking of the Abaconians. But the Abaconians who supported AIM were generally receptive rather than hostile to these ideas. *The Abaco Independent* consistently propagandized these ideas, and also championed local causes.

It called for the construction of a high school in Abaco; it criticized the government for inefficiency and for alleged socialist and communist tendencies.[47] The newspaper grew. Adrian Day, an Englishman with some limited political experience, came from England to become its editor. He used the pseudonym Childe Harold. By September 1974, *The Abaco Independent* was an eight-page newspaper printed by photo offset. It gained stature as a community paper by publishing announcements regarding weddings, births, deaths, and non-political stories of local interest, but it also continued to take every opportunity to fault the government. When electric power was restored to Marsh Harbour only five hours after a fire at the privately owned generating plant, the newspaper lauded private enterprise and criticized the government-run operation at Cooperstown, which had been shut down for four months.[48]

The Abaco Independence Movement had organized as a political party and had announced that it would employ only constitutional means to achieve the separation of Abaco, but by 1973 and 1974 separation by peaceful means was not possible. The government in Nassau opposed dismemberment of the Bahamas and would not condone home rule for Abaco. If the AIM were to achieve a separate Abaco, it would have to be willing to do so by illegal means. Some of its members and supporters were willing. The military-political plan was simple because the Bahamian government had no army, no navy, and no air force—only a fifty man riot police force in Nassau. If independence were declared and the principal airports and docks in Abaco were held by trained military personnel loyal to a new regime for Abaco, the Bahamian government would not be able to land their policemen or respond effectively to the situation. The commissioners, policemen, and other officials of the Bahamas would simply be put on a boat and sent to Nassau. AIM would promulgate a constitution, and Abaco would exist as a de facto independent state by virtue of Nassau's inability to prevent it. A system of government involving neither taxation nor intervention would be established, and the investment capital and people this would attract would shore up the new regime and hasten recognition by the United Nations and by the established nations of the world. This plan for a revolution supported by military action was secret; not even all of AIM's members knew about it. Some of them continued to plan for political action, realizing that there was some planning for security measures going on, but apparently unaware of the extent of the proposed military involvement.[49]

The Abaco Independence Movement and the scheme to separate Abaco from the Bahamas by force was the combined result of the failure of the government of the Bahamas to accommodate the Abaconians and the determination of some of the Abaconians not to subject themselves to Nassau and a black government. It was also the result of foreign money and opportunism, but it was not, as some charged, entirely a foreign import. A large part of the reason for all the earlier separatist movements, and this one as well, was racism. Many white Abaconians were determined not to be ruled by blacks, whom they considered inferior. Some black Bahamians encouraged this kind of vigorous white reaction by the irrationality and excesses of their attack on the Bay Street Boys and other white Bahamians. Although racism on both sides explains a good part of Abaco separatism, it does not explain all of it. Black Abaconians were slow to support the PLP, and many of them supported independence for Abaco, even after 1973. The PLP leadership liked to think that the Abaconian blacks took this position because they were "brainwashed" by the UBP and not yet "politicized" by the PLP. This was only partly true. Many Abaconians—black as well as white—supported Abaco separatism because of traditional center-periphery problems. Bert Williams, a black construction company owner, claimed that there were too many Out Islands for the government to take care of, and he became the Vice-Chairman of AIM.[50]

Many Abaconians said it was unfair that Abaco produced about three million dollars in revenue for the Bahamas government each year (mostly through import duties which averaged 33%), but that the government spent only one million dollars in Abaco each year. The balance, they claimed, stayed in Nassau, and this was why there was no high school and no paved road in Abaco. They also complained that the Commissioner system of administration for the Out Islands gave them no voice in choosing local administrators—that it was a "colonial" system. Others probably supported independence for Abaco because of the hope for rapid economic advancement under a new regime. The foreigners who were financing the Abaco Independence Movement promised that a free market economy in Abaco would bring extremely rapid growth, and even spoke of construction of a hospital in Marsh Harbour. Everyone in Abaco was supposed to benefit by becoming free of the black colonialism centered in Nassau.

Although there was still support for separatism in Abaco in the fall of 1973, the Abaco Independence Movement did not have the strong support which the Greater Abaco Council had enjoyed during late 1972. Part of this erosion, of course, can be explained by the time which had passed and the defeats which had been suffered in the 1972 election, at the Bahamas Independence Conference, in the House of Commons, in the House of Lords, and in the House of Assembly. Much of the erosion of support occurred because those still committed to Abaco separatism became more radical as their options narrowed. What had started as a movement to convince the Queen to continue to hold Abaco as a British Crown Colony was, by late 1974, a movement to declare Abaconian independence, by force of arms if necessary, and to establish a libertarian republic in cooperation with some very conservative swashbuckling militarists and wealthy businessmen from the United States. In 1972 the Abaco separatist movement probably had the support of over two-thirds of the people of Abaco; by late 1975 it was a minority movement kept alive with foreign money. Many Abaconians deserted separatism because it was no longer associated with the Crown, or because they believed Abaco would not be a viable entity on its own, or because they realized that separation could not be achieved without violence. Some opposed AIM because they did not approve of the movement's leaders, who were men of lesser national or regional stature than Leonard Thompson or even Errington Watkins. Although several prominent politicians and attorneys from Nassau were contacted, and some of them considered leading an independent Abaco, no George Washington emerged. Still other Abaconians simply did not trust the "money men" from the United States, and did not want to give them the enclave they desired for a free port in southern Abaco.[51]

Planning for the revolution went forward throughout 1974 even though such an effort lacked support from the majority of Abaco's people. About one hundred Abaconians had volunteered for the Abaco security force and some received preliminary training in Abaco. Mitchell WerBell was to supply arms for the operation. There were reportedly plans to acquire a ninety-foot patrol boat and a few Italian single seat fighter planes for $10,000 each. The Abaco security force was to be supplemented by mercenaries from the United States or Britain. The constitution was written and plans were made to establish diplomatic relations with other countries. AIM was concerned about the potential reaction of the United States to the planned revolution and tried to smooth the road for United States' acceptance and, perhaps, benign support.

The Abaco Independent was mailed to all members of the Senate Foreign Relations Committee, and a United States citizen with a home in Abaco spoke to other Senators. Discreet contacts were reportedly made with the executive branch of the government through appropriate intermediaries. Richard Nixon was President at the time. It is not known who the intermediaries were, but it is well known that Richard Nixon's principal connection with Abaco was through his friend Robert Abplanalp, who owns Walker's Cay as well as a home on Grand Cays in northern Abaco. President Nixon occasionally visited Abaco as Abplanalp's guest. It is said that the contacts reached as high as Henry Kissinger, United States Secretary of State and Special Assistant to the President for National Security Affairs at that time. There is no proof that this actually happened, and there is no information available regarding Mr. Kissinger's response. AIM also tried to do some rudimentary contingency planning. The revolutionaries were worried about the possibility of Jamaican intervention on the side of the government of the Bahamas, or of assistance which might be provided to the government by the Black Panther Party of the United States. Apparently, it was decided that the likelihood of such interventions was not great.

Despite these grandiose preparations, the revolution, which was tentatively planned for 1 January 1975, never happened. The Abaco volunteers were scheduled to go to Power Springs, Georgia, for additional military training, but the decision was reversed at the last moment. Those who were not stopped at the Marsh Harbour airport were greeted in Miami by Constable Smith of Marsh Harbour and a C. I. D. (Criminal Investigation Department) official. Only one trainee arrived in Georgia; he had flown to Florida earlier than the others for personal reasons, and therefore escaped Chuck Hall's reversal and the police roundup. Chuck Hall, it was said, had "chickened out."[52]

The decision to abort was not caused by any single factor; several things had gone wrong. Michael Oliver published information about the impending revolution in his newsletter:

> A free nation is about to be born in the Caribbean, the first nation explicitly committed to the principles of individual liberty and genuine free enterprise. Its name is Abaco.

> The people of Abaco, against their expressed will, were placed by Great Britain in a union with an independent Bahamas. The corruption and socialism of the Nassau government has caused Abaconians to seek a separation from the Bahamas and control their own affairs.

> The ABACO INDEPENDENCE MOVEMENT has contacted us for political, economic, and legal advice and assistance. These are being provided. In return for such aid, a mutually beneficial arrangement which will satisfy our own free enterprise goals has been agreed to. . . Before you read any further, please sit back and reflect on this. Imagine the possibilities . . . It should be obvious that the costs of this movement are enormous . . . we must appeal to you again, in the homestretch, for financing help. We need it now, today. It is in your interests to provide it.
>
> The chance for a truly free country is here—real, actual, at last. Let us secure it. This will be only the beginning[53]

This published appeal ended any hope of surprising the government of the Bahamas and therefore diminished the chances of the success of the revolution.

There were other problems as well. The Bahamians involved in AIM felt they were losing control of the movement and the revolution. Some had deserted AIM as soon as they realized that arms were to be used, and some of those remaining in the movement wondered if they would be able to control the military men. Mitchell WerBell and others involved in the military aspects of the revolution were absolutely essential for its success, but there were misgivings concerning their proper role after the independence of Abaco was achieved. Also, there were problems coordinating various mercenary groups, and Michael Oliver was unable to produce funds in the amounts which were required at the time they were needed. The organization was tied up with money men and military men—"fuzzy libertarians" on the one hand, and "cowboys" on the other—and there was no point, it was decided, of bringing on "possible bloodshed without a very good chance of success."[54] Some others have offered more simple explanations regarding why the revolution never came to be. One observer contended that it did not happen because of the lack of coordination amongst groups on the various islands and cays of Abaco—as he put it—"they couldn't decide whether to have it on Tuesday or a week from Wednesday."[55]

In February 1975, the publication of a sensational article in *Esquire* magazine exposed the association of Michael Oliver and Mitchell WerBell with AIM. Prime Minister Lynden Pindling responded by calling AIM "subversive."[56] AIM protested the charges, claimed innocence, and renamed itself the Abaco Home Rule Movement (AHRM). During the next two years the AHRM kept the spirit of Abaconian regionalism alive and championed decentralization for the Bahamas, but there was no more serious talk of revolution. The idea of limited local self-government for the Out Islands received enough intermittent support to encourage its proponents, but no real changes or reforms were achieved. Michael Lightbourn, an independent member of the House of Assembly from Long Island, moved to establish a committee of the House of Assembly to study the matter, and some members reminded the ruling PLP that more autonomy for local government had been a PLP plank in 1968. Prime Minister Pindling, in response to Lightbourn's motion, said that Abaco might well be ready for more local control. The motion passed unanimously. Despite such widespread support, no changes had been made as the Bahamas approached their first general election as an independent nation in 1977.

The AHRM hoped to play a prominent role in defeating the PLP in 1977, but any chances of victory over the PLP were destroyed by factionalism early in the campaign. Cecil Wallace-Whitfield led the FNM, and stood for election in the Marsh Harbour constituency, but dissident elements broke away to form the Bahamas Democratic Party (BDP). The two opposition groups could not resolve their differences, and this resulted in splitting the anti-PLP vote. In Marsh Harbour the struggle between the two factions was particularly acute. Michael Lightbourn, the candidate of the AHRM and the BDP, defeated the PLP candidate by only four votes. Cecil Wallace-Whitfield was a distant third. Nationally the PLP swept to victory with thirty of the thirty-eight seats in the House of Assembly. The BDP won six seats; the FNM won only two. The AHRM understood the narrow victory in Marsh Harbour and the PLP's triumphant return to power nationally as very discouraging developments. *The Abaco Independent* sent a letter to its subscribers which commenced:

> It is with great regret that we announce the suspension of publication of *The Abaco Independent*.
>
> We hope we will be able to resume publication in the not too near future, and for this reason we do not wish to say too much about the reasons for the suspension. They should be obvious from the enclosed review of election results in the Bahamas and in Abaco.[57]

The letter noted, with disappointment, that the combined vote for the PLP in both Abaco districts was higher than that for all the opposition candidates. For the first time the PLP had won a majority in Abaco. Although Lightbourn had won, Abaco's opposition to the PLP seemed to be weakening rather than growing stronger, and *The Abaco Independent* and the AHRM ceased to exist.

During the late 1970s some observers said that the Abaconians had finally gotten used to Lynden Pindling and the PLP. Mr. Cecil Marche, Senior Commissioner in Marsh Harbour in 1981, went even further. He said that white Abaconians had gotten used to black leadership and that they had learned that the PLP meant equal rights for all.[58] But few Abaconians agreed with Marche's optimistic analysis in 1981. Many still believed that Nassau exploited Abaco by collecting much more in import duties than it returned in services and expenditures. Most were still proud of their unique heritage. Most wanted more freedom to run their own affairs. If Abaconian whites accepted the leadership of the PLP, many of them did so without great enthusiasm. Some may have joined or supported the PLP for purely pragmatic and business reasons and would be quick to desert it if the party seemed to be losing support elsewhere—every ruling party gains this kind of questionable dividend.

Although the Abaco revolution is dead, and the trend has been for Abaconian whites to provide increasing support for the PLP as well as for a maturing Bahamian nationalism, the feeling of many Abaconians that Abaco should have a special place within the Bahamas lives on. The desire for local autonomy has been voiced by Abaconian blacks as well as by whites in recent years and may well continue to find political expression in the 1990s.

END NOTES

[1] Michael Craton, *A History of the Bahamas* (London: Collins, 1968), p. 279.

[2] Charles L. Sanders, "The Bahamas: Newest Independent Black Nation," *Ebony*, 38 (July 1973), 31-34.

[3] Gerrymandering consists of drawing the boundaries of political divisions in such a way that one party gains an unfair advantage.

[4] Craton, p. 290.

[5] Paul Albury, *The Story of the Bahamas* (London: Macmillan, 1975), p. 275.

[6] See Randol Fawkes, *The Faith that Moved the Mountain* (Nassau: Nassau Guardian, 1979), pp. 98-126.

[7] Paul Albury, *The Story of the Bahamas*, p. 275.

[8] A special election, held at some time other than the regular time, to fill vacancies.

[9] Doris L. Johnson, *The Quiet Revolution* (Nassau: Family Islands Press, 1972), p. 67.

[10] For a detailed description of these events see Johnson, pp. 52-55.

[11] *Ibid.*, p. 160.

[12] Candidates and totals were as follows:

Leonard Thompson	UBP	1247
Frank Christie	UBP	1176
John Bethell	UBP	1254
D. B. Archer	PLP	174
Scherlin Bootle	Ind	757
Colyn Reese	Ind	168
Bozwell Sawyer	Ind	107

The top three candidates were elected.

[13] Leonard Thompson, Interview with the author, Marsh Harbour, Abaco, 26 July 1981.

[14] Johnson, p. 139.

[15] In British and Bahamian Parliamentary practice, to table an act means to introduce or move it. This is quite different from the meaning of the term in the United States, where tabling an act postpones action on it.

[16] "UBP Chairman hits out at Racialism Corruption," *The Tribune*, (Nassau), 1 March 1971, p. 6.

[17] Johnson, pp. 144-145.

[18] Leonard Thompson, Interview, and Paul Albury, *The Story of the Bahamas*, p. 281.

[19] According to Leonard Thompson, this plan was suggested by Sir Frederick Bennett, a member of Parliament, who met with Thompson and some other Abaconians at Green Turtle Cay (Leonard Thompson, Interview).

[20] If Dundas Town and Murphey Town had been in the Marsh Harbour constituency rather than in Cooperstorn, Thompson would have polled 450 votes compared to Bootle's 410. Also, the inclusion of Dundas Town and Murphey Town in Marsh Harbour would not have altered Watkin's victory in Marsh Harbour. Therefore, if Dundas Town and Murphey Town had been in the Marsh Harbour constituency, the FNM would have won both of the seats in Abaco.

[21] Leonard Thompson, Interview.

[22] "'I have received threat on my life,' says Watkins," *Nassau Guardian*, 27 January 1973, p. 1.

[23] Leonard Thompson, Interview. Lord Balniel was a Minister of State for Foreign Affairs. He was the Chairman of the Bahamas Independence Conference.

[24] Nicki Kelley, "Council for a Free Abaco is soliciting World Support to stay British Crown Colony," *The Tribune* (Nassau), 12 May 1973.

[25] "New Abaco petition to Queen seeks to rebut UK Contention," *The Tribune* (Nassau), 17 May 1973, p. 1.

[26] "MP takes issue with 'virulent black nationalism' label on Bahamas," *The Tribune* (Nassau), 18 May 1973, p. 3.

[27] "PM flies to London to 'correct misleading opinion' on Abaco," *The Tribune* (Nassau), 21 May 1973, p. 1 and "'Attempts to separate Abaco have one Motive: a massive land grab,'" *The Tribune* (Nassau), 23 May 1973, p. 1.

[28] Mike Lothian, "Opposition FNM split wide over Abaco MP's referendum resolution," *The Tribune* (Nassau), 7 June 1973, p. 1, and "Watkins to be expelled for his 'keep Abaco British' Resolution," *The Tribune* (Nassau), 13 June 1973, p. 1.

[29] Mike Lothian, "Only Respect for the Queen preventing Abaco MP from Burning the Flag," *The Tribune* (Nassau), 18 June 1973, p. 1.

[30] Nicki Kelley, "Council for a free Abaco concede defeat—Will Support Independence," *The Tribune* (Nassau), 14 June 1973, p. 1.

[31] Chuck Hall, Interview with the author, Nassau, Bahamas, 19 July 1984, and "US Arms dealer linked to Abaco's millionaire soldier of fortune," *The Tribune* (Nassau), 8 May 1973.

[32] Mike Lothian, "PM Accuses Watkins of being 'in a conspiracy against government of the Bahamas,'" *The Tribune* (Nassau), 16 May 1973, p. 1.

[33] Mike Lothian, "Watkins decries violence, denies illegality charge," *The Tribune* (Nassau), 16 May 1973, p. 1.

[34] John Marquis, "300 ex-paratroopers volunteer to back Abaco cause to stay British," *The Tribune* (Nassau), 13 June 1973, p. 1.

[35] "Col. 'Mad Mitch' to be security adviser to Abaco?" *The Tribune* (Nassau), 6 June 1973, p. 1.

[36] Andrew St. George, "The New Country Caper," *Esquire* (February 1975), 60-64, 151-154.

[37] Chuck Hall, Interview with the author, Nassau, Bahamas, 20 July 1984.

[38] "Abaco Lost After Gallant Battle," *Palm Beach Post-Times,* 17 June 1973, p. A1.

[39] Nicki Kelley, "Foreign Press Query PM on Vesco, his Rolls Royce, and Discrimination," *The Tribune* (Nassau), 9 July 1973.

[40] Mike Oliver, "Open Letter to the People of Abaco from Mike Oliver," *The Abaco Independent*, 30 March 1975. According to Chuck Hall, the original contact between the Council for a Free Abaco and Michael Oliver was made by Errington Watkins. After this meeting, Oliver travelled to Powder Springs, Georgia, where he met Chuck Hall and Mitchell WerBell. Chuck Hall, Interview, 19 July 1984.

[41] For a detailed but sensationalism account of the involvement and interests of these men, see Andrew St. George, "The New Country Caper," Esquire (February 1975), 60-64, 151-154. Also see "Abaco—The Past," *Bahamas Dateline*, 30 July 1984.

[42] See "Abaco Party Formed," *The Abaco Independent*, Issue 1, c. September 1973.

[43] "AIM Opposes Auto Test Plan," *The Abaco Independent*, Issue 2, c. October 1973.

[44] Hope Town Freedom Proposals, Abaco Independence Movement, 1974 National Convention, An Independent Abaco: Proposals for Public Debate.

[45] The Abaco World Trade Zone, typewritten description probably distributed by AIM, no date.

[46] Proposed Constitution of the Abaco Commonwealth. Fourth Draft. August 1975.

[47] See "PLP Lunges Left," *The Abaco Independent*, Issue 4, c. December 1973.

[48] "Blaze Causes Minor Damage to Power House," *The Abaco Independent*, 30 September 1974, p. 1.

[49] Adrian Day, Telephone interview with the author, Arlington, Virginia, 28 November 1984, and Norwell Gordon, Interview with the author, Marsh Harbour, 9 August 1984.

[50] Outlying rural, or peripheral, regions often resist governments based in far away centrally located capital cities. For more information regarding Bert Williams see "Profile: Bert Williams," *The Abaco Independent*, 30 September 1974, p. 3.

[51] Beryl Patterson, Interview with the author, Lubbers Quarters Cay, 5 July 1981, and C. Percy Gates, Interview with the author, White Sound, Elbow Cay, 30 June 1981.

[52] Hartley Lowe, Interview with the author, White Sound, Elbow Cay, Abaco, 17 June 1979.

[53] Michael Oliver, *The M. Oliver Newsletter*, Carson City, Nevada, no date.

[54] Chuck Hall, Interview, 19 July 1984.

[55] David Gale, Interview with the author, on board *Blue Runner*, January 1975.

[56] "AIM Subversive—Says PM," *The Abaco Independent*, 10 February 1975, p. 1.

[57] *The Abaco Independent*, letter to subscribers, Marsh Harbour, August, 1977.

[58] Cecil S. Marche, Sr., Senior Commissioner in Marsh Harbour, Interview with the author, Marsh Harbour, 24 June 1981.

Chapter Seven —

Contemporary Abaco:
the 1970s through the 1990s

The Abaco of the 1970s and 1980s continued to be a place of striking contrasts. At Man-O-War Cay men sawed through 6" by 6" natural crook logs with hand rip saws to make frames for boats a few hundred feet away from Edwin Albury's shop, where fiberglass hulls were fabricated. In the 1990s Winer Malone of Hope Town was still building Abaco dinghies with only hand tools, while most of the houses surrounding his shed were equipped with television and air conditioning. At Treasure Cay and Marsh Harbour new luxury condominiums were built, and at Hard Bargain many people lived in sub-standard housing. Sponging made a comeback in the 1990s. In some settlements the church maintained its influence and one community continued to prohibit the sale of alcohol and tobacco products, and in some settlements fast money was made by those who ran drugs into the United States. There were large fleets of modern sailing yachts available for charter at Marsh Harbour and Hope Town; there was still one functioning smack boat at Cherokee Sound in early 1982. The older people remember scrubbing pine floors with turbot skins and sand; the younger people sometimes mimicked purposeless fads imported from the United States. Satellite television, direct dial telephones, fax machines and improvement of air, water and land transportation have all opened Abaco to modernization and development—to influence from the outside. But Abaco's distinctive culture survives. For the most part the growth and development of modern Abaco, and the improvement of the living standards of most of its citizens, have been achieved without destroying Abaco's culture or its environment.

TOURISM: ENGINE OF THE ECONOMY

The fastest growing and most productive sector of the economy of Abaco during the past three decades has been tourism. Almost non-existent in the 1960s, it was estimated that 135,000 tourists generated $75 million for the economy of Abaco, or about $7500 per capita, in 1993. Just as tourism has been the "engine" of the Bahamian national economy centered at Nassau during the post-war period, it has become the main driving force for Abaco. But Abaco has not developed the mass tourism which dominates Nassau and Freeport. Some call it "cottage tourism"—it is based in smaller hotels, rental houses and chartered boats—and it is part of what is now called eco-tourism in the travel industry. The attraction for visitors is Abaco's crystal clear waters, pristine beaches, and pro-ductive fishing grounds; tourists come to Abaco to enjoy the natu-ral environment—not to gamble in a casino.

Small hotels and resorts had been built prior to the 1960s— primarily by foreigners on some of the outer cays. The Treasure Cay Hotel, built by Captain Leonard Thompson of Hope Town, opened in 1963 and signalled the beginning of a new era. It called for larger numbers of tourists than the old guest house resorts, and depended on more reliable air transportation to bring visitors to Abaco. During the late 1960s the Conch Inn and Marina opened in Marsh Harbour, and in 1978 Leonard Thompson, who had sold the Treasure Cay Hotel, built the Great Abaco Beach Hotel at Boat Harbour in Marsh Harbour. During the early 1980s Abaco Towns-by-the-Sea, a time-share condominium development, opened next door. By the 1990s it had 130 units.

In Marsh Harbour alone the number of hotel rooms increased from zero in 1960, to 25 in 1970, 50 in 1980, and 190 in 1990. Marina slips increased from zero in 1960, to 50 in 1970, 175 in 1980, and 376 in 1990.[1] There were similar increases in tourist facilities on the outer cays. Small hotels expanded, and foreign visi-tors bought land, built houses, and then many rented the houses to other foreign visitors while they were absent from Abaco. The number of visitors increased from under 60,000 in 1980 to almost triple that number in 1990.[2] These developments fueled the economy of Abaco—the new revenues trickled down through developers and contractors to taxi drivers, fishing guides, and care-

There were several land development projects during the 1960s and 1970s. This brochure is for Bahama Palm Shores on Great Abaco Island south of Cherokee Sound. The photo on the cover of the brochure is not of Bahama Palm Shores—it is Hope Town harbour which is about fifteen miles away. The lots—"none less than 80 X 125 feet"—were offered for $25 down and $25 per month, with total purchase price beginning at $1795. Most of the developments grew slowly during the early years.

takers. It was recently estimated that $55 million of the $75 million total produced by tourism was accounted for by hotel, house rental, and time-share guests.[3]

The largest portion of the balance of revenue generated by tourism is accounted for by those who come to Abaco to cruise. The partial shelter offered by Abaco's reef and string of cays makes Abaco Sound a semi-protected cruising area over one hundred miles long. Well protected overnight anchorages are numerous and interesting—some are at settlements such as New Plymouth and Man-O-War, others are at beautiful uninhabited cays such as Powell and Manjack. Greater numbers of yachtsmen from the United States discovered Abaco during the post-war years, and some returned each year in their boats or built vacation or retirement homes. During the 1960s Abaco Bahama Charters Ltd., was established in Hope Town. The company offered sailboats for charter. This made it possible for sailors from the United States to enjoy a week or two of cruising in Abaco without having to sail their own boats or boats chartered in Florida across the Gulf Stream. Abaco Bahama Charters pioneered bareboat charters[4] in the Bahamas, but it was not until 1972, when Caribbean Sailing Yachts, Ltd. (CSY) moved a fleet of boats to Marsh Harbour, that bareboat chartering

A CSY 39 sailing off Manjack Cay in January, 1973. Caribbean Sailing Yachts (CSY) was the first large bareboat charter company in Abaco, and according to their own claim, accounted for 40% of tourist arrivals in Abaco during 1973. CSY had differences with the Bahamian government and closed its operation in 1978.

became large enough to have a major impact on Abaco's economy. The company claimed that it accounted for 40% of tourist arrivals in Marsh Harbour during its first year of operation there. Bareboat chartering grew rapidly during the next few years, and a fleet of trawler yachts was added to the 30-foot and 39-foot sailboats already in Marsh Harbour, but the terms of doing business in the Bahamas were not acceptable to CSY, which closed its Marsh Harbour operation in 1978.

Caribbean Sailing Yachts failed to survive in Abaco for a variety of reasons. Some were the result of errors made by the company's management; others were the result of actions taken by the government or by government bureaucrats. The company requested relief from customs duties and imported boats with the understanding that duty would not be levied. This was apparently done on the basis of a verbal statement made by a government official. The company was later shocked when duty was levied. Although CSY argued that its request for relief was necessary and reasonable, the demand for exemption from paying import duty in a country with no income tax, and in which the government relies on import duty for more than 60% of its revenue, was not justifiable. Although there are some special exemptions for activities the government wishes to encourage, almost all other business in the Bahamas pay import duty. This was and still is about 33% on many essential household items, but was only 10% on boats and marine supplies during the 1970s. Caribbean Sailing Yachts clearly sought very preferential treatment.

The government of the Bahamas, for its part, subjected CSY to some rather ridiculous regulations. Bahamian law required that large marine businesses be owned by Bahamians rather than foreigners, so CSY had to operate through a Bahamian front. This was CSY (Bahamas) Ltd., which was headed by Gordon Hudson, the unsuccessful Progressive Liberal Party (PLP) candidate for the Marsh Harbour constituency in 1972. Hudson's involvement made the operation technically legal, and he received $2500 annually for playing this role, but he complicated CSY's problems by trying to play a role in management decisions. The situation reached an impasse by 1977. Dr. John Van Ost, President of CSY, wrote: "The government, for whatever its reasons, has kicked our ass pretty regularly since we came to the Bahamas and backed down on one promise after another."[5] Gordon Hudson described the situation differently: "The basic problems are the Dr. wants to operate without duties, to own the licenses, to run the Immigration Department and to advise the Government how to run the Bahamas."[6] By 1978, when CSY left the Bahamas, Dr. Van Ost believed that Gordon Hudson, backed by members of the government, had forced CSY out so they could take over a very lucrative business.[7] By 1980 two charter companies had jumped into the void left by CSY—Bahamas Yachting Services, a company backed by Marcell and Ritchie Albury of Man-O-War Cay, and Abaco for Sail, operated by Gordon Hudson. The latter ceased operations within a few years, but Bahamas Yachting Services was purchased by Sunsail in c. 1990, and was still in operation in 1995. In 1992, encouraged by changes in Bahamian duty on boats which probably would have satisfied Dr. Van Ost, The Moorings, the world's largest sailboat charter company, opened a base in Abaco. Abaco Bahama Charters of Hope Town continued its smaller operation, and a couple of other companies from the United States were placing charter sailboats in Abaco.

Although important to Abaco's economy, sailboat charter arrivals were, in 1994, no where near the 40% of tourist arrivals claimed by Dr. Van Ost for 1972. The level of activity in the bareboat charter sector may well have been equal to that of 1973, but in the 1990s it was a much smaller part of the burgeoning economy of Abaco. One estimate was that it accounted for about $3 million (4%) of the total income from tourism in 1993.

A larger portion of the revenue from tourism is now accounted for by cruisers who bring their own boats to Abaco. This was estimated at $17 million, or 23% of the total, in 1993. Numerous articles about Abaco in boating magazines, construction of top quality marina facilities, changes in government regulations regarding visiting yachts,[8] the publication of new and expanded cruising guides, and the advent of GPS for navigation have all contributed to this. But the principal reason for this growth is that Abaco is such a wonderful place to cruise. Probably half of all boats cruising the Bahamas cruise in Abaco, about half of all slip space in the entire Bahamas is in Abaco. Many boat owners from the United States bring their boats to Abaco and leave them there for months at a time, commuting back and forth to them by air. This is a growing sector of tourism in Abaco, and one for which Abaco provides many excellent resources.

In 1988 a project commenced which many believed would permanently change tourism in Abaco—it was Abaco's entree to mass cruise ship tourism. Ludwig A. Meister, owner of Treasure Cay Limited, developed Baker's Bay, located at the northern end of Great Guana Cay, as a site for cruise ship visitors. This development involved the dredging of a deep channel and mooring basin for the ship, as well as construction of a dock, amphitheater, stores, and other facilities at Baker's Bay, a formerly pristine anchorage which was a favorite for visiting yachtsmen.

Controversy surrounded the project from the beginning. Approval for the massive dredging project was gained from national rather than local authorities, and some local residents opposed the project. A group of these hired Dr. Jack Storr, a marine biologist at State University of New York at Buffalo and a long-time resident of Abaco, to do a study which concluded that dredging and non-containment of the tailings might well adversely affect coral in the area. But others argued in favor of Mr. Meister's project, believing that the economic boom which propelled Nassau to fame and fortune was finally coming to Abaco. Opponents to the project were

A large dredge was brought to Abaco to dredge a channel and turning basin for a cruise ship at Baker's Bay, Great Guana Cay, in 1988-1989 (left). Premier Cruise Lines Starship *Majestic* moored at Baker's Bay (which was re-named Treasure Island) in c. 1990 (below).

scarcely heard, and it went forward. Baker's Bay was converted into "Treasure Island."

The dredging was completed and operations began in April 1989, with Premier Cruise Lines as the lessee. They utilized the Starship *Majestic* for the cruise and advertised it as the "Big Red Boat" and "Abacodabra." It was sold as part of a package tour which included three days at Disney World in Orlando, Florida, and then three days at Treasure Island. The ship left from Cape Canaveral, Florida, and then was moored at Baker's Bay for three days. Advantages of this kind of arrangement were that Premier saved on fuel, and there were probably fewer cases of seasickness. Guests could go ashore at Treasure Island where there were a variety of activities (swimming, sailing, snorkeling, para-sailing, shopping, etc.), or they could take power catamaran cruises to either Treasure Cay, Man-O-War Cay, or Green Turtle Cay.

Residents of the communities to be "visited" responded in different ways. Some opened new businesses or expanded old ones and looked forward to the flow of people and dollars. Others continued to oppose the entire operation. Some argued that cruise ship tourists generally spend very little money ashore because all their meals and even entertainment were provided "free" on the ship.[9] They said that although the cruise ship tourists would not spend money, that they would all probably go to the bathroom on the island, thus leaving something behind. The arguments were not too dis-similar from those which have taken place throughout the Caribbean, where cruise ship companies have been accused of "using" the Caribbean, but contributing little or nothing to it. Some have said that the cruise ship industry is "raping" the Caribbean.[10]

In actual practice the operation of Premier at Treasure Island was not quite as bad as the naysayers had predicted, but it certainly did not result in an economic boom in Abaco. Most business people complained of minimal purchases,[11] and some began to stock inexpensive trinkets made in Asia which the cruise ship tourists seemed to favor. Many hoped for residual benefits—they hoped that some of the visitors would return to Abaco on their own. Some did, but not in numbers which were impressive. On balance, a few well- positioned entrepreneurs profited significantly from the cruise ship, but most Abaconians did not.

The people of Abaco were not the only ones who were not 100% satisfied with the arrangement. In 1992 Premier Cruise Lines pulled out. Sea conditions in Loggerhead Channel—even with the dredging—often made it impossible for the cruise ship to enter, especially during the winter months. This necessitated a last minute change of schedule and some unhappiness amongst the passengers when they discovered they were going to Nassau or Freeport instead of Treasure Island. Knowledgeable Abaco seamen had said from the very beginning that Loggerhead Channel would often be too rough to guarantee safe entrance and egress for a cruise ship. In the end they were right, and Abaco's experience with mass cruise ship tourism came to an end.

Tourism in Abaco suffered another blow when Treasure Cay Limited closed the original Treasure Cay Hotel building in 1991. Operations continued at the Harbour House building at the marina, and the marina and the golf course and all other parts of the operation remained open, but a *New York Times* article incorrectly reported that the entire resort had closed, and business suffered even though the hotel continued operations at Harbour House. A malaise settled in at Treasure Cay. Stafford Symonette explained that Treasure Cay was always a "marginal operation," and that "it didn't take much to screw it up." Berkeley Evans, who managed Treasure Cay during the 1970s and early 1980s did a good job of re-investing and making it work, according to Symonette, but Ludwig Meister, the new owner who took over in 1982, eventually hired various managers and administrative advisors from the hotel chains. Each came with an agenda—to reform Treasure Cay by implementing programs and systems similar to those used in the hotel chain which formerly employed them. These ideas did not work well at Treasure Cay. Ludwig Meister, who lacked experience as a hotelier, needed "to be guided, but he was mis-guided."[12] Treasure Cay had serious problems.

The solution was Sandals. Shortly after the hotel building was closed, Treasure Cay Limited announced that Sandals Inc., a very successful company operating all-inclusive, adult-only, "cruise ship style" vacation packages in land-based facilities in Jamaica, had purchased the hotel and would soon renovate it and open it as a Sandals Resort. But then the hotel was not renovated. Throughout all of this, the marina and retail stores and restaurants at Treasure Cay remained open, and the home owners, numbering over 600, continued to visit, and Treasure Cay survived, but it did not flourish. By late 1994 it was obvious that Sandals was not going to reopen the old hotel, so Treasure Cay Limited exercised its option to re-gain ownership. The building was still for sale. The reduced number of visitors to Treasure Cay has resulted in some economic hardships for people in Green Turtle Cay and Cooperstown and other surrounding communities as well as in Treasure Cay. Many residents are puzzled by Treasure Cay Limited's actions, and hope that someone will soon refurbish and re-open the hotel building which was the foundation on which Treasure Cay was built.

CRAWFISHING: A BONANZA FOR THE COMMON MAN

Second only to tourism as a principal prop in the economy of Abaco is crawfishing. It has been a consistent producer of revenue since the 1930s, and employed about 1000 persons during the early 1990s. In 1992-93 Abaco's fishermen caught 1.5 million pounds of crawfish, accounting for 30% of the total Bahamian catch, and contributing $12 million to the local economy. Crawfishing is big business now, and usually involves a fairly large "mother" boat which serves as a base of operations and provides living accommodations and freezers. The crawfishermen venture out from the mother boat in smaller boats and dive to get the crawfish.

Crawfishing is hard work but provides a good livelihood. In late 1994 a crawfisherman in Fox Town said he was able to harvest about 50 pounds of crawfish a day, and that this was bringing about $10 per pound on the market. Another crawfisherman from Cooperstown reported that a good year for a crawfisherman would yield earnings of $120,000. per year to be split by the two-man team. A "medium" year would bring $100,000., and a bad year $60,000., or $30,000. each.

Since the 1970s Abaco crawfishermen have used traps and compressors. The "traps" do not actually confine the crawfish, but rather simply provide shelter for them. Only the crawfisherman who put out the trap knows exactly where it is—so he visits it periodically to spear the resident mature crawfish. This is generally more productive than exploring the reef looking for crawfish. Also, compressors are used aboard small boats to allow crawfishermen to dive deeper in search of crawfish. During recent years many crawfishermen use sophisticated global position system (GPS) devices to find their traps. A good crawfish crop in 1993-1994 was followed by a generally poor catch in 1994-1995, leading some to speculate that the crawfish were over-exploited. Some blamed foreigners, and some over-fishing by Bahamians. But the reduced catch led to higher prices—20% fewer crawfish produced 50% more money—according to a crawfisherman from Cooperstown.[13]

AGRICULTURE: WAVE OF THE FUTURE?

Agriculture is another important sector of Abaco's economy, but it has yet to fill the grandiose predictions often made for it. Abaco is large enough to provide extensive fields, and has sufficient sunshine and rainfall (about 50" per year) for most crops, but The Bahamas continues to import most of its food, wasting its hard-earned foreign exchange on agricultural goods it should be able to supply from domestic sources.

After the failure of Owens-Illinois' sugar cane venture in southern Abaco (see chapter 5, pp. 100-101), and the failure of the government to find another sugar grower to buy the operation, the Bahamian government bought out Owens-Illinois in 1979. The sugar refinery was sold to a Venezuelan company for a substantial portion of the government's purchase price for the entire complex, and some of the fields were leased to Florida citrus grower B. J. Harmon. Harmon had a variety of difficulties, and later sold its interests in Abaco to other Florida growers. The Abaco citrus groves were viewed as insurance crops during these early years. In good years for Florida it was expected that the Abaco operations would lose money, but a frost in Florida would drive prices up, and the Abaco groves would turn a good profit. An established vegetable farm in northern Abaco was also converted to citrus.

The Key-Sawyer farm north of Treasure Cay has been described as the most successful farm in The Bahamas. It was established in 1972 as a partnership between Edison Key and Morton Sawyer of Marsh Harbour. Morton's experience in farming and Edison's knowledge of heavy equipment and land preparation helped to make the operation successful. During its first five years Key-Sawyer Farms associated with Gulf and Western, but this arrangement was dissolved in 1977 when Gulf and Western closed down all its vegetable operations in Florida. The farm continued to be successful on its own. Its principal crop was cucumbers, with the United States as the principal market. There was no import duty on cucumbers during the winter months, and the warmer climate of Abaco made it easy for Key-Sawyer to compete with Florida growers. But the cucumber operation was labor intensive, and there were difficulties with the large Haitian labor force. During the 1980s there was a shift to citrus, and in the late 1980s the farm was sold and renamed Bahamas Star Company.

Citrus production continues to be a central feature of agriculture in Abaco during the 1990s, with 6000 acres under cultivation. Bahamas Star accounts for about half of this total, and exports grapefruit, lemons, limes, and oranges to Fort Pierce, Florida. Other producers include Bahamas Citrus Groves with 2000 acres, Bahama Palm Groves, Rainbow Groves, and some others. Though citrus continues to be a very important sector of agriculture in Abaco, there is a trend toward experimentation and diversification in the 1990s.

Sugarland Farms is operated by Bahamian Jimmy Albury of Man-O-War Cay. He grows cucumbers, tomatoes, and squash, and is producing the same volume of cucumbers as Key-Sawyer Farms did on one-third the acreage by using drip irrigation. This new technology results in lower labor costs as well. Abaco is much better suited to cucumber production than Florida, and the only real competition is from Mexico. Sugarland Farms is also experimenting with livestock; it has 40 acres of alfalfa hay, 69 black angus cows and a bull, 300 sows for pork production with a goal of 6000 carcasses a year, and a poultry production project with a goal of 5000 per week. The success of these projects could move The Bahamas closer to its goal of self-sufficiency in foodstuffs.

Another interesting new operation is Bahama Neem, which is planting Neem trees on a 150 acre tract in southern Abaco. The Neem tree originates in southeast Asia and is the source of some herbal medicines and azodoractin, a substance which prevents the normal development and therefore reproduction of insects. The first commercial harvest will not take place until 1997, and full production will not be reached until 1999 or 2000. If successful the Neem will be Abaco's first industrial crop since sisal.[14]

Bahamian agriculture undoubtedly has the potential to produce more than it has during the past forty years—and it is very important for The Bahamas to supply more of its own food in order to conserve valuable foreign exchange. Abaco seems well suited to play an important, perhaps even central, role in this effort because it has an abundant supply of water. But by 1995 there was no great change in agriculture's role, though there were many optimistic predictions and projections.

DRUG TRAFFICKING: A DISEASE OF THE 1980s

During some years of the 1980s the income produced by trafficking in illicit drugs, primarily marijuana and cocaine, bound for the United States, was probably greater than that produced by any other sector of the economy except tourism. The Bahamas are ideally situated to serve as a transshipment point for drugs moving from South America to markets in the United States. It is also well configured for such a purpose—there are thousands of small cays and little harbours to serve as hiding places for caches of drugs on the way to the United States. And it is impossible for the Bahamas Police and Defence Force to adequately patrol 700,000 square miles of ocean and islands with twenty-six boats and two planes.

At one time it was the fashion for certain United States leaders to blame The Bahamas for the United States' drug problem. They accused The Bahamas of not policing their borders. It should now be obvious to all that even with the assistance of the United States Navy and the United States Air Force, the United States—the world's greatest power—cannot effectively police its own borders. If it could do so, drug imports would cease. So it was ludicrous for the United States to expect The Bahamas to be able to stop all drug transshipment to the United States. Some Bahamians took issue with the fact that the United States blamed The Bahamas for its drug problem. They said that the root of the problem was not drug runners in The Bahamas—the real root of the problem was that the society and culture in the United States could not, or would not, eliminate the demand for drugs by individual citizens. The United States, they said, concentrated on interdiction of the drug traffic rather than on education and other social programs to curtail the actual demand. There is, of course, logic to this view.

Just as Bahamians made money running the Union blockade into the Confederacy during the Civil War, and just as they profited from prohibition, many Bahamians moved into the drug transshipment business. It was a fast track to big money. But most Abaconians who became involved were not drug organizers; they did not arrange for deliveries of drugs from Colombia and then carry the drugs to the United States for resale. Typically, they became drug traffickers because they found marijuana or cocaine which was landed or dropped by airplanes from Colombia or Jamaica. Some found "square Grouper"—bales of marijuana—floating in the sea. They hid the merchandise and waited for buyers from the United States who came to Abaco in fast cigarette-type ocean racing boats. Then they paid off the Colombian supplier. It started this way during the middle to late 1970s. Outlying and more isolated areas with good sea and air transportation were more favored than population centers such as the Marsh Harbour area. Sandy Point was well situated, and during the early 1980s the new Treasure Cay airport was used while it was still under construction. The air strips on Scotland and Spanish Cays were used. Although Abaco was active as a drug transshipment center, it was certainly not the main center in The Bahamas. More isolated areas such the Exuma Cays were better positioned for that. But as time went by, some Abaconians became drug organizers, arranged for deliveries, transshipment, and paid off local police and government officials.

The money which could be made was big money. Cocaine worth $5,000-$15,000 a kilogram (kilo) in Colombia sold for $50,000-$90,000 wholesale in the United States, and could be worth up to $120,000 retail. Bahamians could buy a kilo for about $20,000-$30,000 and sell it to United States buyers for $40,000-$70,000 without even leaving Abaco. By carrying the cocaine to a "fix" for transfer, or even into the United States, they could sell for up to $90,000 per kilo. One deal or trip with just one kilo was sufficient to support a very comfortable life-style for more than a year, and some people who were quite poor became millionaires within a few months.

The economy of Abaco boomed. Massive amounts of United States dollars flowed through the system. A Central Bank of the Bahamas regulation requiring a full report for cash deposits of over $5000 was regularly ignored by "every bank." The grocery stores reportedly accepted the money and automobile dealers accepted the money—"nobody turned the money down . . . I don't know what the churches did, but everybody else held their hands out and said 'I'm the best buy in town.'" And the money seemed to be everywhere. One resident of Green Turtle Cay recalled that a friend approached him and said: "I think everyone in Abaco is involved with drugs except you and me, and I'm not so sure about you."

The banks had such large holdings of US dollars that some lacked the physical space in their safes to store the cash, and, in any case, the dollars could not all be spent or invested in Abaco,. The money had to be moved to parent banks in Nassau. The amounts were so large that during the middle 1980s the banks in Marsh Harbour collaborated and chartered a plane once a week to carry money to Nassau. When the drug trafficking abated during the late 1980s, the plane flew only once every two weeks.

The Reagan administration's response to the burgeoning drug problem in the United States was interdiction, but at first there was very little cooperation from The Bahamas. Drug money bought protection from local police and customs officials. In the Exuma chain of islands and cays south of Nassau, Carlos Joe Lehder, a Colombian drug lord, ran a transshipment center with planes arriving from Colombia and planes departing for the United States on a daily basis. When Vice President George Bush presented evidence to the Bahamian government showing over thirty take-offs or landings per day, he reportedly referred to Norman's Cay in the Exumas as the "O'Hare Field of the Caribbean."[15] Official United States pressure on The Bahamas to cooperate with the United States was complemented in 1983 by popular pressure. On September 5, 1983, NBC correspondent Brian Ross aired a story which claimed that high officials in the Bahamian government, including Prime Minister Sir Lynden Pindling, were accepting payoffs to allow Carlos Lehder's operation at Norman's Cay to function. The *Miami Herald* followed up on the story with a series of articles titled "A Nation for Sale," and the *Sunday Times Magazine* (London) published an extended piece called "Paradise Lost."[16] Lynden Pindling professed his innocence, hired F. Lee Bailey to sue NBC, and appointed an official Commission of Inquiry to study the entire matter of drug trafficking and payoffs. None of these were completely convincing, nor did anyone ever prove that Sir Lynden had accepted drug money. The Commission of Inquiry discovered that Pindling had received large amounts of money as "gifts from constituents" and that he had built an extravagant multi-million dollar house on a salary of only about $100,000 per year, but fell short of proving that the money had come from drugs.

The United States government insisted on cooperation. Carol Boyd Hallet, the newly appointed Ambassador to The Bahamas in 1986, arrived in Nassau in a Drug Enforcement Agency plane. Her top priority was to stifle drug trafficking. By this time more than half the cocaine entering the United States was coming through The Bahamas and 10% of the Bahamian economy was said to be based on drugs. She urged the Bahamian Government to sign the Mutual Legal Assistance Treaty, which she said the United States had been ready to sign since 1985. The United States brought pressure to bear on the Bahamian Government by initiating a procedure which called for foreign nations to be certified each year if they cooperated in the campaign to stop the flow of illicit drugs to the United States. Although the Reagan administration recommended certification each year, some members of Congress challenged that determination. De-certification would have meant loss of all United States aid, of the United States Customs pre-clearance center at Nassau which was considered to be a boon for tourism, and limitation of visas issued by the United States for Bahamians. De-certification was unthinkable for a small nation with so many important ties to its large neighbor.

The Bahamas began to cooperate with the United States during the early middle 1980s. Operation Bahamas, Turks and Caicos (OP-BAT) was launched in 1984 and involved extensive cooperation between The Bahamas Police and Customs on the one hand and the United States Coast Guard and Drug Enforcement Agency on the other. United States agencies were allowed "hot pursuit" of drug traffickers into Bahamian waters, with arrests made by Bahamian officers who travelled on the United States vessels. Eventually aerostat radar balloons were installed on Grand Bahama Island, Exuma, and Inagua. Monitored by special personnel at the United States Embassy in Nassau, the United States was able to detect almost all aircraft and boat activity in The Bahamas. In 1988 Ambassador Hallet announced that drug seizures in 1987 were up 300% from 1986.[17] Seizures were again high in 1988, but in 1989 they were only a little more than half the record of 10,500 kilos of cocaine in 1987. The Bahamian Minister of Foreign Affairs proudly proclaimed that "drug trafficking has been pressured away from our islands and, from the standpoint of drug eradication, it is getting better in the Bahamas."[18]

Although there was still some drug trafficking through The Bahamas and through Abaco during the 1990s, the level of activity was much lower than it was during the middle 1980s. A Cooperstown resident said: "You don't see traffic anymore, just some users." This is the legacy of drug trafficking. For almost ten years in The Bahamas it was easy to get cocaine—almost anyone could buy it, and they could buy it "wholesale." The major drug traffickers may have been able to remain non-users, and they may have been able to legitimize themselves by investing in various other business ventures, but others, sometimes their younger brothers, sometimes their sons or daughters, became users, and The Bahamas developed massive drug abuse problems of its own. It was often said during the late 1980s that there was not a single extended Bahamian family which had not been adversely affected by drugs. The Bahamas was slow to act against drugs because of the flow of money that drug trafficking brought, and the money found its way into unusual places and corrupted many normally honest people. Bankers and lawyers were in the forefront; they helped to launder money. Some entire communities showed a predilection for drug money rather than law enforcement because there were some very visible results of the flow of dollars.[19] The individuals who were directly involved had huge amounts of cash, and some of this wealth stayed in their communities. Some are still wealthy men. Some who used to sail Abaco dinghies to the reef to fish for grouper for a living, now go to the reef in well equipped sportfishing boats to fish for pleasure. Many others wasted the money; some who used to light their cigarettes with $100. bills have nothing left to show for their involvement in drugs. Others built unnecessary shopping centers or condominiums. But some of the money was spent or invested wisely. Some communities experienced more rapid modernization than would have occurred without the flow of dollars from drugs. But gradually many realized that the legacy of drug trafficking might well cost more than it produced. The diminished capacity of individuals addicted to drugs and the enormous social and business costs of that harm the entire society. The benefits were clearly offset by the damaging social and economic impact of drug abuse by Bahamians. Abaco and The Bahamas will not escape the scourge of drug running for quite some time—it is a legacy of fast money, materialism, deficiencies of moral and social standards, the end of idyllic innocence in remote communities, and a few addicts in every town. It continues to change The Bahamas permanently.

HAITIAN IMMIGRATION:
AN ECONOMIC AND SOCIAL CATCH 22

Another "economic opportunity" developed into a problem for Abaco and for The Bahamas during the 1970s, 1980s, and 1990s. Haitian labourers were first brought to Abaco by Owens-Illinois in 1962. They were desirable because they were willing to work for minimal wages. Haiti is the poorest nation in the Western Hemisphere; its per capita income was $58. in 1961 and only $440. in the early 1990s.

During the 1970s many more Haitians came to Abaco to work at Key-Sawyer Farms. They did manual labor shunned by both white and black Bahamians. Working and living conditions were poor, and there were some protest strikes.[20] The dramatic expansion of tourism, and construction of second homes by foreigners during the 1970s and 1980s, brought Haitian labourers into menial jobs at hotels and other tourist facilities as well as in the construction industry. Here they also provided hard work for low wages while Bahamians filled more desirable jobs.

By the middle of the 1980s it became clear that The Bahamas faced a major problem. Large numbers of illegal Haitians, variously estimated at from 20,000 to 60,000, had migrated to The Bahamas. In 1980 the Bahamian population was only about 200,000, so the Haitians comprised from 10% to 25% depending on the estimate used. Bahamians became very aware of the fact that there were over six million Haitians in Haiti—many of whom wanted to leave. Clearly, the Bahamians could be in danger of becoming a minority in their own country—of losing it to Haitian immigrants. But it was also believed that The Bahamas' modern economy needed at least some Haitian labourers to function efficiently.

There were other problems as well. The Haitians at Key-Sawyer Farms lived in wretched conditions, but they were far from view. The Haitians who established squatter settlements in vacant sections of Marsh Harbour were in plain view—their barrios were called Pidgeon Peas and The Mud. In 1990 it was estimated that 45% of Marsh Harbour's population was Haitian.[21] Ramshackle housing and inadequate sanitation were common. Some residents feared contamination of the city's water supply and/or outbreaks of epidemics resulting from inadequate sanitation. On Elbow Cay Haitians squatted in the woods off the Centerline Road, and in some cases they rented land from Bahamian owners to build their

Haitian immigrants provide labour in The Bahamas, but often live in sub-standard housing with inadequate sanitation. A squatter's residence on crown land in The Mud is shown above. Monty Albury said the problem is a difficult one—"we need a work force and they're willing to work—it is hard to get anyone else who will do what they are prepared to do." But he also said that The Bahamas has to take a firm position with Haitian immigrants. Victor Patterson believes that The Bahamas does not need Haitian labour. If those who hire Haitians had to bear the full cost of maintaining their employees in legal and acceptable conditions, they would no longer be induced to hire Haitians. "The only real attraction," Victor says, "is the opportunity to employ someone who will accept a lower standard of living." If the standard of living were raised, there would be no advantage to Bahamian employers to hire a Haitian rather than a Bahamian. Victor believes that repatriation of Haitians will lead to a higher level of employment for Bahamians. The Marsh Harbour Town Planning Committee took a firm position when it announced, in 1993, that new construction of unauthorized buildings would not be tolerated (see notice at right).

NOTICE

Any new building constructed without approval of the Town Planning Committee in the Mud, Pigeon Peas, Charlie Boo Yard, Elbow Cay (Hope Town) or elsewhere will be TORN DOWN and the person or persons responsible will be PROSECUTED - as authorized under statute laws of the Bahamas, Chapter 236, Town Planning, Sections 7 & 8.

Town Planning, Marsh Harbour

NINPORTE

CAY NOUVO CAP BATI NAN
POUA-GONGO NON SALINE NON
CHARLI-BOU OU NONPORTE COTE KI
PA GIN PERMISION COMITION NON AP
CRASE AVAN 24 IN DE TEMJS PA BATE
CAY ANKO,
BAHAMAS LAW
CHAPTER 236, SECTIONS 7 & 8.

A sub-committee of the Marsh Harbour Town Planning Committee chaired by Victor Patterson recommended the destruction of unoccupied Haitian residences in 1993. This was done in order to prevent re-occupation. Victor is shown above with the wrecking crew. To the left, a puzzled child watches.

shacks. Some communities banned them; no Haitians were allowed to settle in Murphy Town. There were fewer Haitians in the communities of northern Abaco than there were in the central region, probably just twenty at Cooperstown and twenty on Little Abaco Island. They rented houses but squatted on land for farming.

Some of the Haitians in The Bahamas intended to stay permanently—others were just on their way to the United States, but stayed for several years. Some had no plan but just moved on whenever the Bahamian government cracked down on illegal immigrants. By the 1980s The Bahamas had some second and third generation Haitian immigrants. Many of them maintained regular contact with friends and family in Haiti, and sent money home to support family members, or to buy farmland, or a business, or a truck which could be used some day to make a living at home.[22] Many Haitians demonstrated their intelligence by learning English quickly and by learning new skills on the job, and some Haitian children excelled in the Bahamian schools.[23]

Despite their contributions, they strained the system. Many Haitians were unemployed or underemployed. Their children overcrowded the schools and they taxed health services, but the government did very little during the 1980s. The official opposition Free National Movement (FNM) Party said it would move toward a solution to the Haitian problem in its 1992 platform, and after taking power in August 1992, it made some moves to do so. After some Haitians were returned to Haiti, the Marsh Harbour Town Planning Board, a unit of the new local government, decided to demolish the empty housing units to prevent new migrants from occupying them. This was proudly described as the first positive act to turn the tide of Haitian migration in Marsh Harbour, and it was, but there was also an element of human tragedy as Haitian men, women, and children watched the destruction of their former neighbor's homes.

Bahamian Haitian policy got a boost from President Clinton's decision to overturn the Haitian dictator Raul Cedras and return the elected President Juan Bertrand Aristide to office in September-October 1994. In Nassau the Bahamian government announced that all illegal Haitians should register for return to Haiti by 15 November or risk jail terms. Employers of illegal immigrants were also put on notice—fines would be up to $10,000. The timing was excellent; some Haitians were willing to return because Aristide was back in office. The economic realities are that even with the democratically elected President back in Port au Prince, the likelihood of a rapid economic turnaround for a nation which has been poor for two hundred years is not bright. But the Haitians who do return from The Bahamas to Haiti will return with new skills and with good educations—they may well play an important role in building a new Haiti.[24] For Abaco and The Bahamas, it is an opportunity to solve a major social problem.

RELIGION

Religion has always been a very important part of the lives of Abaconians. Perhaps it is living so close to the elements of nature—having constantly to adjust one's life to the vagaries of wind and waves, or to the sequence of tides and the phases of the moon—that makes it extremely difficult for Abaconians to ignore God. Vernon Malone, a lay preacher at the Methodist Church at Hope Town, said, "I do not know of a Bahamian atheist, and I have only met one agnostic."[25] The people may "...not necessarily be church-going, but they are God-fearing,"[26] and their beliefs are strongly held, even if they don't regularly attend services. During the nineteenth century the Anglican and the Methodist Churches were dominant. Hope Town's old Methodist Church seated about 600, and New Plymouth's could accommodate 1200. During the twen-

Church of God, Great Guana Cay

The Roman Catholic Church has gained members in The Bahamas during the twentieth century and serves Haitian immigrants as well as Bahamians. St. Francis de Sales Church in Marsh Harbour is one of that community's few architectural treasures; it was designed to fit in well with the surrounding land.

tieth century the religious situation has become more diverse, with the Brethren and the Assembly of God Churches playing major roles in some communities. The Baptists have also made gains in Abaco, and the Roman Catholics have been active during the past forty years. The Catholics serve the needs of the Haitian as well as the Bahamian population; masses in Abaco are recited in Haitian French as well as in English. The churches in the black Bahamian communities generally tend to be more evangelical than their white counterparts, whether they are Anglican, Methodist, or Brethren. At Man-O-War Cay the Brethren dominate. They recently split as a result of a disagreement regarding the discipline of a member, so now there are two Brethren churches at Man-O-War. The Methodist church building there was sold to Man-O-War Hardware and is used to store carpeting and padding. But the Methodist Church is dominant in Dundas Town, where the average Sunday attendance is seventy. At Green Turtle Cay the Anglican Church and the Church of God are most prominent. At Great Guana Cay, with a population of under 100, there are two churches—the Brethren and the Church of God. On a pleasant weekday evening several years ago the Church of God was nearly full, with a black man rhythmically and methodically preaching the gospel to his white congregation— "De Lord," he said, "who put the sun in the sky; De Lord," he said again, his voice rising in tone and dwelling on the word Lord to provide greater emphasis, "who put the fish in the sea; He loves ya brother, he loves ya."

POLITICS

The religious beliefs and commitment of most Abaconians have not been matched by a patriotic commitment to the Bahamas national government in Nassau. Nationalism has gained precedence over regionalism very slowly. The spirit of political separatism still lives in Abaco, and even during the 1990s some wanted to revive the Abaco Independence Movement (AIM).[27] But this was wishful thinking rather than a realistic basis for political action. The plan to separate Abaco from The Bahamas had clearly failed to gain the support of a majority of Abaconians, but that did not mean that the majority of Abaconians supported Prime Minister Lynden Pindling and his Progressive Liberal Party (PLP). For many years Abaco remained a center of activity for opposition political groups which were generally ineffective because of internal quarreling and splits.

In 1977 the first post-independence election for a new House of Assembly was held. The Cooperstown constituency, which still included Dundas Town and Murphy Town, and was therefore safe for the PLP, elected Hubert Ingraham to the House of Assembly by a very wide margin. In the Marsh Harbour constituency there was a three-way race. Cecil Wallace-Whitfield, head of the Free National Movement (FNM) ran, but Michael Lightbourne, a member of a splinter opposition group called the Bahamas Democratic Party (BDP) and the recipient of support from the Abaco Home Rule Movement (AHRM), also ran. The PLP passed over Gordon Hudson, who had lost in 1972 and then had been accused of wrongdoing in regard to a government contract to pave the Abaco Highway, and nominated Edison Key, a white man from Marsh Harbour who had joined the PLP in 1971 and was one of the owners and operators of Key-Sawyer Farms. The election was close. Edison Key polled 503 votes to Michael Lightbourne's 507. Cecil Wallace-Whitfield won 280 votes. Although Lightbourne had won, the fact that the PLP had come within 4 votes of winning in the Marsh Harbour constituency dashed the hopes of the old separatists. Polling divisions which had previously been overwhelmingly opposed to the PLP, such as Man-O-War Cay, provided twenty-two votes for Edison Key, compared to just three votes for Gordon Hudson five years earlier. Michael Lightbourne and the rest of the political opposition were ineffective during the next five years. Edison Key, the loser in the election, was appointed to the Senate by Prime Minister Lynden Pindling. Although the Bahamian Senate is not a geographically representative body and can only delay legislation, Edison Key's access to the highest ranking members of the government enabled him to be much more useful to many Abaconians than Michael Lightbourne. He became, along with Hubert Ingraham, Abaco's man in Nassau.

By 1982, when another election had to be held, it was generally believed that the Progressive Liberal Party (PLP) faced its toughest challenge since first gaining power in 1967. Labour actions by teachers and Bahamas Telephone Company (BATELCO) employees during the previous two years underscored the fact that all was not well with the economy, which suffered as a result of the recession in the United States. There was lingering opposition to the PLP's proposed constitutional amendment restricting citizenship, which some church and labour groups opposed. There were the inevitable newspaper reports regarding corruption in the government, and a House of Assembly investigation. Some of these charges were made against the Prime Minister. Most important in the minds of hopeful opposition supporters was the fact that the Social Democratic Party (SDP), successor to the Bahamas Democratic Party (BDP), dissolved itself early in the year, leaving only one reasonably unified opposition group, the Free National Movement (FNM), headed by Kendal Isaacs. Also, many pointed with glee to the fact that in each election since 1967, the percentage of the vote won by the PLP had declined. In 1977 the PLP had won only 55% of the popular vote, and some predicted it would poll less than 50% of the vote in 1982.[28] Although the total number of constituencies was increased from 38 to 43, Abaco's two districts remained essentially unchanged. The Cooperstown seat was handily won by Hubert Ingraham, the PLP incumbent. Michael Lightbourne, who held the Marsh Harbour seat from 1977 to 1982, retired from politics. The FNM chose Roscoe (Ross) W. Thompson, Jr., nephew of former House of Assembly member Leonard Thompson, to run against Senator Edison Key, who had lost to Michael Lightbourne in 1977 by only 4 votes.

The campaign was heated and intense; the result was that the PLP won the Marsh Harbour constituency for the first time. Edison

Key won 833 votes to Roscoe Thompson, Jr.'s 727. Key won large majorities in black settlements such as Spring City, Crossing Rocks, and Mores Island. Sandy Point and Marsh Harbour were almost evenly divided. White settlements at Cherokee Sound, Hope Town, and Man-O-War Cay provided solid two-thirds majorities for Roscoe Thompson, Jr., but larger minorities than ever before voted for Edison Key and the PLP. In Hope Town there were 45 votes for the PLP. In 1977 there were only 7. At Cherokee the PLP had won only 4 votes in 1977; in 1982 they won 34. The increase for the PLP was not quite as great at Man-O-War Cay. At Great Guana Cay, Roscoe Thompson won 51 votes to Edison Key's 6, but those 6 votes represented a 50% increase over the 4 votes Key had won on Great Guana in 1977. Although Great Guana remained one of the opposition's most secure bastions in the nation, Abaco as a whole had voted to support the ruling PLP. Some of this support was genuinely enthusiastic, but some of it was born of resignation rather than commitment. Opposition had not gained benefits for Abaco, and some felt that if the PLP could not be defeated, it would be better to join it. Many of those who continued to support the FNM were very critical of these "turncoats," and there were some minor disorders associated with the election. Within a few days the rancor began to subside, and one resident of Hope Town predicted that there would soon be 90 claimants for Hope Town's 45 PLP votes.[29]

Nationally, the PLP scored its fifth successive victory. Thirty-two of the forty-three seats were won by the PLP, and the party won 55% of the vote, the same percentage as in 1977. The PLP ran on its record—it had provided stable government, empowered black Bahamians, achieved independence, and presided over steady economic growth as a result of tourism. Even a cursory comparison with the governments of other small developing nations is enough to convince most skeptics that the PLP and Lynden Pindling provided some good leadership during these years. But critics said the growth would have occurred with or without the PLP, and said that the government wasted resources which could have been used to produce more growth.

Although the PLP had consistently advocated a greater measure of self-government for the Family Islands,[30] nothing was done to change the system of centralized control. The commissioner system had deep roots in the colonial past, and the PLP government, despite its anti-colonialism, had no greater inclination to distribute political power regionally than the British did. Although the structure of government was decidedly opposed to local control and was resistant to change, there was an informal system which provided for some local government. The power wielded by members of the House of Assembly within their respective constituencies, and their ability to influence the bureaucracy in Nassau as well as in their own constituencies, provided a significant measure of local government. Edison Key and Hubert Ingraham played roles similar to those of elected local officials such as mayors and governors in alternative structures of government. And it was a new experience for Abaco to have two Members of Parliament from the ruling PLP; many Abaconians looked forward to a new era of development with this new access to the government in Nassau.

Those who went over to the government's side expecting an array of road-building, dock-building, and other development projects, were probably disappointed during the middle 1980s. The government money which did come to Abaco continued to be concentrated in the north—the Cooperstown constituency of Hubert Ingraham. The Treasure Cay Airport was up-graded into a jet port. Marsh Harbour Airport received a new terminal building which was too small to handle the traffic on the day it opened. The Great Abaco Highway from Treasure Cay north to Cooperstown and the small communities on Little Abaco Island was paved by 1988, but the road between Treasure Cay, Marsh Harbour, and Sandy Point in the south were still just gravel and were infrequently re-graded. Edison Key did become the head of BATELCO and brought direct dial telephones to most of Abaco as well as most of The Bahamas during the 1980s. But many Abaconians were still resentful of the fact that the burgeoning economy of Abaco produced steadily increasing revenue for the national government, only a small portion of which was returned to Abaco. More than half of it, they said, was "squandered in Nassau."

Hubert Ingraham, who won the elections of 1977 and 1982 easily, soon became one of the leading young men in the PLP. After the 1982 election he became Minister of Housing and National Insurance. He pursued ambitious projects designed to provide meaningful benefits for the Bahamian people. Ingraham was serving his constituency well, had risen to become one of his party's emerging leaders, and some viewed him as a possible future successor to Prime Minister Sir Lynden Pindling. But in late 1984 he was dismissed from the Cabinet, and in 1985 he was evicted from the party.

Brian Ross of NBC news aired a story about drug payoffs in The Bahamas and Pindling's possible involvement in September 1983. The FNM called for Sir Lynden's resignation, and demanded a general election. Sir Lynden professed his innocence, ignored the call for an election, and established an official Commission of Inquiry to investigate the entire subject. Its hearings dominated the Bahamian news media throughout 1984. The evidence presented against Pindling was damaging, but not conclusive.[31] Ingraham and some others in the party took the position that Pindling should step aside to limit the damage to the party and its ability to govern. But Pindling was not ready to quit.

In October 1984 he accepted the resignations of two cabinet ministers who had been implicated in drug payoffs by testimony before the Commission of Inquiry. George Smith, Minister of Agriculture and Fisheries, had accepted a BMW as a bribe, and Kendall Nottage, Minister of Youth, had been involved with money laundering. But on the same day as he announced these resignations, he fired Hubert Ingraham and Perry Christie, the Minister of Tourism. Arthur Hanna, Deputy Prime Minister, resigned. Smith and Nottage were out because they were tainted; Ingraham, Christie and Hanna were out because they opposed the continued leadership of a partially tainted Pindling. The incident resulted in much political confusion; some thought the Government was going to fall. Ingraham fought back with hard hitting speeches in the House of Assembly criticizing the Pindling administration, and by the end of 1985 he was an independent. The FNM was the official opposition to the PLP, but it mounted only cautious and measured attacks on government policy during these years. Hubert Ingraham was not cautious, and he did not relent—he delivered major speeches against the government on an almost weekly basis. He blasted away at the PLP, but he did not join the FNM. He mounted an independent crusade, and was an amazingly effective one-man opposition.

The 1987 election loomed. Pindling and the PLP had been discredited by the revelations of the Commission of Inquiry, and the FNM campaigned hard on the issue of corruption. But the PLP had two and one-half years between the release of the Commission's report and the election. The matter dragged on. There were some indictments made as a result of the Commission's investigation,

In 1987 Sir Lynden Pindling and the Progressive Liberal Party continued to control the government by winning 31 seats in the House of Assembly to the FNM's 16. Hubert Ingraham, who had been evicted from the PLP, won re-election as an independent. Photos show Albert Albury of Marsh Harbour, an ardent FNM supporter (upper left), a PLP supporter with a tee-shirt bearing the PLP slogan "Steady as she Goes—PLP All the Way (upper right), and Lowell Edgecombe, whose tee-shirt declares his support for Hubert Ingraham.

but no prominent individuals went to jail. Sir Lynden emphasized his international role: he went to Chicago where he spoke out against apartheid in South Africa and also met Stevie Wonder. And the economy was robust. The result was that Pindling's PLP won 54% of the popular vote and thirty-one seats in the House of Assembly to the FNM's sixteen. Two independents were elected—Perry Christie and Hubert Ingraham.

Ingraham's re-election in the Cooperstown constituency was an easy one. The FNM did not run a candidate against him, and he defeated the PLP's Wesley Campbell 1307 to 684. And Edison Key was defeated in Marsh Harbour where Frederick Gottlieb, son of a German immigrant who was Marsh Harbour's only medical doctor for many years, polled 1031 votes to Key's 927. The PLP retained power in the nation, but they lost both of the Abaco seats.

During the next five years the issues for Abaconians were the same as what they had been for the preceding five to ten years. The failure of the Government to pave the Great Abaco Highway was holding back economic development and causing numerous problems for Abaco automobile owners. The Government was gaining about $25 million from Abaco in import duties and other revenues, but spending only a very small portion of it in Abaco. Abaconians regularly complained about roads, docks, and other infrastructure, but the government was slow to respond.

In April 1990, important political events occurred in The Bahamas. Cecil Wallace-Whitfield, leader of the FNM, died. The week before Wallace-Whitfield's death Hubert Ingraham ended his long vigil as an independent by joining the FNM, and the week after Whitfield died Hubert Ingraham became the new leader of the FNM. The FNM finally had a truly charismatic and energetic leader. Ingraham organized a hard-hitting campaign for the 1992 elections, and the FNM issued a detailed *Manifesto* as its platform. Pindling postponed the election as long as he possibly could, hoping for an economic recovery. The PLP did not devise a platform; the party ran on its record. When the election was finally held, on 19 August 1992, the FNM won thirty-one seats to the PLP's eighteen. The popular vote was 55.7% for the FNM and 44.2% for the PLP. Sir Lynden Pindling, who some thought would try to retain power by fraud, simply announced that "the people have spoken, and the voice of the people is the voice of God." Hubert Ingraham of Cooperstown, Abaco, became the Prime Minister of The Bahamas.

168

Hubert Ingraham, Member of Parliament for Cooperstown, leader of the Free National Movement, and Prime Minister of The Bahamas.

Ingraham had won election in his Cooperstown constituency easily over Lionel Evans, polling 1045 to Evans' 793. And in a new Abaco constituency called Hope Town and including all the off-lying cays, Robert Sweeting of the FNM trounced Gary Sawyer of the PLP 989 to 472. But in a gerrymandered Marsh Harbour constituency Frederick Gottlieb lost to Edison Key, 728 to 883, so Marsh Harbour continued its contrarian trend.

The FNM Government immediately implemented various initiatives. It proposed construction of new airport facilities at Marsh Harbour, but then deferred to local preference for paving the South Abaco Highway first. This work was well under way by late 1994. Installation of a new water main and construction of a storm sewer system necessitated tearing up the main roads of Marsh Harbour and caused great inconveniences, but new paving was already scheduled and was to be done as soon as the underground work was completed. Construction of a new port or expansion of the existing port was being studied. The FNM Government made a decided move toward local government with the creation of a Town Planning Council in Marsh Harbour, and by giving new authority and funds to local Boards of Works. And elections were scheduled for summer, 1995, to choose representatives for new Town Councils, which will send representatives to a new Abaco Island Council. These new councils will be the first true local government in The Bahamas. The new FNM Government seemed to be responding to many of Abaco's needs, and Robert Sweeting predicted that the goals of the FNM's *Manifesto* would be achieved during the five-year term of the Government. He listed numerous public works projects which would be done, including a new airport, a new port, electrification of Cherokee Sound, and he said he thought there was a new sense of freedom in The Bahamas as well.[32]

CONTEMPORARY MARSH HARBOUR

The communities of Abaco are sufficiently diverse to make separate treatment of their recent history and present condition desirable. Marsh Harbour is the largest settlement. The population of the town, including its two black satellite communities, Dundas Town and Murphy Town, was 3611 in 1990, up from about 2700 ten years earlier. It is The Bahamas' third largest metropolitan area. It is a sprawling community with businesses and residences spread along the three-mile road which encircles the harbour, as well as along the two-mile road to Marsh Harbour International Airport, a single runway without a control tower. Unlike towns of 4000 in the United States, which usually rely on larger nearby towns for retail and other services, Marsh Harbour is the regional center in Abaco, and attracts consumers from forty or fifty miles away. There are three supermarkets and at least five liquor stores, two hard-

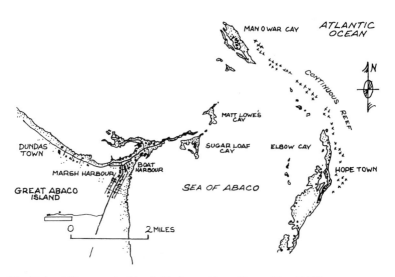

The Hub of Abaco is the Marsh Harbour, Hope Town, Man-O-War area.

The *Deborah K II*, operated by Captain Garnet Archer of Marsh Harbour, is Abaco's mail boat, and makes a round trip to Nassau each week.

ware stores, several large modern marinas and restaurants, two lawyers, four doctors, and numerous other businesses and services. There is a medical clinic, a post office, and Marsh Harbour is the seat for the Senior Commissioner for Abaco. Marsh Harbour has two gasoline stations and two auto parts stores, one of which also sells homemade conch salad. The Great Abaco Beach Hotel on the southeast shore and the Conch Inn on the harbour cater to tourists from the United States, Canada, and Europe. The harbour is just as spacious as Nassau's, but it cannot accommodate deep draft vessels, and will therefore never be on a large cruise ship's itinerary. There is constant small boat traffic in the harbour—outboard speedboats, visiting yachts, charter sailboats, fishing boats, and dinghies.

Despite the advent of airplane service to Abaco during the past fifty years, Marsh Harbour as well as other Abaco communities are still dependent on ships for freight service. Modern island freighters—the *M. V. Biak, M.V. State Challenge,* and others—make the trip to the Port of Palm Beach in Florida each week, arriving back in Marsh Harbour on Thursday or Friday. Marsh Harbour is also the principal terminus for the *M.V. Deborah K II*, which is Abaco's mailboat. The *Deborah K II* leaves for Nassau every Sunday or Monday morning, and returns to Marsh Harbour on a night run depart-

THE ABACOS

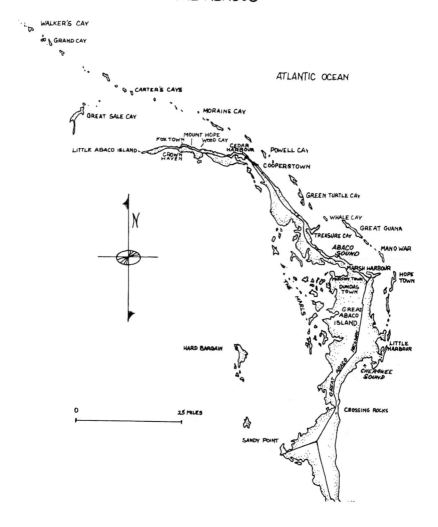

ing from Nassau late Wednesday afternoon. The fare from Marsh Harbour to Nassau is $25, up from $16 in 1982. It includes lunch, which is usually pork chops and traditional Bahamian peas and rice.

Bahamas Electricity Corporation (BEC), a government corporation, took over the privately-run Marsh Harbour Power and Light Company during the 1980s. They built a new power plant and lowered the rates, which are still about double the United States average. Bahamas Telephone Company (BATELCO) installed a modern phone system during the 1980s, and in 1994-95 Marsh Harbour was finally getting a modern storm sewer system and

172

new roads. Also, the road south to Sandy Point will be paved by the end of 1995. The power/communication/transportation infrastructure is finally catching up to development in Marsh Harbour.

Marsh Harbour's taxi cabs are probably among the highest priced in the world, but the service usually matches the cost. Victor Russell initiated local taxi service in Marsh Harbour during the early 1950s, and when the Marsh Harbour airport first opened, he was in charge of immigration and customs, as well as being airline ticket agent and taxi cab driver. The airport provided the market for a fleet of taxis. Whereas the seaplanes of Bahamas Airways had carried passengers direct to the settlements on the cays, the new land-based aircraft deposited passengers several miles from downtown Marsh Harbour. A distribution system involving both taxis and ferries was required. The business activities of Owens-Illinois on Great Abaco, as well as increased tourism throughout Abaco, supported a growing number of cabs.

The taxi fleet was originally owned and operated by whites. Delgano Newbold, black owner and operator of taxi 17 in Marsh Harbour in 1982, said that no blacks applied for taxi plates because, at first, they "didn't know it was happening." Later, when some white taxi operators employed blacks to drive additional cabs for them and the blacks realized how lucrative the business could be, they applied for taxi plates on their own. The white UBP government did not approve their applications, and control of the taxi industry remained in white hands. After the PLP gained power in 1967 the situation changed—"they got plates and every one was driving for himself."[33] The white drivers, however, still dominated the system. Because they had became acquainted with many of the foreign residents, those foreigners pre-

In *Marsh Harbour*, it's

SPOTTY'S TAXI SERVICE
Marsh Harbour, Abaco

This early (1964) advertisement for one of Marsh Harbour's first taxi services appeared in *Sun 'n Sixpence,* a travel guide to the Out Islands. It is reproduced here with the permission of Etienne Dupuch Jr. Publications, Nassau.

ferred to use the white drivers. Many of the foreigners who rented their homes recommended these same white drivers in brochures used to advertise their homes. This made it difficult for the black drivers to break into the market. During the early 1970s the government stepped in to regulate the taxis. It was determined that taxi stands would be established at the airport, the ferry dock, and at all hotels and government docks. The first cab in line would get the first fare. This made it possible for blacks to compete on an equal basis with the established white drivers. Taxi service was probably the first business in which blacks were successful at competing with whites—the required capital investment was within the reach of many blacks, and the return on the investment and the work was very good.

The government actions which made black-owned taxis possible won new support for the PLP in the black communities, because it helped to break down the barriers which had prevented the blacks from achieving economic gains. Many of the whites, and especially the white taxi drivers, resented the changes and regarded the blacks as upstarts. Even as late as 1982 some white drivers were still angry about the intrusion of the blacks, and some blacks still harboured latent hatred for racist regulations which had been off the books for over a decade. The introduction of so many new taxicabs made it less lucrative for all drivers, and this created new tensions. In general, however, fair-minded people of both races recognized that the situation was much more equitable and humane in 1980s and 1990s than it had been in 1960s.

Delgano Newbold of Dundas Town drove a taxi for many years, but now runs Express Cleaners in Dundas Town.

As of 1982, Delgano Newbold had been driving a taxi cab in Marsh Harbour for five years. Prior to that he operated a bulldozer at Key-Sawyer Farms, and he lived in Freeport for two years while driving a tractor-trailer rig for Tropical Shipping Company. He was born and raised in Dundas Town and is pleased to live there now. He decided to become a taxi driver because he became ". . . tired of working for people for nothing." He liked the idea of working for himself—"whatever I make, I'm

satisfied with." He has twelve living children. His son Trevor earned
a scholarship to go to Queen's College in Nassau while he was a
student at Dundas Town School, and he later went on to study
chemistry at a Canadian university in Halifax, Nova Scotia. He
worked for Syntex in Freeport for many years. Delgano's home is
modern and is nicely furnished; he grows bananas, sugar canes,
thyme and some other crops on his own property and occasionally
sells some to local grocery stores. He is a fair and reasonable man
with no grudges and no hard feelings for the white community. He
supports the PLP government. He is a lay preacher in the Methodist Church and always had a Bible handy on the front seat or the
dashboard of his taxi cab. He recently gave up driving his taxicab in
Marsh Harbour—maintaining a taxi was not an easy task, and the
cost of repair parts and gasoline was very high, and the government, he said, allowed too many taxicabs. "They should have limited it, even if they had done it before I got mine." The government did not want to say no to anyone who applied, because they
would lose votes—"it was all politics," Delgano said. Too many
taxis came on the line, so it "made it hard for those who were
there, then nobody makes anything because there are so many."
Delgano gave up driving a taxi and opened a dry cleaning business—Express Cleaners in Dundas Town—with one of his sons.
He is proud that he has been able to establish another business of
his own, and that he is still working for himself. He remains loyal to
the PLP even though the present Prime Minister, Hubert Ingraham,
is his first cousin. "I think they (the PLP) did a good job. Some
people don't think so, but I think they did." And he finds fault with
Ingraham's increase in the gasoline tax because "when you go up
on gasoline, that's everything." "Its not the man with the money
who's hurting, its the poor people who are hurting, and I think any
leader should look out for the small man." He is doing a lot of
things which needed doing; we do need new roads, and new schools.
But Delgano believes the small man was better off with the PLP,
and says that too many people are losing their houses, their cars,
and their boats.[34]

Mother Merle's Fishnet Restaurant has been open at the same
location in Dundas Town for twenty-three years. Like Delgano,
Merle Williams had grown tired of working for somebody else.
She had done some cooking, and decided to "do something on my
own." Her business was slow in the beginning and required much
hard work. "It is still a lot of hard work," she said, but the business
is now well established and a significant portion of the clientele are
tourists. It is a family affair—three of Mother Merle's children work

Godfrey, Merle, Angela, and Shirley Williams at Mother Merle's Fishnet Restaurant in Dundas Town, one of the first businesses in Dundas Town to gain a share of the tourist market.

in the restaurant. Her son Godfrey, who works for BATELCO, also serves as the restaurant's manager. Her daughters Angela and Shirley help in the kitchen and wait on tables. Mother Merle is obviously proud of her cooking, pleased that her chicken, fish, and conch are known throughout the Marsh Harbour area, and proud that her business has prospered.[35]

One of Marsh Harbour's leading citizens is Edison Key. Son of Bunyan Key, owner and operator of Key's Bakery, Edison was one of the principals who developed Key-Sawyer Farms, which successfully exported cucumbers to the United States. He sold the farm several years ago, and now he devotes most of his time to political activities and public service.

He was one of the first whites to join the PLP—he became a member in 1971, just four years after Lynden Pindling and the PLP came to power, and two years before Bahamian independence. It was a courageous act for any white man, but especially for one from Marsh Harbour, which was soon to be the headquarters for a movement to separate Abaco from the rest of the Bahamas. He went to London with Prime Minister Lynden Pindling in early 1973 to argue in favor of passage of the Bahamas Independence Act in the House of Commons without separation of Abaco. Many in

Marsh Harbour viewed him as a
turncoat for this. He has served in
the Bahamian Senate, as the Chairman of BATELCO, and as Marsh
Harbour's Member of Parliament,
a position he continued to hold in
1995.

When asked to describe
Abaco, he said quietly and sincerely
that Abaco ". . . is one of the finest
islands of the Bahamas," and that
Abaconians are good people. They
are gradually, he believes, coming
to understand that the old govern-

Edison Key, MP for Marsh Harbour,
1982-87, 1992-present

ment (UBP) lied to them about the PLP. He said that the people of
the Bahamas—white and black—are gradually moving away from
racism. He was proud to say, in 1982, that the Bahamas had enjoyed a stable government for fifteen years, that there had been a
long and healthy dose of prosperity, and that his country was ". . .
probably the most peaceable country on earth."

Edison Key is confident of what the future holds for Abaco.
He believes Abaco will play an important role in feeding the Bahamas, and predicts other types of economic growth as well. He is
confident that one day Marsh Harbour will challenge Freeport for
the position of the second largest city in The Bahamas. He is so
optimistic about the growth of Abaco and the Bahamas that he
foresees—or perhaps just hopes for—a flourishing free and open
economy, which would be so buoyant that foreigners could be
allowed to compete with Bahamians in businesses and for jobs so
that, he said, ". . . there would be no difference in people."[36]

Patrick Bethel of Marsh Harbour is one of the most amazing
men in Abaco. The first thing that strikes anyone meeting Patrick is
the extremely high level of energy he exudes. He is a dynamo of a
man, and always seems to have at least three things going on at the
same time. And he is clearly a leader—in his church, in the business sector, in service organizations, in the community, and in the
nation.

He was born and raised in Cherokee Sound, Abaco, now connected to Marsh Harbour with a new road, but when Patrick was
growing up, Cherokee was a very isolated place which could be
reached only by boat. Jack Ford, a schoolteacher from England,

befriended him while he was a student. Patrick decided to become a teacher. From 1954-1958 he was the teacher at Hope Town, and then he went to England to study because the Bahamas Teacher's College was closed. There he lived with the Ford family. When he returned to Abaco he taught at Lake City, Abaco, for several months, and then at Harbour Island (Eleuthera) for two and one-half years. He went back to the United Kingdom, this time to Edinburgh, Scotland, specifically to prepare himself to be a teacher and administrator at the Bahamas Teachers College. He returned to the Bahamas in 1965 and was at Bahamas Teacher's College until 1974, serving as its principal until 1972. In 1974 Bahamas Teacher's College became the College of The Bahamas. Patrick stayed on for a short time, and then moved on to become Deputy Director in the Ministry of Education, a position he "retired" from in 1977. He returned to Abaco and soon was involved in several businesses in Marsh Harbour—an insurance agency, a travel agency, and a real estate agency. He said that it took him awhile to learn how to work in the business world—that he "brought too many of my civil service qualities" to the business world. But he succeeded—he built up all three businesses into thriving enterprises. He became active in Rotary, the Methodist Church, and in the community at large. Over the years he contributed much to Marsh Harbour and to Abaco, but most remember him primarily for one thing. Throughout the 1980s Patrick wrote letters to the newspapers to complain about the condition of Abaco's roads, and the fact that the government did not return to Abaco a fair share of the revenue generated by Abaco's growing economy. No one dared argue with him; he made his case and made it well. He did not write just one letter, or two, but dozens of them—perhaps hundreds. He kept the issue in the forefront when others had given it up for lost. He was consistent—he was persistent—some in the government undoubtedly thought he was obnoxious. But it worked—virtu-

Patrick Bethel of Marsh Harbour was born and raised in Cherokee Sound.

ally everyone in The Bahamas knew that Patrick Bethel was the man who wanted paved roads in Abaco—and he wore out his opponents.

The government finally decided to pave the Great Abaco Highway, but began with the segment serving the small towns of Little Abaco Island rather than with the center of commerce, Marsh Harbour. Some attributed this to politics. But then finally, in 1992, paved highway finally reached Marsh Harbour, and it was possible to drive to Treasure Cay and beyond in a fraction of the time it required previously. And then, by 1994, work was underway on paving the road south of Marsh Harbour all the way to Sandy Point. Patrick's persistence paid off. He says he is pleased with the role he played—especially with the establishment of the Abaco Concerned Citizen's Committee (ACCC) which was formed on 1 April 1990. Some of the members of this group refused to buy license plates for their vehicles unless the government promised to build roads in Abaco. Some were arrested and went to jail. Patrick said: "This sent a message right across The Bahamas."[37]

Now that the road is built or is under construction, what does Abaco need next? Patrick says an enlarged airport, which is already on the drawing board, and larger port facilities for Marsh Harbour, a subject already under study. He predicts new development in South Abaco—not only real estate and tourism—but he foresees a commercial deep water port and a new industrial city at Cross Harbour to provide a place for The Bahamas' growing population. Finally, he says he has a dream that one day the island of Abaco will have a "truly local government system which will meet the social and economic needs of the people—that the revenue produced by Abaco will be used responsibly for the people of Abaco."[38] Now retired again, Patrick Bethel stays very busy with a variety of public service work, as well as doing occasional real estate appraisals. He has a home at Bahama Palm Shores, a development just south of Cherokee Sound where he was raised. He maintains close ties with many people at Cherokee, and plays an important role in the life of the town. Though his horizons extend far beyond Cherokee Sound, Patrick Bethel is a man who knows where he came from—and shows his appreciation and his love for Cherokee Sound and its people. He plans to retire to Bahamas Palm Shores sometime within the next few years.

HOPE TOWN, MAN-O-WAR CAY, AND GREAT GUANA CAY

Albury's Ferry Service provides passenger transportation between Marsh Harbour, Hope Town (population - about 300), and Man-O-War Cay (population - about 220). Though Hope Town and Man-O-War are only a few miles from Marsh Harbour and within four miles of each other, they are as different as Italy and Switzerland. Hope Town is more casual and less disciplined than Man-O-War Its population is only a fraction of what it was fifty to seventy-five years ago when it was the home port for a fleet of spongers, when large schooners were built and sailed by her men, and when the commissioner ruled South Abaco from his office across the harbour from one of the most impressive light houses in the Bahamas. Hope Town was important when Marsh Harbour and Man-O-War were not, and Hope Towners can remember the glories of the past. In contrast, Man-O-War Cay was never more prominent than it is now. At Hope Town there is more reminiscing and more lethargy, though one is not necessarily related to the other. Some men sit in the shade of a palm tree all day long; at Man-O-War everyone appears to be occupied and there is a more businesslike atmosphere.

Both Hope Town and Man-O-War are white communities, but Hope Town has consistently had two or three black families in the settlement. Until recently, blacks who worked at Man-O-War were not permitted to stay on the cay overnight. Racial restrictions such as this are now a thing of the past, and there is greater tolerance in both communities, though both are still primarily white and are dominated by the whites. The head schoolteacher provided by the government to each community is black, and at Hope Town the lighthouse keepers, who are also employed by the government, are black. Both communities have Haitian labourers. On Elbow Cay Haitians live in shacks they have built themselves. Some may be squatters, but some live on land rented to them for that purpose by Bahamians. In most cases the housing does not meet Bahamian code, and some efforts have been made in recent years to force compliance or demolish the housing. Haitians also work at Man-O-War Cay, but most of those do not live on the island; they commute from Marsh Harbour daily.

Hope Town was visited by members of the Baltimore Geographic Society in 1902, who contended that the in-breeding of whites in the small settlement had led to genetic deficiencies such as idiocy and blindness.[39] Some other authors, using the information provided by the Baltimore Geographic Society, have implied that Hope Town whites could have avoided genetic problems if they had given up their racism and inter-married with the blacks. These contentions are less than popular with Hope Town whites, and it appears that the Hope Towners have some good reasons to find fault with the report of the geographic society.

There may have been some problems which resulted from close inter-marriage, but the Baltimore Geographic Society's report was inaccurate and overly sensational. A chart showing the lines of descent from the widow Wyannie Malone was titled "Family Tree of Degenerates at Hope Town, Elbow Cay, Abaco, Bahamas." The chart and the written report tentatively and inaccurately attributed the presence of leprosy, a disease caused by a bacillus, to genetic causes. The chart implies that a death resulting from cholera was caused by close inter-marriage. Some of the factual information in the chart is also incorrect. It appears to be quite likely that the scientists from Baltimore were so thrilled and excited to have discovered an experiment in human genetics that they misinterpreted, exaggerated and even fabricated the results.[40] Further, recent studies seem to indicate that the deleterious results of inter-marriage, even of first cousins, have been grossly exaggerated, and that actually very few problems occur.[41] The report of the Baltimore Geographic Society tells us more about the intellectual, social, and religious quirks of the "scientists" from civilized Baltimore than it does about the people of Hope Town. Also, because of their concentration on this one issue during their visit to Hope Town, they failed to contribute more to historical knowledge by describing other aspects of life in the town. There is still resentment in Hope Town regarding the Baltimore Geographic Society ninety years after they visited, and it seems to be justified.

Any problems of degeneracy which may have resulted from inbreeding have been mitigated during the twentieth century in small communities such as Hope Town by improved transportation and communication amongst the settlements. Technological innovations such as the outboard motor may well have played a role by making transportation from one cay to another faster and easier.

Hope Town is still dominated by a few families—the Bethels, the Sawyers, the Russells and the Lowes—but no family is more prominent than the descendants of Wyannie Malone, the widow from South Carolina who was one of the town's founders. Rudy Malone operates the Hope Town Marina and Club Soleil Restaurant and Resort. He is deeply involved in the Friends of the Environment organization. His brother Robert is proprietor of Malone Estates, a real estate firm, and the only liquor store in town. Another brother, Beltron, was a fisherman who died in 1993, Ivor is retired, and still another brother, Vernon, owns and operates Vernon's Grocery Store and the Upper Crust Bakery. Vernon is thin and wiry. His voice is melodic and deadpannish at the same time; he is quick witted, and he has a good,

Vernon Malone at work at the Upper Crust Bakery.

robust sense of humour. Vernon's small restaurant and party catering service developed into a grocery store several years ago. In small towns like Hope Town, grocery stores and their owners play more central roles than they usually assume in larger communities. Vernon Malone works very hard in his store, and he also works very hard for Hope Town. He is a lay preacher in the Methodist Church, where he regularly and competently conducts service. He picks up street litter while walking through town, and he re-built one of the town's older homes. On Saturday evenings during the 1980s he often was found running the projector for the movies shown at the ball field. He has served as a member of the local Board of Works, and he was one of the original backers of the Wyannie Malone Historical Museum.

The museum started as a result of a conversation between Byrle Malone Patterson and Vernon. Both were interested in the heritage of Hope Town. They had found an artifact of some sort which they wanted to preserve, but had no place to keep it. They considered trying to turn the rarely used Hope Town jail into a museum. One thing led to another, and within a few months Byrle's sister had helped to arrange for the free use of an old house in Hope Town. The structure was repaired and painted, members and volunteers were recruited, furniture and exhibits were collected, and the Wyannie Malone Historical Museum was born.

Vernon remembers acquiring an old bed for use in the museum hours before it was to become a crawfish trap.* Other exhibits were collected in similar fashion; many were found beneath houses in Hope Town, a traditional storage place for items too good to discard, but not good enough to use.

Vernon is not without criticism for his home town. He says it is a far easier place in which to vacation than to live, and he is probably right, but his love and pride in Hope Town show through. Recently, after a flying tour of all of the Abaco Cays, he said: "After seeing all those other places, I still think there is something special about Hope Town . . . it was more than just coming home . . . it even looked greener than the others."[42]

Both Hope Town and Man-O-War have a substantial number of houses owned by foreign residents, and both derive a significant portion of their prosperity from building and maintaining these homes. By 1980 Hope Town's 115 foreign owned homes outnumbered 79 native owned homes. These homes are scattered throughout the community and throughout Elbow Cay. At Man-O-War foreigners were excluded from the settlement itself, but were allowed to develop land located elsewhere on the island. This was a conscious decision of the town fathers and was done to insulate the settlement from foreign influence. At first the plan worked, and the settlement was preserved, but as business grew at Man-O-War more and more of the old houses in the settlement were transformed into stores or tourist gift shops, and as the affluence of the natives increased, they began to build more modern homes at the periphery of the old settlement. The result is that the settlement, though still devoid of foreign residents, has nevertheless changed dramatically over the past twenty years as a result of Man-O-War's economic mini-boom, and native residents are moving out to join the foreigners rather than vice versa.

Man-O-War Cay, located four miles northwest of Hope Town, is about two and one-half miles long and one-third of a mile wide. The settlement is located on the southwest side of the cay at about its mid-point; the harbour is formed by Dickie's Cay, a long, narrow cay which lies parallel to Man-O-War's western shore. The harbour front bustles with activity—boats are hauled out, bottoms scraped and re-painted, fiberglass runabouts are under construction, power saws whine from the marinas and boat storage facili-

---

* A crawfish trap does not actually confine crawfish, but serves as a shelter on the bottom of the sea and attracts a resident community. Various discarded items have been used as crawfish traps.

ties along the waterfront, and motor bikes and golf carts (rather than automobiles) zip to and fro along the main road. There is an intense local pride amongst the inhabitants of Man-O-War They are proud that their community has become more prominent, and proud that they have been economically successful. One native of Man-O-War who lived in Nassau during his working years and returned to Man-O-War to retire, explained that his boat had been broken into three or four times during the last years that he was in Nassau and kept the boat in Nassau Harbour. At Man-O-War he didn't even bother to lock the boat—"at Man-O-War everyone has everything they want," he said.

Man-O-War is known throughout the Bahamas not only for boat building, but for providing high quality marine maintenance services at reasonable rates. Some boats from the United States are regularly hauled out and painted at Edwin's Boat Yard on Man-O-War while they are in Abaco. Man-O-War is also known as the home of Albury's Ferry Service, which was founded after Owens-Illinois opened the airport in Marsh Harbour. Marcell Albury, who had returned to his home, Man-O-War Cay, in 1958 after working for eight years on a farm in Wisconsin, decided to develop a scheduled ferry service. He bought a used forty-foot lobster boat on a time payment plan. She had been brought to the Bahamas from the United States, and she was named *Junonia*. He and his wife, Christine, ran the boat, and they handled freight as well as passengers. The business was so successful that Marcell's brother Ritchie came into it the following year. Ritchie took over running the ferry, and Marcell helped the boat yard build another ferry boat. Additional boats were added about every three years.

The Ferry service now operates seven boats. The *Donnie VII*, their newest boat, acquired in November 1991, can carry eighty passengers, and represents an investment of over $150,000. Marcell is proud that despite increasing costs, they have been able to hold the fares on the ferry down. In 1969, when the service

Marcell Albury, founder and owner of Albury's Ferry, Man-O-War Cay.

started, the fare was $3.50; in 1982 it was $6.00, and in 1994 it was $8.00. This has been made possible by the rapid growth of tourism, which has dramatically increased the volume of passengers.[43] The operation of the ferry has provided a steady influx of money to Man-O-War Cay and has provided jobs for the young men of Man-O-War Without Albury's Ferry Service, the prosperity which Man-O-War has experienced would not have been possible.

Man-O-War is different from the other settlements for other reasons as well. It is a more disciplined community than most. Alcohol has never been sold on the island, and a few years ago, when the town fathers decided that too many young people were smoking, they convinced the local grocers to cease the sale of tobacco products on the cay. The Gospel Chapel, which is affiliated with the Brethren Church, plays a very important role in the community. A recent schism has resulted in a second Brethren Church in the community, with the old Gospel Chapel the smaller of the two. People from Man-O-War are, for the most part, honest, religious, and industrious.

Great Guana Cay is several miles northwest of Man-O-War and is also served by Albury's Ferry, but the service is limited to one day of the week—Friday. The largest business on the island, the Guana Beach Resort, recently began a daily ferry service of its own to supplement this infrequent service. The settlement is quite small. The population was about 110 in 1980, and had declined to about 80 in 1990. The settlement is located on a harbour which does not offer full protection, but the island has one of the most beautiful ocean beaches to be found in the Bahamas. The people

Eldred Pinder of Great Guana Cay grew tomatoes, green peppers, broccoli, onions, bananas, and other crops. He is shown here in his dinghy with his son, Milo, sculling.

live by fishing, farming, working at the Guana Beach Resort, or by caring for the foreign owned homes on the cay, which numbered fifty-five by 1995. Eldred Pinder, now retired, was probably the best known farmer from Guana. His ties to the soil seem to be emotional and almost mysterious, as well as economic. One foreigner described him as a man whose appearance and demeanor gave one the impression that he was endowed with the power to bless or curse the land. He is a small, wrinkled, pixie-like man who is happiest when talking of planting or harvesting or of grafting citrus. When the weather permitted, he travelled to his farm in an Abaco dinghy with a small inboard engine. He grew all kinds of vegetables and citrus and sold to grocery stores and supermarkets from Marsh Harbour to Green Turtle Cay. His farming ended in 1992 when he was partially crippled by a stroke, but he was still active and alert in early 1995, and willing to talk about farming in the good old days. His son Milo operates a small store in Guana, and his son Edmond is Guana's sole real estate agent.

Edmond is confident of the future of Great Guana Cay. The number of foreign owned homes is increasing, and there is more economic activity. In late 1994 he reported that a new restaurant and resort was under construction on the ocean side of the cay, and he outlined his own plans for the construction of a marina on the Sea of Abaco side. In the more distant future Guana may well change even more. Carleton Ritz Hotels has purchased a large part of the land on Guana to the southeast of the settlement, and is holding it for possible future development.[44]

NEW PLYMOUTH AND COOPERSTOWN

New Plymouth and Hope Town are both much larger communities than Guana, and they are similar to each other in many ways. Both are located on cays of similar size a few miles from the mainland of Abaco. Both were much larger one hundred years ago than they are now. New Plymouth, with a population of about 415 in 1980, and 475 in 1990, is only one-fifth of what it was during the late nineteenth century. Like Hope Town, New Plymouth has been stripped of its role as seat of the commissioner, and has adjusted to its more secondary position. Both settlements were once prosperous centers for boat building and home ports for fleets of smack boats and spongers. Both suffered through several decades of poverty before the advent of modern crawfishing and tourism brought a new period of prosperity. Their present economies are similar—some men fish and crawfish, some are involved in house construction and caretaking, some do marine maintenance, and others are involved in various aspects of tourism—from working in local hotels or resorts to serving as fishing and diving guides. Both communities have narrow streets and beautiful, quaint, Cape Cod style cottages. Both have attracted a number of foreign residents and enjoy buoyant economies based on tourism, but have, so far, avoided intensive development of tourist facilities such as large hotels or time-share condominiums, which would be so inconsistent with their small town characters.

Growing up in New Plymouth was very exciting for Bahamian artist Alton Lowe because, he said, ". . . my father was a shipbuilder and he always had boats, and I was always able to get any one of my father's boats, and we would go exploring the islands, and go crawfishing—of course, you know I was only six or seven when I was allowed to take them out,. . . we had lots of games; we played soccer. The biggest day of the entire year for all the young people was what was called Empire Day—now called Commonwealth Day—it was the Queen's birthday and everybody celebrated—because back when I was a child we all thought we were British, not Bahamian; to us the Bahamian was the Arawak Indian." The town was very poor, but ". . . we didn't know it was poor," Alton said, "because we didn't have anything to compare it with."

The prosperity which the town now enjoys has improved its appearance, but has not made the people happier, Alton said, because much of the cooperative spirit of helpfulness has disappeared. In the old days, if someone needed a roof shingled, everyone pitched in to help. Today, he said, the only way to get a roof shingled is to pay to have it done.

Alton started to draw when he was very young—his father often drew pictures of ships he had sailed on and Alton made copies of the drawings. He learned to paint when he was twelve. A resident from the United States—an amateur painter—gave him some lessons at New Plymouth, and he took a correspondence course before leaving Green Turtle Cay at the age of sixteen to study with United States' artists Alden and John Baker Smith for five years. He then studied in New York. After going through several stages—painting religious themes, mountain scenes, and female nudes—he decided to return to the Bahamas in 1969 to paint

This painting by Alton Lowe shows his father Albert rigging a model of a smack boat he built on the beach at New Plymouth Harbour. Reproduced with the permission of Alton Lowe.

the Bahamian life-style. His first show at Nassau was a sellout and he has had successful shows each year since. His paintings are realistic. He portrays the beautiful blues and greens of the waters of the Bahamas with extraordinary skill. His paintings of the people as well as the land and water of the islands reveal a deep sensitivity, respect, and love. He has become the national painter of the Bahamas, and has played an important and unique role in the cultural life of the new nation.

After living in Miami for about fourteen years, Alton built a house on Green Turtle Cay and moved back to his home town in 1983. The house is at the top of a hill east of New Plymouth from which the ocean as well as the Sea of Abaco can be seen. It was designed to resemble homes of the nineteenth century, and the dormers are exact replicas of those found on an old New Plymouth home. Alton is committed to preserving the beauty and heritage of New Plymouth and helped his father, several years ago, to establish the Albert Lowe Historical Museum. Albert's ship models highlight the exhibits, which also include artifacts, photographs, and brief descriptions of Abaco's heritage.[45]

The closest native mainland settlement to New Plymouth is Cooperstown, which is located on the northeastern coast of Abaco about fifteen miles north of the Treasure Cay resort. It is a barren roadstead without any harbour, chosen by the original settlers for its agricultural rather than its maritime potential. They came from Grand Bahama Island after emancipation, and the town, except for some foreign residents, is exclusively black. It has grown tremendously during the past forty years, with the population increasing from about 400 to over 1200. This growth has been achieved without significant migration, and is the result of natural increase. Cooperstown is one of the fastest growing communities in the Bahamas. This growth, and the prosperity which accompanied it, is due primarily to the dramatic increase in the price of crawfish. The average crawfisherman in Cooperstown made about $30,000. during the 1981 season and $50,000 or more per year during the early 1990s. This was enough to convince young men to stay at home rather than look to Nassau or Freeport for job opportunities. The town is neat and clean; many of the houses are freshly painted, and some have brand new automobiles parked outside. Another reason for Cooperstown's growth and prosperity is its proximity to Treasure Cay, where thirty to forty people are employed on a regular basis.

Medious Edgecombe is the owner of a fuel dock at Cooperstown. His business has grown with the town and with the increase in touring by yachtsmen from Florida. Thirty years ago he sold only 40-50 gallons of gasoline each week; he now sells 2000-3000 gallons a week—sometimes 4000—plus 600-800 gallons of diesel fuel. Medious has done his part to increase the local population—he had eight children by his first wife and fourteen by his second. He likes living in Cooperstown, and he is proud that it is growing in importance. About twenty years ago the government moved the seat of the Commissioner from New Plymouth to Cooperstown. This centralized the administrative services in the district, and recognized that New Plymouth, like Hope Town, had declined in importance. A modern school was built in Cooperstown shortly after the PLP came to power in 1967, and the local constable was replaced with two full-time policemen. Medious looks forward to further growth in Cooperstown. He hopes the day will soon come when there will be a supermarket and a bank in town, because residents now must drive to Treasure Cay or Marsh Harbour to use these services. He believes that more foreign residents might come to Cooperstown to build vacation homes. The best thing about Cooperstown, he believes, is its people. He described them as "friendly, spiritual, and respective."[46]

Cooperstown in late 1994. At top, a curious young girl walking past a campaign sign for Hubert Ingraham from the 1992 election. In the middle, school children walking home from school with Prime Minister Ingraham's home in the background. Above, Everette Bootle, crawfisherman and early supporter of Ingraham. And at right, the new government clinic in Cooperstown.

Everette Bootle is a crawfisherman in Cooperstown. He started at age nineteen and has two hundred traps located in the region from Ambergris Cay, just east of Cooperstown, to Mantanilla Reef, beyond Walker's Cay seventy miles northwest of Cooperstown. He works the traps with his helper twice a month, using a seventeen-foot Boston Whaler. In late 1994 he was in the process of acquiring a mother boat—a larger vessel with accommodations and large freezers to serve as a base of operations for several crawfishermen in smaller boats like his present Whaler. Everette Bootle is pleased with his life and his town, and he is especially proud that Cooperstown is the home of Hubert Ingraham, Prime Minister of The Bahamas. Everette said Hubert Ingraham was always somewhat different—when other boys were shooting marbles or playing other games, Hubert was reading. Once Hubert's cousin had arranged for him to go on a crawfishing boat, but C. A. Portier, a grocery store owner in Cooperstown, convinced his mother that he should not go. Mr. Portier believed there were greater things in store for Hubert Ingraham than crawfishing, and he did not want him to be lured away from them by relatively easy money to be made crawfishing. He was right, of course, but Hubert wanted to go—his clothes were already packed—and he cried when he was told he was not going.[47]

When Hubert was thirteen or fourteen years old he worked as a messenger for BATELCO, and then did office work for BAIL, Owens-Illinois' sugar operation. Then he went to Nassau to attend Government High School. He worked for BATELCO, took night classes, and studied law. In 1972 he was called to the Bahamian Bar, and in the same year he returned to Cooperstown to manage Scherlin Bootle's successful campaign for Member of Parliament from the Cooperstown constituency.

Five years later Scherlin Bootle retired from political life and Everette Bootle was one of those who suggested that Hubert Ingraham be the PLP's candidate for Cooperstown. Hubert won the election easily in 1977, and has been re-elected every five years since then—once as a member of the PLP (1982), once as an independent (1987) after he was evicted from the PLP, and once, in 1992, as a member and the leader of the FNM. He has a lot of support from his home town, but there are some who deserted him when he joined the FNM—Medious Edgecombe said: "I like him, but I don't like the idea of the FNM." On the other hand, an FNM supporter said, "He come over to me" with great pleasure.[48] Everette Bootle is probably representative of the majority in Cooperstown—he moved to the FNM with Ingraham. Bootle's respect for Ingraham's leadership abilities and for his integrity are obvious, and he places higher priority on these than on party labels. Cooperstown is justifiably proud of Hubert Ingraham.

LITTLE ABACO ISLAND AND THE NORTHWESTERN CAYS

The northern tip of Great Abaco Island is about five miles north of Cooperstown. Little Abaco Island lies directly to the west of it. This island is about fifteen miles long and a mile or two wide, and is connected to Great Abaco Island by a causeway and the Scherlin Bootle Highway. There are five settlements on Little Abaco Island, all of which are inhabited by blacks. Most were settled by people who moved from Cooperstown. From east to west they are called Cedar Harbour, Wood Cay, Mount Hope, Fox Town, and Crown Haven. Before the construction of the paved highway linking them to Cooperstown, they were all extremely isolated. Seventy to eighty years ago, when there were sisal plantations on Little Abaco, regular employment was available, but the sisal plantations have been closed since the end of World War I. Since then most of the residents of these communities have made their living from the sea, even exporting sea cucumbers to China at one point. As in many other such communities, crawfishing is now the economic mainstay. There have been many big changes in these small towns during the past fifteen years. Government services are much more accessible now that the Commissioner is in Cooperstown. The government has improved the schools and there is bus service to the high school in Cooperstown. Some people have jobs at Treasure Cay and commute daily.

Just as much remains unchanged in these settlements. None of them have a good deep

Allan Mills is a leading citizen of Cedar Harbour on Little Abaco Island.

Merlin McIntosh and C. Sawyer at the Zion Baptist Church in Fox Town (above). Charlin Johson, a young lady of Fox Town (right).

water harbour, and are therefore not often visited by yachtsmen or tourists of any kind. At Cedar Harbour, population - 110 (down from 125 ten years ago), Allan Mills is the leading citizen and businessman. He is the minister of the local Zion United Baptist Church which has twenty-six members (down from twenty-seven ten years ago), plus several followers. He is also the proprietor of the only gasoline station in the town, the only grocery store in town, is in charge of the branch post office, served as the local constable until 1992, is the Pepsi-Cola distributor, and buys and sells crawfish. Clearly, he plays a role in just about everything that happens in Cedar Harbour. He is pleased with most of the changes that have occurred during the past few years, but is disappointed that so many members of the younger generation ignore the church. In 1994 he was encouraged by the fact that a young man in his twenties was ready to become a deacon. He attributes part of the well-being of the past few years to the fact that mortgage money is available to young men to build houses now, whereas in years past, people in isolated places such as Cedar Harbour could not borrow money at all. He was pleased to be able to say that there are no problems with crime or violence in Cedar Harbour; "the young-sters," he said, "are very peaceful."[49]

Gersil Edgecombe lives in Cooperstown but manages Fox Town Shell in Fox Town. He also drives the school bus between Fox Town and Cooperstown each day. He is very interested in developing Fox Town as a boating and diving center. In this photo Gersil is holding his daughter Keva.

Fox Town is the largest of the communities on Little Abaco Island. Its population is 600. There is an office for the Commissioner there, and it is open on a regularly scheduled basis. There is also a government clinic with a nurse at Fox Town. Merlin McIntosh was born in Cooperstown, but had lived in Fox Town for forty-nine years by 1994. He started out fishing, and then established a little restaurant, and then a grocery store, a motel, and a gasoline station. The complex of these businesses is the main center of activity in Fox Town. Merlin also buys crawfish from local fishermen for Floyd Lowe of Green Turtle Cay, and he is Deacon at the Zion Baptist Church. "I like to be at Fox Town," he said. "Fox Town is a very nice place. It is close to the sea and we get the sea air. It's kind of like quiet—no violence—nothing like that yet." He could not think of anything he would change about it.[50] Harold Saunders, a crawfisherman, is also pleased to live in Fox Town. He makes a good living from crawfishing, and during the off-season he sells fish, conch, and sponges. Sponging has made a comeback in recent years because natural sponges are preferred for bathing and skin care.[51]

Fox Town is the only one of Little Abaco's communities which has the potential to become a yachting/tourist center because it has reasonably deep water and offers reasonably good protection. It could certainly be an overnight stop for boats travelling between Abaco and Florida. Merlin McIntosh and his son-in-law Gersil Edgecombe, who runs Fox Town Shell for Merlin, both recognize this potential. But large capital investments would have to be made to realize it, and the decline in activity at Treasure Cay has hurt the entire area of north and central Abaco. Gersil worked at Treasure Cay as an accountant at the hotel for thirteen years, but is pleased to be working in Fox Town now. In addition to running Fox Town Shell, he drives the school bus between Cooperstown and Fox Town. He likes being his own boss—"there were one hundred bosses at Treasure Cay."[52]

The most visible and probably most important recent changes in the six black settlements on northern Great Abaco and on Little Abaco are that the government is providing services (electricity, water, telephone, roads, and health care) which were never before available or accessible to the inhabitants, and crawfish continued to bring good prices.

There is only one permanent native settlement on the cays of northwestern Abaco. It is on Grand Cay and has a population of 320. Located in the heart of one of the best areas for crawfishing in the Bahama Islands, many of the men are involved in this business. Others are employed by the exclusive sport fishing resort and marina located on Walker's Cay, and commute by boat from Grand Cay daily. Walker's Cay is at the northwestern end of the chain of Abaco Cays. Beyond Walker's Cay about forty miles to the northwest lies Mantanilla Reef, and beyond that is the Gulf Stream and the North American coastline.

CHEROKEE SOUND, LITTLE HARBOUR, CROSSING ROCKS, AND SANDY POINT

There are not as many settlements south of the Marsh Harbour/Hope Town/Man-O-War hub of Abaco as there are to the north. The string of off-lying cays ends a few miles south of Elbow Cay, and there are no large harbours on the mainland south of Marsh Harbour. There are three settlements—all on Great Abaco Island—Cherokee Sound, Crossing Rocks, and Sandy Point.

Tallmadge Sawyer, one of the last smack boat captains of Cherokee Sound, and his wife, Ruth, at their home at Cherokee Sound in 1982 (left). Michael Bethel, resident of Cherokee Sound in the 1990s, is the captain of the *M. V. Biak*, which makes a weekly trip between Marsh Harbour and West Palm Beach, Florida.

Cherokee Sound is the most geographically isolated settlement in Abaco. Located on the eastern shore of Great Abaco Island south of the long barrier reef and string of cays which protects the northern half of the island, its harbour is difficult to enter and affords protection for small shoal draft vessels only. The mailboat, the *Deborah K II*, stops regularly at Cherokee, but she cannot get to the dock because of shallow water. She lies off and goods and passengers are lightered off. Most yachts cruising the Abaco cays do not stop at Cherokee Sound. The town was not directly connected by road to Marsh Harbour until 1990; it was necessary to cross a shallow bay in a small boat before driving fifteen miles on a gravel road to Marsh Harbour. The new road from Cherokee to this road is dirt and is in poor condition, but it is a vast improvement over the old days. Despite these difficulties, many of the residents of Cherokee are employed in Marsh Harbour and commute daily. Some men from Cherokee crawfish on boats which operate out of Marsh Harbour. Others crawfish in small boats and sell their crawfish to the fish house in Marsh Harbour for export. Cherokee has a population of about 170, and until quite recently was a very important boat building and fishing center. The

Tallmadge Sawyer's smack boat *Victory*.

settlement is neat and clean, and the people are as warm and friendly as can be found anywhere in the islands. In 1982 Tallmadge Sawyer lived across from the schoolhouse with his wife Ruth. He started fishing when he was seventeen years old, in 1920. During Cherokee's peak as a fishing village, thirty to forty years ago, about ten smack boats operated out of the town. Each was manned by about ten men, who set nets out with Abaco dinghies. The smack boats went out for four to six weeks at a time, and usually fished near the Berry Islands or off Andros. They kept the fish in a large live well in the hull of the smack boat, and carried them to market in Nassau. Tallmadge Sawyer owned the *Victory* for about twenty years. She was 32' on the keel and about 40' overall, and was built by Jim Lowe at Cherokee Sound. "Sometimes it was pretty hard . . ." to make a living by fishing, Tallmadge said, "After we got the motor, . . . it wasn't so hard, but with the sail, it was tough."[53] Most of the smack boats were powered by the end of the 1960s, but it was still hard work and none of the fishermen became wealthy men. Tallmadge's boat was swept ashore in Marsh Harbour during hurricane Betsy in 1965. He sold the boat shortly after that, and retired. He died during the 1980s. The *Victory* is still in use at Long

Benny Sawyer built twenty-two boats in his career as one of Abaco's master builders. He made no more than a meager living from his skills. He used a V-8 engine to power a planer because the town had no electricity. His wife Viola said "They were hard years, but they were good years too." Photo taken at their home in Cherokee Sound, November 1994.

Island, Bahamas. The smack boat fleet at Cherokee has steadily decreased in size, and Leland Albury, the last smack boat captain at Cherokee, sold his boat during the summer of 1982.

Cherokee has experienced many changes during the past twenty-five years, but because it is less accessible than New Plymouth or Hope Town, it has been less affected by tourism and the United States. More of the old Bahamian life-style survives in Cherokee, but this too is changing. Benny Sawyer, a master shipwright, gave up building boats in 1978, and then built houses until he retired during the 1980s. Benny built 22 boats during his career, and many of them are still in service. Reflecting on his work in 1994, he said that boatbuilders now seem to command a good income, but that all he did was make a living.[54]

Many of the old skills as well as the traditional Bahamian life-style at Cherokee Sound will soon be lost. The community is gaining access to the world outside and is losing its self-sufficiency. It is relying more and more on external sources for employment and goods. Even boats are imported. Its economy is moving toward tourism. In 1982 there were nine or ten foreign owned homes in Cherokee. Some of these were rented to vacationers occasionally; tourism had reached Cherokee Sound. Despite this, the modernization of Cherokee will almost certainly lag far behind the more accessible settlements such as Marsh Harbour and Cooperstown.

About ten miles north of Cherokee Sound there is a small circular harbour with a narrow, shoal entrance called Little Harbour. There is no native settlement there, though there is a light house. Before 1990 there was no land access to Little Harbour from any Abaco settlement except by foot path. When the road to Chero-

Randolph Johnston lived and worked at Little Harbour, Abaco, from the 1950s to the 1990s. His bronze castings were sold throughout the world. The photo to the left was taken in January 1981. His "Everyman Running from Death"was photographed in January 1975.

kee was built, a branch road was cut to Little Harbour, so it is now possible to drive there. A sand beach forms the eastern side of the harbour, and rock cliffs with caves are on the western side. It is a serene and fully protected anchorage for small boats.

In 1952 no one lived at Little Harbour except the lighthouse keeper and his family. A middle aged sculptor who had left his Massachusetts home and an Assistant Professorship at Smith College sailed into the harbour that year and decided to spend the remainder of his life there. Randolph Johnston wanted to escape from the "megamachine" and everything it stood for. As a young artist he had struggled to make a living. He had only sold a "half dozen or so" of his bronze sculptures during his entire artistic life, and had failed to win fellowships or commissions to decorate public buildings for which he had applied. The goal of his life was to make sculptures in bronze, but he had to teach college to support his family. He had become convinced, during World War II and the post-war years, that the continuous military build-up in the West was not beneficial to either the West or to humanity: "After the destruction of Hiroshima and Nagasaki, it became clear to me—although I could find no one who agreed with me—that humanity was bound for extinction unless a collective will could be aroused to head off the Gadarene panic."[55] Randolph and his wife Margot decided to build a homestead and studio at Little Harbour to escape from the meaninglessness of modern Western life. They sought a place where Randolph could work and where they could raise their sons—Bill, Denny, and Pete—free from "regimented society" in which "they could hardly escape being molded into conforming consumers or passive escapists."[56] Randolph and Margot lived at Little Harbour for forty years. He cast his bronzes in a beach side studio and foundry. He became a well known sculptor in North America as well as in Europe. His artistic and financial success did not dull his message—he was a voice crying for the survival of man in the wilderness of weapons of mass destruction. He feared deeply for the future of the human race; he hoped buoyantly that his art would awaken men to the new morality of survivalism. His work, he said,

> describes the Megamachine and the way people are inadvertent accomplices in the process of manufacturing mass murder. I call this mass effort the death futures business. But we know that just as the ultimate *evil* of delivery of the commodity, extinction, will have been made possible by law-abiding, good people, so Survivalists say that conformity to traditional religious and legal mores will not ensure humanity's survival. . . . we must create new virtues; Living-kindness, Joy-In-Beauty, Responsibility and Clear Eye all must work together to expose the sins behind the masks of respectability.[57]

At eighty years old during the middle 1980s, Randolph Johnston still displayed the exuberance and impatience of a child with a secret to share. He continued to work, for there was much he wished to say to mankind. During the early 1990s Randolph suffered a stroke, and then died. Margot is only at Little Harbour part of the time now. Their son Pete does bronze casting in his father's foundry studio, and many of Randolph's works were still on display in 1995. Randolph Johnston played a special role in the history of modern Abaco—he had a philosophical justification for living at the periphery of the modern world, and a special vision of what should truly concern mankind. He spoke to Abaco and to the world from the relative isolation of Little Harbour.

Like Cherokee and Little Harbour, Sandy Point is far from the megamachine. It is a peaceful community of about 407 blacks located on a peninsula projecting from the west side of Great Abaco Island. It is about thirty-eight miles southwest of Marsh Harbour, and is connected to Marsh Harbour by a poorly maintained gravel road. The settlement is well laid out in a neat grid pattern with a main road running through the center of the peninsula and other roads running perpendicular to it, and is shaded by hundreds of coconut palms. Most of the houses are neat and well painted, and the people are open and friendly. Sandy Point's prosperity is based almost entirely on fishing and crawfishing. Boats line the waterfront and nets are spread out to dry every place. A weigh-out station is located at the main public dock. Scale fish are shipped to Marsh Harbour for export, and crawfish are frozen and taken directly to the United States. Some men fish from locally built, small, planing outboard runabouts. There were still two smack boats based in Sandy Point in 1979, but they were no longer in operation in 1982. Large power boats with freezers on board dominate the lucrative crawfishing industry. Captain Ernest Dean runs the mailboat to Nassau and Mrs. Dean operates one of the local grocery and dry-goods stores—"E and E Grocery and Dry Goods—All Under One Roof"—the sign declares. J. Dean, their son, operates several crawfishing boats. Mrs. Dean is very proud of him, and explained that they go so far to catch crawfish that they can see "Cuba lights." Mrs. Dean was raised at Cherokee Sound, but had lived at Sandy Point for forty-five years by 1982. She belonged to the Assembly of God Church, and said that occasionally she went back to Cherokee Sound to participate in a joint church service. The church building at Sandy Point was relatively new in 1982, and the school and radio-telephone station were freshly painted. Though there were a couple of foreign owned homes in Sandy Point and a limited amount of tourism, the well being of the village and its people clearly depends upon its ability to harvest fish, crawfish, and conch from the sea surrounding it, just as in times past. Although the people often shop at Marsh Harbour, none of them are regularly employed there. Sandy Point is sufficiently remote to have its own commissioner, but, for purposes of representation in the House of Assembly, it is in the Marsh Harbour constituency. Sandy Point is independent and it is prosperous, and the road to Marsh Harbour which was under construction in 1995 promises more development for Sandy Point.[58]

Crossing Rocks is located between Sandy Point and Marsh Harbour at a spot where Great Abaco Island is quite narrow. The settlement is very small, consisting of about three dozen structures. Most of the people, like those in Sandy Point, make their living from the sea. There are no settlements on Abaco south of Sandy Point, but there is a lighthouse at Hole-in-the-Wall and houses for the lighthouse keepers. The light marks the extreme southern tip of Abaco and the entrance to the northeast New Providence Channel. It is one of the most important lights in the Bahama Islands.

The communities and people of Abaco present a variegated pattern to the contemporary observer—there has been change and there has been progress, but there are still places where certain things are done in much the same way as they were done one or two hundred years ago. Some of the changes have been good for the land and the people, but not all have been beneficial. In the future there will be more change and more progress; it will occur at different rates in each community. Some old customs will survive it, some communities will embrace it, and others will shun it. The old will continue to mix with, change, and moderate the new. It is difficult not to be optimistic about the future. Abaco has a robust economy now, but could serve additional tourists and could play a large role in making the Bahamas self-sufficient in food production as well. The future of Abaco, like the future of any land, is tied to its resources and its people.

THE ALBURYS OF WHITE SOUND, ELBOW CAY

Monty Albury is one of the next generation of Abaco's men. In 1982, when the first edition of this history was published, he was the handsome, nineteen year old son of Belle Lowe Albury of Hope Town and Floyed Albury of Man-O-War Cay. He lived with his parents at White Sound on Elbow Cay, several miles south of Hope Town. His mother was one of the best cooks in Abaco, and his father was a fine carpenter and building contractor. Both worked very hard, and their example served Monty well. He finished at the Hope Town Public School, where he had been the "head boy," when he was sixteen years old. He took some correspondence courses to prepare for the examinations leading to the General Certificate of Education of the University of London (G.C.E.), the equivalent of a high school diploma in the United States, but he did not complete these courses, and did not receive the G.C.E. Instead, he found a job.

Monty had been employed since he was eleven or twelve years old—at Vernon's Grocery Store in Hope Town, as a waiter at a local restaurant, for his father building houses, and as a fiberglass repair man and outboard mechanic at a marina. When he was about fifteen, he purchased a lot on the ocean beach near his parents' home. It is an old Abaco tradition that young men build their own houses before they seriously court a girl. Monty's two bedroom cottage was built during the winter of 1981-1982; he was renting it to tourists during the summer of 1982 to help him to pay for the cost of materials. He used the best woods available—cedar, cyprus, and pressure treated pine—and his father helped him to build the house well. During the summer of 1982 Monty Albury, then eighteen, became engaged to Ruth Albury, a beautiful and mature fifteen year old girl from Man-O-War Cay. Though both were young by modern North American standards, marrying early has been a common practice in Abaco throughout its history. They were married in 1984.

In 1982 Monty said he never wanted to live anyplace other than Abaco. He had travelled to Nassau, Freeport, and the United States, but saw his future in Abaco. Twelve years later, as the second edition of this book was in preparation, Monty had fulfilled his desire to stay in Abaco. He was living with his wife Ruth and sons Bradley and James in a house next door to his parents. He was the

Ruth, Bradley, Monty and James Albury of Sea Spray Resort and Marina, White Sound, Elbow Cay, Abaco.

operator of a marina and resort complex built as a family effort. His and Ruth's success was the result of their skills and their hard work, and the encouragement, support, and work of a closely knit family unit.

In 1982, when Monty and Ruth were engaged, the plan was for them to join Ruth's brother Michael and her sister's husband Ben in running an existing marina operation at Man-O-War Cay. Ruth's father, Ritchie, a part owner of Albury's Ferry at that time, planned to help to oversee the business. But Monty changed his mind. He decided he did not want to live and work at Man-O-War Cay. He explained the decision ten years later by saying that Man-O-War was already well developed, and there was little room for physical expansion of the facility. He wanted to build something for himself. He decided that he and Ruth would make their home next to his parents at White Sound. When Ruth was asked about this decision over ten years later, she said that she was only sixteen at the time and didn't have much to say about it—"I used to go along with everything he said, but now I don't." She said it was "hard at the beginning to live here" because it was so isolated, but she is happy living at White Sound now. At first Monty rented boats, and then he built fiberglass boats. He continued to manage the rental of the two cottages on his parents' property, and he rented the house he had built. At some point it was decided to develop the property he and his parents owned into Sea Spray Resort and Marina. Floyed stopped building houses for others and shifted full time to White Sound to build the marina and resort. He built the docks, the office, the rental units, and kept things in good repair. Ruth's father Ritchie provided capital. Her mother Sylvia chose decorating schemes and bought furniture for the rental units. Monty and Ruth managed the new facility. Belle baked bread and catered meals for guests. The entire effort was a family project, with each one contributing what he or she did best. Together the Alburys have built one of Abaco's finest small resorts and marinas.

As an Abaconian white in 1982 Monty was sympathetic with the plight of many Bahamian blacks, but he did not believe that all of the government's policies to help the blacks had been fair to young whites: "From what I know of Bahamian history," he said, anything the blacks do to the whites, the whites deserve it—but not my generation—my grand daddy's generation." By 1994 he believed that the country had "matured tremendously" during the previous twelve years, and that the government "genuinely has the interests of all Bahamians at heart." He included both recent PLP and FNM Governments in this judgment, despite the fact that he had become, during the 1980s, a very strong partisan of the PLP.

He had supported PLP candidate Edison Key in the 1982 election, and he went on to become a devoted and enthusiastic member of the PLP. During the middle 1980s he defended Prime Minister Lynden Pindling from charges of corruption, and he was campaign manager for Gary Sawyer, the PLP's candidate for the Hope Town constituency in 1992. He was such a strong supporter of the PLP that some wondered what he would do if the PLP lost. When that happened in 1992 he handled defeat well and put it into perspective. In fact, he said he now believes that the FNM's victory was the "best thing that could have happened" for the country, because it brought new people and new ideas to power. It nurtured the maturing of The Bahamas. The government changed hands without violence; The Bahamas is truly a working democracy. He now says that there are no major philosophical differences between the two parties, but admitted that he did not believe this during the 1992 campaign. He supports some of the policies and programs of the new FNM Government—"I support any program which will lead to a better Bahamas." But he has not gone over to the FNM; he is still PLP. The FNM gives no credit to the PLP for doing anything right. That, he contends, is not fair. "We did some things right," he said.

In 1983 this book concluded by saying that the future looked bright for Monty and Ruth, and that Abaco would be enriched by what they have to contribute to their native land. This is even more true in 1995. Though they are most certainly exceptional rather than average people, they have shown that Abaco offers more than ample opportunity to its young people to build futures for themselves and their families, and to contribute to the development and modernization of Abaco and The Bahamas. Monty and Ruth Albury, their parents Floyed, Belle, Ritchie, and Sylvia, and their children Bradley and James, still have much to contribute to their native land.[59]

END NOTES

[1] Patrick Bethel, *The Economic, Physical and Social Growth of the Town of Marsh Harbour,* unpublished manuscript, table IX.

[2] Patrick Bethel, *The Economic, Physical and Social Growth of the Town of Marsh Harbour,* "Boom of 80s," p. 3.

[3] Victor Patterson, "Abaco: The Year in Review," in Steve Dodge, *The Cruising Guide to Abaco: 1994 - Supplement* (Decatur, IL: White Sound Press, 1993), p. 2. Most of the economic statistics in this chapter come from Victor Patterson's annual reviews of developments in Abaco published in *The Cruising Guide to Abaco,* or from Patrick Bethel's unpublished manuscript, *The Economic, Physical and Social Growth of the Town of Marsh Harbour.* It should be understood that these are estimates rather than tabulated totals.

[4] The term bareboat charter applies to a sailboat chartered without a captain or crew and sailed by the charterers themselves.

[5] John Van Ost, letter to Gordon Hudson, Tenafly, New Jersey, 31 October 1977.

[6] Gordon Hudson, letter to Hubert Ingraham, M. P., Marsh Harbour, 3 March 1978.

[7] See John Van Ost, letter to Hubert Ingraham, Tenafly, New Jersey, 25 July 1978.

[8] During the early 1990s the government decided to allow visiting boats one year in the Bahamas and to provide a one year renewal at reasonable cost. Under the old rules, visiting boats were allowed six months only, at which time they had to pay duty or leave the Bahamas. For boats which would stay in the Bahamas permanently, import duty was reduced on large boats and completely eliminated on mega-yachts.

[9] In c. 1990 the numbers for Nassau showed that the typical "stopover" visitor (air arrival) spent about $500.-600. in the Bahamas, whereas the cruise ship visitor spent only $50.

[10] Some residents of Key West have resisted cruise ships and complain about the quality of the tourists who arrive on them. Key West does not allow them to stay offshore overnight because they would obstruct the view of the sunset from Mallory Pier. See "Invasion of the Cruise Ships—Key West: Locals are Fighting Attack by Sea *Newsweek* (January 17, 1994), p. 49.

[11] Lois Albury, Sail Shop, Man-O-War Cay. Marguerite Sawyer at the Loyalist Rose Shop at Green Turtle Cay claimed that about 30% of her business had been cruise ship visitors. Lawrence Higgs of the Sand Dollar Shop at Green Turtle Cay said that the percentage varied from month to month, and that the real benefit of the cruise ship was that it continued even during the normally slack months. Lawrence Higgs, interview with the author, Green Turtle Cay, 11 November 1994.

[12] Stafford Symonette, interview with the author, Treasure Cay, Abaco, November 17, 1994. Gersil Edgecombe independently expressed almost identical views regarding hotel operations at Treasure Cay (Gersil Edgecombe, Interview with the author, Cooperstown, Abaco, 17 November 1994).

[13] "Sea Resources Declining: Local Fishermen Upset with Catches," Abaconian 2:8 (August, 1994), 1,11. Also Everette Bootle, Interview with the author, Cooperstown, Abaco, 17 November 1994, and Harold Saunders, Interview with the author, Fox Town, 17 November 1994.

[14] Much of the information for this section on agriculture in Abaco was gained from Simeon Pinder, Assistant Director of Agriculture and Officer in charge of Abaco, Interview with the author, Marsh Harbour, 18 November 1994.

[15] "Paradise Lost," The Sunday Times Magazine (London), 29 September 1985, p. 35.

[16] The six-part series in the Miami Herald was written by Carl Hiaasen and Jim McKee and published from 23-28 September 1984. The Sunday Times Magazine published "Paradise Lost" in September 1985.

[17] Robyn Adderley, "Seizures of Drugs up 300%," Nassau Guardian, 22 February 1988, 1,3.

[18] Charles Carter, Minister for Foreign Affairs, "Foreword," Bahamas Narcotics Control Report: 1989, Nassau: Ministry of Foreign Affairs, 1990.

[19] Report of Commission of Inquiry, quoted by Colin Archer, "Alcohol and Drug Abuse in the Bahamas," in Dean Collinwood and Steve Dodge, eds., Modern Bahamian Society (Parkersburg, IA: Caribbean Books, 1989, 252-264.

[20] See pages 102-103.

[21] Athena Damianos, "45 Per Cent of Marsh Harbour Now Haitians," Tribune, 17 November 1990, pp. 1,16.

[22] Niles Timothy, interview with the author, White Sound, Elbow Cay, Abaco, 24 July 1986.

[23] In 1993-1994 Brenda Louidor, a Haitian girl who lived in Pidgeon Peas, was Head Girl of Abaco Central High School in Marsh Harbour. She was also selected by the Ministry of Education as Bahamian Student of the Year. See "Interview of the Month," Abaco Journal (Treasure Cay) 8:87 (June 1994), 2, 14-15.

[24] "The Editor's Comments," Abaconian 2:10 (October/November, 1994), 2.

[25] Vernon Malone, interview with the author, Hope Town, 21 July 1982.

[26] Gay Chambers, Interview with the author, Hope Town, 21 July 1982.

[27] For a complete discussion of AIM and Abaco separatism, see chapter 6.

[28] "Election is Called for Next Month," Bahamas Dateline (21 May 1982).

[29] Belle Albury, Interview with the author, White Sound, Elbow Cay, 11 June 1982.

[30] The Government of The Bahamas has officially changed the name of all islands other than New Providence from the Out Islands to the Family Islands.

[31] See more complete discussion on pp. 152.

[32] For more detailed summaries of recent developments in Abaco see the annual reviews written by Victor Patterson in Steve Dodge, The Cruising Guide to Abaco, 1994 and 1995

editions. Also see "FNM Improves Abaco: MP Sweeting Outlines Two Years of Progress," *Abaconian*, August 1994, pp. 1,7.

[33] Delgano Newbold, Interview with the author, Marsh Harbour, 24 July 1982.

[34] Delgano Newbold, Interviews with the author, Marsh Harbour, 24 July 1982, and 16 November 1994.

[35] Merle Williams, Interviews with the author, Marsh Harbour, 26 July 1982, and 17 November 1994.

[36] Edison Key, Interview with the author, Marsh Harbour, 21 July 1982.

[37] Patrick Bethel, Interview with the author, Marsh Harbour, 16 November 1994.

[38] *Ibid.*

[39] George B. Shattuck, ed., Geographic Society of Baltimore, *The Bahama Islands* (New York: Macmillan, 1905), pp. 410-414, plate LXXVI.

[40] Shirley Higgs, Interview with the author, Hope Town, 9 July 1982.

[41] Several studies reported at the American Association for the Advancement of Science indicated that inbreeding did not necessarily produce damaging results. See "Study finds little risk in Inbreeding," Decatur Herald and Review, 15 February 1993, p. A10.

[42] Vernon Malone, Interviews with the author, Hope Town, 21 July 1982 and 16 November 1994.

[43] Marcell Albury, Interview with the author, Man-O-War Cay, 19 July 1982; and Ralph Albury, Interview with the author, Man-O-War Cay, 10 November 1994.

[44] Eldred Pinder, Interview with the author, Great Guana Cay, 26 July 1982, and Edmond Pinder, Interview with the author, Great Guana Cay, 11 November 1994.

[45] Alton Lowe, Interview with the author, White Sound, Elbow Cay, 31 July 1982.

[46] Medious Edgecombe, Interviews with the author, Cooperstown, 22 July 1982 and 17 November 1994.

[47] Everette Bootle, Interview with the author, Cooperstown, 17 November 1994.

[48] Medious Edgecombe, Interview, 17 November 1994; and Merlin McIntosh, Interview with the author, Fox Town, 17 November 1994.

[49] Allan Mills, Interviews with the author, Cedar Harbour, 22 July 1982 and 17 November 1994.

[50] Merlin McIntosh, Interview with the author, Fox Town, 17 November 1994.

[51] Harold Saunders, Interview with the author, Fox Town, 17 November 1994.

[52] Gersil Edgecombe, Interview with the author, Cooperstown, 17 November 1994.

[53] Tallmadge Sawyer, Interview with the author, Cherokee Sound, 27 July 1982.

[54] Benny Sawyer, Interviews with the author, Cherokee Sound, 27 July 1982 and 18 November 1994.

[55] Randolph Johnston, *Artist on his Island: A Study in Self-Reliance* (Park Ridge, New Jersey: Noyes, 1975), p. 6.

[56] *Ibid.*, p. 7.

[57] Randolph W. Johnston, *Survive Man! or Perish* (Marsh Harbour: Little Harbour Press, 1980), pp. 112-113.

[58] Mrs. Dean, Interview with the author, Sandy Point, Summer, 1982.

[59] Monty and Ruth Albury, Interviews with the author, White Sound, Elbow Cay, 15 July 1981 and 6 January 1995.

Appendix -
Boat Building in Abaco

Boats were necessities rather than luxuries in Abaco. They were needed for getting to the reef to go fishing, to go to the fields, or to carry harvested crops to other communities to sell. They were the only means of transportation and communication with the capital of Nassau, and the only carriers for goods to be imported or exported. They were essential for individual and communal survival, and the knowledge and skills necessary to build boats was a vital community resource. A continuous supply of small boats was necessary to catch local fish which sustained the community. And sometimes boatbuilders supervised grand building projects requiring the coordinated work of many skilled craftsmen over months and even years, to build vessels on which the hopes and aspirations of their communities depended. Their special talents and skills played a central role in a society which relied so greatly on the sea for its livelihood.

The sailboat is surely one of man's greatest inventions. Prior to the development of the steam engine and its application to wagons and boats, the sailboat was the only vehicle man had devised which did not rely upon human or animal muscle for power to propel it, and until quite recently, sailing boats and ships were among the largest and most complex things which men dared to build, and subsequently control. Sailboats and sailing ships are complex and ingenious devices which utilize the interface between the atmosphere and the sea. They are buoyed up by one element and use the natural forces of another for propulsion. They must be able to cope with this often tempestuous zone where wind and waves generate complex forces which must be utilized rather than suffered. The problems which the designer of a modern vessel copes with are very much the same as those every boatbuilder has had to deal with for centuries, and all boats are compromises -- one must trade stability or carrying capacity for speed or seaworthiness, etc. Though the Abaconian boatbuilders lacked the sophisticated testing tanks and computers which are utilized by naval architects to-day, they developed boats which became famous throughout the Bahamas and the eastern United States for their sailing ability and seaworthiness. Abaco became the premier boat building center of the Bahamas; from 1855 to 1864, 108 of the 234 boats built in the Bahamas were built in Abaco.[1] The superiority of Abaco boats was generally recognized throughout the islands, and it is still common for old Abaco-built boats to bring premium prices, even in today's fiberglass boat market. Abaco's boats continue to prove themselves worthy of their reputation. A boat built at Man-O-War Cay participated in the Tall Ships Race in 1976, and William F. Buckley's trans-Atlantic crossing, which was the basis for his popular book, *Airborne*, was made in *Cyrano*, a boat built at Cherokee Sound, Abaco.

The loyalists who emigrated to Abaco knew they would need boats and ships. Their goal was to build a commercial hub in Abaco which would grow to rival New York and Boston. The United States, they believed, would languish outside the protection and privileges offered by the British Empire. They believed they would be the heirs of the burgeoning economy of British North America, which they would simply transplant to the Bahama Islands. In order to achieve this they needed ship's carpenters who would fashion the timber of Abaco into vessels which would carry their goods to ports throughout the world.

Although the agricultural sector of the early settlements failed to live up to expectations and caused the failure of the grandiose schemes for a new British Empire in the Bahamas, the ship's carpenters did their jobs and did them well. *Huaibras*, a sloop of twenty-one tons, was launched in 1785, and the *Fair Abaconian*, a sloop of seventy-four tons, and the *Recovery*, a snow* of one hundred fifty-five tons, as well as some smaller sloops, were launched in 1786. A schooner of one hundred nineteen tons, the *Ulysses*, was built in 1787. But the failure of Abaco to develop an economy which could produce exports meant that once these ships were launched they rarely, if ever, returned to Abaco. Cotton production did not develop, and other agricultural production did not grow beyond the subsistence level. The dream of establishing an integrated commercial-agricultural-maritime colony in Abaco was defunct by 1790. Many of the new settlers left and became emigrants once again. Those who remained were joined by Bahamians from Harbour Island and Spanish Wells, Eleuthera, and a new style

---

*A snow was very similar to a brig.

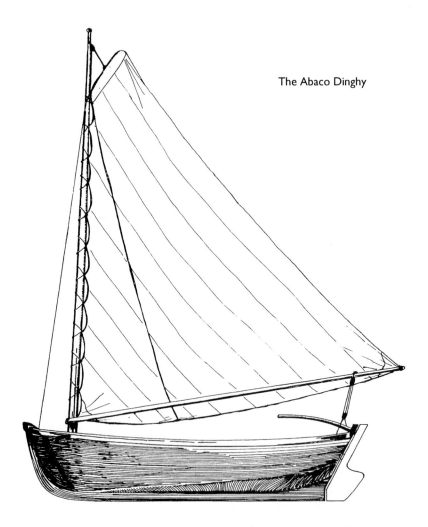

The Abaco Dinghy

of life, as well as a new boat building tradition, was born. The dreams of international commerce gave way to the realities of subsistence fishing and farming and a very limited trade with Nassau.

Different kinds of vessels were required for this more humble life-style. Small fishing dinghies or sloops which could be handled by one or two men were probably developed. When the economy changed, different boats were needed. Later in the nineteenth century, when goods such as pineapples or sisal were exported from Abaco to the United States, schooners were built to carry these goods. In the twentieth century large lumber-carrying schooners were built. The basic designs for these vessels were developed by trial and error, and were not committed to paper. Many of the dimensions were extrapolated from the length of the keel, but the formulae, or rule-of-thumb, was different for each type of boat and for each builder. Despite this lack of uniformity, most of the boats built in Abaco during the heyday of boat construction between 1800 and 1940 can be placed in one of three or four general categories.

The Abaco dinghy was the Bahamian Model T. They ranged in size from 9 to 20 feet long and were used for fishing, sponging, conching, and general inter-island transportation.[2] They had a round bilge with a great deal of deadrise and had a long, straight keel with deadwood aft. The rudder was outboard, hung on the sternpost and the transom. The sheer had a beautiful curve. Dinghies had a single mast with a single sail of the leg-of-mutton type. The sail was bent to the mast with lacing line, but was loose footed. The boom was quite long, with about one-fourth of its length over-hanging the transom. A notch in the upper port side of the transom made it possible to scull the boat when there was no wind. The long keel provided the directional stability necessary for effective sculling. Dinghies intended for fishermen were equipped with live wells through which sea water flowed, making it possible to carry live fish home or to the market. After the advent of gasoline motors in Abaco in about 1950, many dinghies were equipped with small two-cycle Stuart-Turner inboard engines rather than rigged for sailing. Later, dinghies were built to use outboard motors. Many old Abaco dinghies are still in use, and dinghies are still built in several places in Abaco.

Smack boats had lines which were similar to those of dinghies, but the boats were larger. They were from 18 to 40 feet long "on the keel"—the way boats are usually measured in the Bahamas. Overall length was somewhat greater. Their beam was about one-third of their overall length, and they were shoal draft. Smack boats had a single mast which carried a leg-of-mutton mainsail similar to the dinghy sail, as well as a jib, the tack of which was bent to a bowsprit. Smacks were generally built for fishing and had live wells. There was no cockpit; the entire hull was decked over and a hatch provided access to a cargo hold located forward. There was usually a small trunk cabin aft, but the crew of seven to ten men on a smack boat cooked, ate, and slept on the open deck rather than below. Overall length was somewhat greater. Their beam was about one-third of their overall length, and they were shoal draft.

Smack Boat

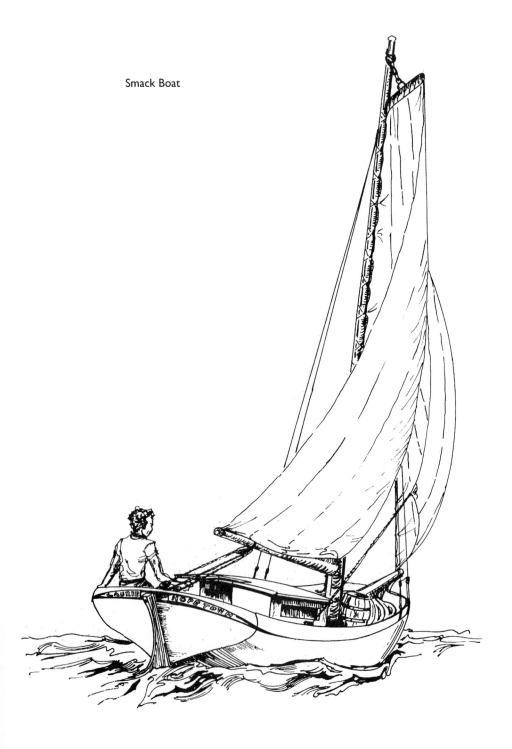

Sponge Schooner

Smack boats had a single mast which carried a leg-of-mutton mainsail similar to the dinghy sail, as well as a jib, the tack of which was bent to a bowsprit. Smacks were generally built for fishing and had live wells. There was no cockpit; the entire hull was decked over and a hatch provided access to a cargo hold located forward. There was usually a small trunk cabin aft, but the crew of seven to ten men on a smack boat cooked, ate, and slept on the open deck rather than below.

Sponging schooners also utilized some of the same basic hull lines as dinghies and were typically 35 to 38 feet on the keel, 50 to

55 feet overall, 16 feet wide, and drew about 5 feet. They were two-masted vessels, and were usually gaff-rigged with topmasts and topsails. They carried a foretopmast staysail and a jib bent to a long bowsprit and jib boom. Sponge schooners carried a crew of up to 20 men and served as mother ships for fleets of 8 to 10 dinghies, which searched for and hooked the sponges and then returned to the schooner. Sponge schooners were also used for carrying cargo, especially during prohibition in the United States (1920-1933).

Fruit-carrying cargo schooners were built during the late nineteenth century, and lumber-carrying schooners were built during the early twentieth century. The latter were 130 to 150 feet long, and were the largest ships ever built in Abaco. Only a few were built. Various special purpose vessels have also been built in Abaco. These included powered freight boats, tug boats, barges, and passenger ferries. During and after World War II yachts were built for sailors from the United States, and during the 1950s and 1960s high speed round bilge planing outboard powerboats were developed by builders at Man-O-War Cay. The versatility as well as the woodworking skills of Abaco's boatbuilders clearly contributed to the survival of the industry in Abaco long after it had failed on some of the other Bahamian Islands.

Like New England, Abaco had resources appropriate for boat building. Abaco's forest of Caribbean pine provided excellent wood for planking and masts, and madeira or horseflesh could be acquired for frames. Excellent well-protected harbours provided good construction sites. Unlike New England, Abaco's economy did not usually produce goods which could be profitably exported on the ships. Without local demand for ships and shipping, the industry slumped, but even during the decade or two after 1790, when Abaco's population was very small and very poor, dinghies were undoubtedly built for fishing. When new economic pursuits became available and communities became more prosperous, larger vessels were built. According to Haziel Albury of Man-O-War Cay, dinghies were built there at an early date, and the first larger boat (19' on the keel) was launched around 1850. It was used as a lighter, carrying pineapples from the shore of Great Abaco to cargo schooners from the United States which anchored offshore. In the early 1860s a fishing sloop with a live well which was 29' on the keel was built, and she was later replaced with a schooner, which was 35' on the keel.[3]

Comprehensive and detailed accounts of the numbers and kinds of boats built in each of the settlements of Abaco do not exist, but based on the fragmentary information which is available,[4] several generalizations can be made. Boats were built in all of the white and integrated settlements of Abaco beginning in the early nineteenth century and ending, in some settlements, within the past twenty to thirty years. Boats are still built at Man-O-War Cay, Sandy Point and Hope Town. Though Man-O-War is the most prominent boat building center now, it was overshadowed by Hope Town, as well as Cherokee Sound, fifty or sixty years ago. Some have said that Hope Town became more prominent than New Plymouth during the late nineteenth century because Hope Town's economy was based on boat building and seafaring rather than agriculture. This is, in part, true, but many fine boats were built at New Plymouth and many of its men were seafaring men. A few boats were probably built in the black settlements of Abaco, but most often dinghies were purchased from builders in the white or integrated communities.[5] It is interesting to note that although few boats were built in the black settlements, some blacks living in Marsh Harbour and New Plymouth became boatbuilders.

Boats were built based on immediate and usually short-lived economic opportunities. Dinghies sufficed when the communities engaged only in subsistence fishing. When it became known that fish could be sold in Nassau, smacks were built. When fruit was exported to the United States, schooners were built to carry it. When this business collapsed, the vessels were soon sold. Sponging sloops and schooners were built after good seasons, sold after bad ones. Lumber schooners were only profitable during and just after World War I, when freight rates were high. In brief, the number and types of boats built in Abaco during any given year served as a rather accurate measure of the health of various sectors of the economy of Abaco. For example, in 1912 the commissioner at Hope Town reported that 3 schooners, 6 sloops, and 140 dinghies had been built in his district during the year, and that at year's end one three-masted schooner, one smaller schooner, and two sloops were on the stocks. He also reported a very good year for sponging, with about £20,000 realized by thirty-two vessels, "one vessel alone selling sponge to the value of between £900 and £1000."[6]

Abaco dinghies are still built only at Man-O-War Cay and at Hope Town. Maurice Albury of Man-O-War was probably the best known builder of Abaco dinghies when he died in 1978. Dinghies

216

Winer Malone

are now built at Man-O-War by Joe Albury, who also builds planing outboard boats and half models. Joe was one of The Bahamas' representatives at the Folklife and Culture Exhibition sponsored by the Smithsonian Institution during the summer of 1994. He built an Abaco dinghy on the Mall in Washington, D. C.

Winer Malone of Hope Town is the only boatbuilder in that settlement. He is about sixty years old, and has been building dinghies for over forty of those years, except for the period from 1965-73, when he was a caretaker for several homes owned by winter residents from the United States. He also tried house construction for a short time. Winer returned to boat building and boat repair because, he says, it suits him better. He is his own boss and plans his own work, it is what he knows and does best, and it is what he enjoys.[7]

He recognizes that dinghy construction is a dying sector of the economy of Abaco. Just thirty-five years ago almost every Bahamian who needed a boat to go fishing wanted an Abaco dinghy; now few Bahamians buy Winer's boats. Foreign visitors are his primary market. Bahamians buy either planing power boats built at Man-O-War or foreign fiberglass boats. "Bahamians are getting away from Bahamianism. Bahamianism is dying a slow death—not so slow really," Winer said while caulking the seams of a very old Abaco dinghy built at Marsh Harbour. Someone had pulled the boat under some coconut palms several years ago and deserted it. Winer was trying to save her—"I don't know why they just left her. I suppose a few things may have needed fixing and they decided she wasn't worth it to them." He planned to use the boat himself—for his own pleasure sailing on Sunday afternoons.

Winer is a thin, small man with sharp features and pale complexion. He wears glasses and appears to be rather frail, except for his arms and hands. He prefers to build ordinary work dinghies rigged for sailing, but doesn't get the opportunity to do so very often. Most of his boats are now built for use as recreational boats only or as tenders for large yachts. A small dinghy he built as a

tender for *Cyrano*, the Cherokee Sound-built schooner in which
William Buckley crossed the Atlantic, was typical of his recent work.
It was fastened with brass screws rather than with galvanized nails,
and was stained and varnished rather than painted. The carpentry
had to be precise if the boat were to look good. Winer calls this
kind of boat a pleasure boat, and would prefer to build ordinary
workboats. "In the old days," he said, "we didn't even use sandpa-
per—just planed them off and painted them, and we just put cotton in the seams and painted it. Today they all go modern; now we
putty over the seams."

In 1979 Winer's son stopped by to watch him caulk the seams
of the old dinghy—"Aren't you going to do this one, Daddy?" Roddy
asked, pointing to a seam well above the water line and still filled
with putty from years before. "No," Winer said, "I don't have to
do that one. You should know more about boat work; you don't
come around enough; you're playing all the time." He was sad but
not angry. He accepted the fact that he was an anachronism in the
world of the 1980s, and could not expect his son to become one
also.

He knows that Abaco dinghies are dying; he doesn't receive
very many orders for new boats, nor does he make the amount of
money that his skills and labor would justify. He estimates that he
makes only a common laborer's wage, because a carpenter who
uses only hand tools must put in extra time.

Winer lacks the capital to buy power tools, and he doesn't
think the investment would be a sound one (because he lacks orders for new boats) unless he decided to build some other kind of
boat more in demand in today's market. He thinks about this sometimes, but not often—"I'm prejudiced about boats. I don't like many
boats except Abaco dinghies. I like 'em." He hopes Abaco dinghies
will come back—"I'll just try to keep 'em alive for as long as I can."

Winer sold the first boat he built in Palm Beach, Florida, for
$65.00—"a good price, a very good price." In 1982 a 10' keel (about
12' overall) ordinary workboat sailing dinghy could be built for
about $1,000. A pleasure boat cost more. By 1995 he no longer
quoted a price for workboat models—all he built were pleasure
boats. Commenting on how his market had changed, he said "The
Abaco dinghy used to be a poor man's workboat, now it is a rich
man's toy." The cost in 1995 was $350. per foot, plus $600. for the
mast, boom, and rudder. The sail and special sailing hardware were
not included.

Boatbuilding Woods

The first step in building an Abaco dinghy is, of course, to acquire the lumber. In the old days, crews of men went to Great Abaco Island to cut madeira (mahogany), horseflesh, or dogwood for frames, and Caribbean pine for planks. Winer doesn't build enough boats to make such an expedition economically viable, and he acquires his own lumber for frames right on Elbow Cay. There are a good number of dogwood and madeira trees on Elbow Cay, but most of these are now inaccessible because the land in the interior of the cay, which used to be Crown land, has been sold to foreigners who don't want their trees cut down. Winer now uses mostly corkwood for frames; these trees are very salt tolerant and

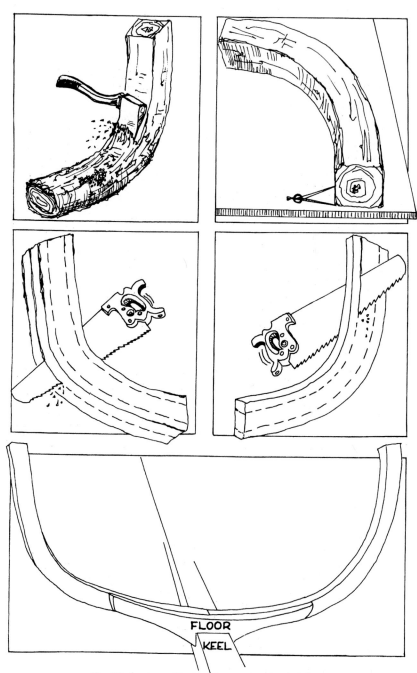

FLOOR

KEEL

The fabrication of frames from natural crook logs

thrive in low, swampy areas. Corkwood is significantly lighter than dogwood or madeira, but it is a tough wood.[8] Crooks of trees are selected so that the grain of the frames will curve in the same way as the shape of the frames to provide maximum strength.

Once Winer determines the size and type (power or sail) of dinghy he is building, he determines the dimensions of the middle frame* and the transom. All these dimensions are based on the length of the keel and determined by what Winer calls "mother's wit." There are no plans; each builder does it a little differently. Winer makes a 10' keel sailing dinghy 4'2" wide at the middle frame and 3'4" wide at the transom. A 10' keel dinghy intended for outboard power would be 4'4" wide at the middle frame and 3'4" wide at the transom, Also, the power dinghy would have fuller sections at the after end.

The shape of the middle frame is determined by mother's wit. A natural crook log is selected to match the shape of the ribs. The log is rough hewn with an axe until it is roughly 4" X 4". It is then laid on the table and scribed with dividers at its midpoint and then

* Some builders call this frame the rising frame.

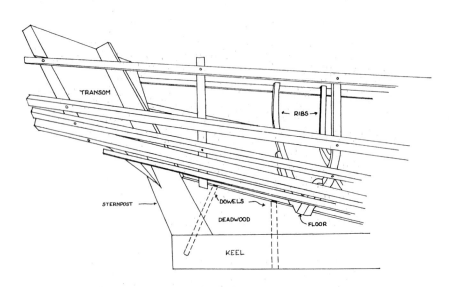

Construction details of the aft portion of the Abaco dinghy

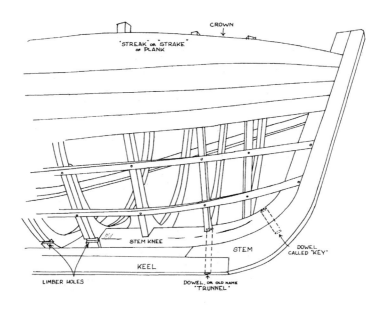

Construction details of the forward portion of the Abaco dinghy

ripped by hand. The flat surface of each piece is then laid on the table, and it is again scribed and ripped to produce two pieces with smooth, flat sides for the ribs. The shape of the rib is then drawn on one of the pieces and it is sawed and planed. A spokeshave is used to shape the concave curve on the inside; a spokeshave or regular plane is used to trim the convex curve on the outside. A floor, which is the straight, horizontal member which holds the two sides of the frame together, is sawed out and planed, and the completed frame can then be assembled.

The sternpost is shaped from a straight corkwood log. The deadwood is cut from 1½" clear stock, usually imported fir. The keel is cut to its appropriate shape from the same material, as are the transom planks. The shape of the transom is determined by eye, and the boards are hand cut and trimmed to the appropriate bevel.

The stem is sawn from a natural crook corkwood log and scarphed to fit the keel. The stem lining is similarly fashioned and a

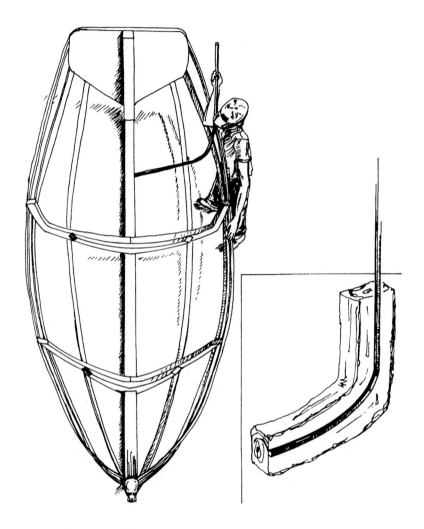

Winer Malone uses a homemade lead batten to take the shape desired for a frame from the ribbands. He then traces the shape onto boards ripped from natural crook logs.

rabbet is cut into it to receive the planks. This piece is screwed to the stem. A stem knee is also sawn from corkwood and is used to secure the entire assembly to the keel.

Next, the keel is laid. The sternpost, transom, stem, and middle frame are plumbed and secured to the keel. The sternpost is screwed to the keel. The deadwood is secured with screws and two dowels, or trunnels. The stem is fit into the scarphed notch in the keel and the stem knee is drift fastened through the overlap of the stem and the keel. A dowel which Winer calls a key is fitted at the joint between the stem lining and the stem knee to resist twisting of the assembly.

Several ribbands, which are temporary longitudinal stringers about ½" by I" in cross section, are then secured to the middle frame, transom, and stem. The extent of bend in each ribband, which determines the fullness of the hull, is determined by the eye of the builder, who provides fuller bow sections for a dinghy to be used for conching, because a man up forward with a water glass requires extra stability, or finer sections for a boat designed primarily for sailing. The ribbands are secured to one side of the boat only.[9] The position of the "quarter" frames is now determined— the aft one is usually placed just forward of the deadwood—the forward one just aft of the stem. A homemade bendable lead batten, or spline,[10] is used to take the shape of the quarter and other intermediate frames from the ribbands. This lead batten is sufficiently pliable to permit bending it by hand around the curve made by the ribbands. The batten retains this shape, is removed, and its curve is traced onto boards cut from natural crook logs. These are sawn in the same manner as that described for the middle frame, except that their outer sides must be beveled to fit flush against the ribbands. The inner side is also beveled. Next, floor pieces are cut, the components are assembled, and the complete frame is secured to the keel. The remainder of the frames are built and secured in similar fashion, using the lead batten to determine the shape of each one. Frames are placed every 10-12"—a 10' keel boat has 12 frames, a 12' keel boat has 14-15 frames. When all the frames have been installed, the boat is ready for planking.

Abaco (Caribbean) pine, cut on Great Abaco Island, was used for planking prior to the middle 1960s. It is a hard, resinous pine which is very resistant to rot. This pine, however, was cut by the Owens-Illinois company for pulpwood between 1959 and 1969. Abaco boatbuilders now must import their planking. Winer some-

224

times uses pine from the United States, but he does not like it because he was told the growing trees in the United States are bled of their sap to produce turpentine. The resultant wood, he says, lacks resin and resistance to rot. He contends the sap and resin are processed and sold as turpentine, which is then used to thin the paint which is applied to the wood to preserve it, implying that it would be better and less expensive for the consumer (but not for the lumber and turpentine companies) if the resin were simply left in the wood. If his customer is willing to bear the cost of a better wood, he uses red or white cedar. The planks must be spiled before they can be sawn to the appropriate shape.

Spiling is the process which enables the builder to determine the shape of the planks, which will be wider at the middle than at the ends. The shape of the top, or sheer plank, is determined first. The top ribband, bent in its natural curve around the frames, is used to determine the shape of the top of the plank. Either its natural bend determines the curve of the sheer, or the builder alters the curve to suit his own taste. The contour of the bottom of the plank is determined by the builder, and is limited by the

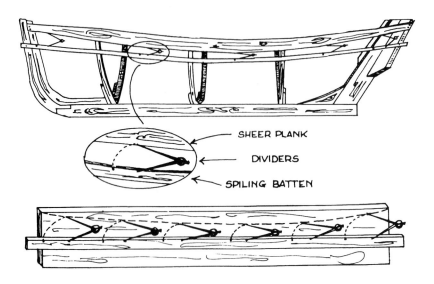

SHEER PLANK

DIVIDERS

SPILING BATTEN

Spiling involves tacking a spiling batten to the frames and measuring the gap between the batten (a straight edge) and the bottom edge of the plank above. The measurements are transferred to a board, the points are connected, and the plank is sawed out. The shape of the bottom of the plank is simply determined by the builder.

width of the planking lumber and by the need to make the ends wide enough to receive fastenings and still retain strength. After the plank is sawn to shape and the edges are planed smooth, a duplicate is traced, sawed out, and planed for the opposite side of the boat, and the planks are fastened to the frames.

A spiling batten (or rod), which looks like a wide ribband, is then tacked or clamped to the frames a little below the lower edge of the top plank, the gap between the straight-edged spiling batten and the bottom edge of the top plank is curved. By carefully measuring the gap at every other frame, Winer can reproduce this contour on the second plank so that a perfect butt joint will be achieved. A pair of dividers is used to measure the gap, and these distances are then marked (pricked) on the spiling batten itself. The batten and the dividers can now be used to transfer the curve of the bottom of the top plank to a board which will become the next plank. The batten is laid on the board and clamped in position.

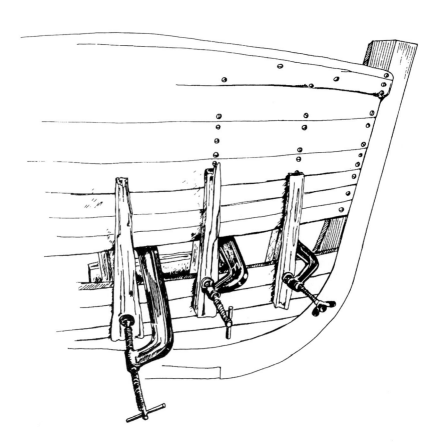

The dividers are used to prick the board and the points are connected by using a flexible wood batten to draw the line. The shape of the bottom edge is determined by the builder in the same way as was done for the top plank; it is determined by the width of the lumber and the need for sufficient strength at the ends. After the plank is sawed out and planed, a duplicate plank is made for the opposite side of the boat. The second plank may now be fastened to the frames. Each additional plank is spiled in similar fashion, but the middle of the planks must be made narrower as the builder approaches the sharper curves near the waterline. This is done because each plank must be planed concave on the inside and convex on the outside to fit the frames, and a wide plank would become too thin at its center. Winer determines the width of each plank based on his previous experience. When the planks from the sheer to below the curve of the bilge are spiled, sawn, planed, and secured, Winer spiles the garboard plank (the plank next to the keel). He then works up from the garboard toward the planks which are already installed. The last plank is usually made in two pieces and is butted on a frame to make installation easier.

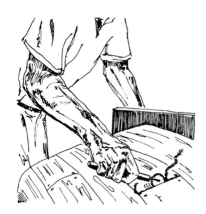

Rolling cotton into seams.

Tamping cotton tightly into seams.

Transom knees, the breasthook, and the sheer clamps are shaped and secured to strengthen the hull. A false keel is secured to protect the keel of the boat when it is beached. The seams between the planks are opened to a uniform width and a slight "v" shape with a homemade reaming tool. Cotton is then pressed into the seams with another homemade tool—a roller made from an old English penny. The cotton is then tamped tightly into the seam. Paint is applied over the cotton, and caulking compound is used over the painted cotton to finish the seams.

Although the basic hull is complete at this point, much work remains for the builder. Seats and floorboards must be made, and the mast, boom, and rudder fabricated, if the dinghy is a sailing model. Finally the hull must be sanded and then painted or stained. The finished product is a thing of great beauty, incorporating native woods to the extent possible, and the talents of a builder who designed the boat to suit its owner's needs, and who hand-fashioned every member of it. Winer Malone of Hope Town, Abaco, who still builds Abaco dinghies in much the same way as it was done over one hundred years ago, is a skilled and talented man— a first class boatbuilder. He is one of the last heirs of a great boat building tradition which commenced with the arrival of the loyalists two hundred years ago.

Even the names of many of the nineteenth-century boatbuilders are probably irretrievably lost. The same is true of information regarding the vessels they built. More is known about the boatbuilders of the early twentieth century. Mr. Dickie Roberts of Green Turtle Cay was a well known boatbuilder who built the *Albertine Adoue*, a schooner which served as Abaco's mailboat until the 1920s. The *Albertine Adoue* was 60 feet long on the keel and had a beam of 20 feet.* She was built with timbers from a wrecked vessel of the same, or similar, name. Edgar Albury of Man-O-War Cay made the sails for her. Henry Augustus Fisher was another well known builder. He was from Green Turtle Cay and later lived at Hope Town and on Man-O-War Cay. He built many fine sponging schooners, including the 65-ton *Columbia* in about 1906. Fisher's sons were boatbuilders also.[11]

The most famous of all the Abaco boatbuilders was Jenkins Roberts. Born in Hope Town in 1886, he learned his first boat building skills from his father, who was a builder of dinghies and

---

*See p. 88, for a photograph of the *Albertine Adoue*. Also, she is shown in the painting on the cover.

smack boats. Jenkins Roberts was able to become the premier boatbuilder of Abaco because of what he learned from local builders, and because when he was twenty or twenty-five years old he "sent away" for a six-volume set of books on ship designing. He digested the information in the books, and became the only boatbuilder in the Bahamas capable of producing detailed plans as well as half models and building from them.[12] In 1914 Jenkins Roberts built the *Perceler*, a 150-ton, three-masted cargo schooner. In 1917 he built the 266-ton *Abaco* at Man-O-War Cay. The *Abaco* was 130 feet overall and had a beam of 33 feet. In 1922 Jenkins Roberts launched the *Abaco, Bahamas*. This 484-ton vessel was the largest ship ever built in Abaco, and the second largest in all the Bahamas, exceeded only by the *Marie J. Thompson* (696 tons), which

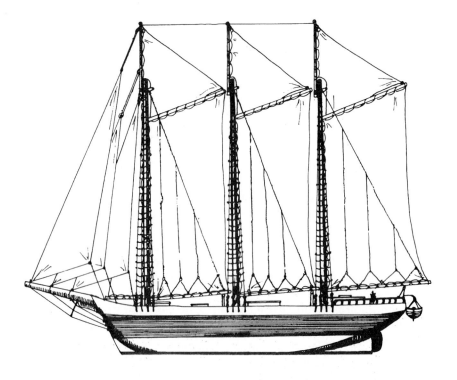

The *Abaco, Bahamas*, launched in 1922 at Hope Town, was the largest vessel built in Abaco, and the second largest built in the Bahamas. She was 150 feet long and was used to transport lumber cut on Great Abaco Island to Cuba and Florida.

was launched at Harbour Island, Eleuthera, in the same year. The *Abaco, Bahamas* was 150 feet long and had a draft of only 8 feet. The mainmast towered 80 feet above the deck, and the topmast 30 feet above that. She was planked with 4-inch by 6-inch Abaco pine with very few butts, and was able to carry about 500,000 board feet of lumber.

The ships built by Jenkins Roberts were conceived by the builder during and just after World War I, when freight rates were very high. The *Perceler* and the *Abaco* earned profits for their owners, but the *Abaco, Bahamas* was uneconomic by the time she was launched. She could not compete with powered vessels during the post-war boom in the 1920s. Jenkins' son Dawson said that "they got carried away with it"; that they built one, and then a larger one, and then still a larger one.[13] It is unfortunate that these great vessels were not more economically successful, but that sad fact certainly does not tarnish the accomplishments of Jenkins Roberts and the men of Hope Town and Man-O-War who built them. They were ships in which any seafaring people could take pride.

Jenkins Roberts moved from Hope Town to Nassau in 1925 in search of work. There he was employed by the Symonette Shipyard for over twenty years, where he designed and built several freight boats as well as doing maintenance and repair work. He was accredited by Lloyds of London and by the American Bureau of Shipping as a surveyor; he conducted surveys and assessed damages after mishaps on ships located all over the Caribbean. He died at the age of eighty-eight in 1974.

William H. Albury was also the son of a boatbuilder. His father, Richard Albury, built dinghies, smack boats, and schooners. He learned skills from his father and from Jenkins Roberts, whom he helped during the construction of the *Abaco*. William Albury was Jenkins Roberts' junior by sixteen years. He was born in 1902, and was fifteen years old when the *Abaco* was completed. Jenkins Roberts taught young William how to use plans in boat construction.[14] Though he developed into a fine boatbuilder very quickly, there was little demand for boats during the 1930s, and William became a crawfisherman. In 1938, a cruising sailboat from the United States arrived in Abaco, and Ted Zickes, one of the sailors on board, commissioned William to build a boat for him. The *Sweetheart*, a 30-foot sloop, was soon launched. During World War II William Albury accepted contracts from the Abaco Lumber com-

A boat under construction at Mr. Wissie's (Mr. Wilson Albury's) boat yard in Marsh Harbour during the 1950s. Photo courtesy of Dave Gale.

Basil Sands' boat yard at Man-O-War in the 1950s. Photo courtesy of Dave Gale.

The *William H. Albury*, named for her builder, drawn while on the ways at Edwin's Boat Yard, Man-O-War Cay.

pany to build the *Joyce Roberts*, a freight boat, and the *Donald Roberts*, a 60-foot tug boat, as well as a 130-foot barge. These were probably the largest vessels built in Abaco since the lumber schooners of the 1920s. After the war, people from the United States arrived at Man-O-War War Cay in greater numbers, and many of them ordered boats. In 1946 *Wynne*, a sloop, was built, and in 1948 William H. Albury built a 57-foot motor sailor named *Lucayo*. These boats were sold to their buyers from the United States at bargain prices relative to their value in the United States, but this was of little concern to the men of Man-O-War, who were pleased to have found reasonably steady employment. One of the most interesting of the boats built by William H. Albury during these years is now named for him. Launched in 1964, the *William H. Albury* was built to the plans of a United States pilot schooner of about 1810. She is 56 feet long on deck and 70 feet overall. She has a beam of

16 feet, draws 6 feet, and carries 2100 square feet of sail. The *William H. Albury* represented the Bahamas in the Tall Ships Race and Op Sail '76 in 1976, and at the celebration commemorating the 350th anniversary of the founding of Boston, held in 1980. She is a fine example of the boat building skills of William H. Albury and the men of Man-O-War Cay.

Benny Sawyer of Cherokee Sound is surely one of the finest master shipwrights and boatbuilders Abaco has produced. He is now retired, and during his last working years he was involved in house and building construction because there was little demand for large wood boats, and because house construction was much easier. Benny built 22 boats in his lifetime, ranging in length from 18 to 102 feet. Most of his boats were smack boats built for fishermen in Spanish Wells, Eleuthera. Prior to the 1960s, the smacks were sailing vessels, but after that Benny built powered smacks. In 1966 he built *Blue Waters*, which was 81' on the keel and 92' overall. She was built for Captain Willie Johnson. Roosevelt Sweeting of Spanish Wells is her present owner, and she is still in use. Benny drew his own plans for the boats he built. In 1965 he built a yacht for an American named Leech. She was 32' on the keel, had two spars, and cost her owner about £600 ($1400.). Six men worked on the boat, and she was completed in only five months. The last boat Benny built was also his largest. She was 92' on the keel and 102' on deck. She was started as a small freighter, but during construction it was decided that she would be a fishing boat. She was launched as a powered smack boat with a live well about 35' long and 14' wide. The well was capable of carrying about 15,000 pounds of fish. Her frames were doubled (lapped) natural crook hardwood 4" X 4" from local forests on 18" centers. The frames were sawn by hand and the bevel was cut with a hatchet after the frames were in place. She was planked with Abaco pine. Skill saws were used to rip the planks, and Benny used a 22" planer powered by a V-8 engine.[15]

Benny Sawyer gave up boat construction in 1968 and became a house builder. William H. Albury died four years later in 1972. Boat building continued in Abaco, but it was not as diverse. Dinghies were still built, and occasionally a sailboat of 20 to 25 feet was built, but the carpenters who were busiest were those who built the Man-O-War powerboats. Ranging in length from 16 to 24 feet, these unique round bilge, deep-V, planing hulls were well adapted to the waters of Abaco and the Bahamas. Ben and Willard

Launching of *Pinocchio* at Cherokee Sound. *Pinocchio* was one of twenty-two boats built by Benny Sawyer.

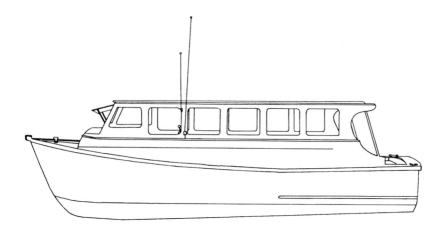

Junonia was built for Albury's Ferry Service by Edwin's Boat Yard at Man-O-War Cay to replace the original *Junonia*, which was a New England lobster boat.

Albury of Man-O-War Cay succeeded in achieving a remarkably smooth riding boat, even in a stiff chop. The building process for these planing hulls was very similar to the process used for the Abaco dinghies.

During the 1970s and 1980s several sailing boats have been built in Abaco to compete in the Out Island Regatta held in Georgetown, Exuma, each spring. This regatta is for Bahamian work boats and dinghies, and has been an annual event since the 1950s. Although the regatta was started as a contest for Bahamian workboats, many of the recent entries are racing boats built with lines similar to the old smack boats for the specific purpose of participating in the Out Island Regatta. Abaco's first entry was in 1975, when the *Abaco*, which was built at Man-O-War Cay, came in seventh in a fleet of eleven. The boat was rebuilt during the next year and fitted with a taller mast and a larger sail. She was renamed *Rough Waters,* and won several races in the 1977 regatta. Three other racing boats have been built at Man-O-War for the Out Island Regatta—one was named *Abaco*, another *Man-0-War*, and the third, *Abaco Rage*. Also, the first-place winner in the dinghy category at Georgetown in 1981 sailed a boat built by Winer Malone of Hope Town.

During the late 1970s Edwin Albury of Edwin's Boat Yard at Man-O-War Cay, who had built small sloops as well as ferries, racing boats, and planing hulls, made a mold from one of his 16'

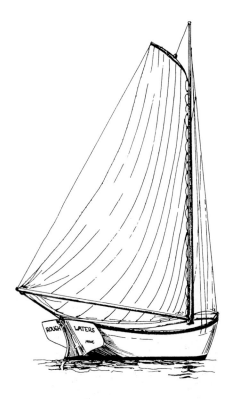

Rough Waters was the first of several boats built since 1975 at Man-O-War Cay to compete in the annual Out Island Regatta at Georgetown, Exuma.

wood hulls and began to produce fiberglass hulls. He immediately received enough orders to keep his shop working at capacity for over two years, and soon expanded operations by making a mold for a 22' model. Darwin Sands, manager of Edwin's Boat Yard #2, was in charge of the operation throughout the 1980s. He eventually decided to sell the molds and get out of the business because he feared toxic contamination from working with the fiberglass and the ever-present fiberglass dust. But by the time Edwin's Boat Yard was out of fiberglass construction, Ben and Willard Albury's shop had shifted to glass. They began in 1985, and by the 1990s were making both an 18½' and a 20' model. They accept orders only for what they can build during the next twelve months. Their fiberglass hulls are built with solid fiberglass rather than cored with balsa or foam, resulting in heavier boats built for rugged use. They are in high demand throughout The Bahamas, and demonstrate, once again, the versatile skills of the boatbuilders of Abaco.

END NOTES

[1] Rawson W. Rawson (Governor of the Bahamas), *Report on the Bahamas for the Year 1864* (London, 1866), p. 65.

[2] Much of the information in this section about dinghies, smack boats, and schooners was gained from William R. Johnson's beautifully illustrated book, *Bahamian Sailing Craft* (Nassau: Explorations Ltd., 1974).

[3] Haziel Albury, *Man-O-War: My Island Home* (Hockessin, Delaware: Holly, 1977), p. 53.

[4] Annual reports of the Resident Justices and Commissioners frequently list the number and type of boats built during that year in the district.

[5] David Cornish, Interview with the author, Dundas Town, 10 May 1979. Winer Malone confirmed this, but indicated that a black boatbuilder from Grand Bahama who moved to Sandy Point, Abaco, built boats there (Winer Malone, Interview with the author, Hope Town, 11 June 1979). Also see Norman Albury, Interview, Man-O-War Cay, 28 August 1973 (tape recording at National Archives of the Bahamas, Nassau).

[6] Report of Commissioner, Hope Town, 1912.

[7] Winer Malone, Interviews with the author, 6 June and 11 June 1979, and 18 March 1995.

[8] The cork tree which grows in The Bahamas is not the same as the cork oak which grows in the Mediterranean area, the bark of which is used to make plugs for wine bottles.

[9] One or two ribbands may be fastened to the other side to hold the frames straight, but only one side is used to determine the shape of the other frames.

[10] Winer made his lead batten by cutting a groove measuring approximately ¾" wide and ½" deep in a board. Lead was melted on a stove and poured into the groove in a single, steady pour. The batten must be free of bubbles and other voids. The cooled lead was then removed from the board and planed with a regular plane until its edges were smooth and fair.

[11] See Norman Albury, Interview, and Iris Lowe, "New Plymouth," *The Tribune* (Nassau), 17 February 1975, p. 5.

[12] Most of the information about Jenkins Roberts in this section was gained from Dawson Roberts, Interview with the author, Nassau, 2 July 1979.

[13] *Ibid.*

[14] Much of the information about William H. Albury in this section was gained from Haziel Albury, Interview with the author, Man-O-War Cay, 18 July 1979.

[15] Benny Sawyer, Interview with the author, Cherokee Sound, 27 July 1982.

An Essay Describing Selected Sources

Several articles were the most useful sources for information regarding the geologic origins of the Bahama islands and banks. For a general understanding of tectonic plate theory see Robert S. Dietz and John C. Holden, "The Breakup of Pangaea," *Scientific American* 223:4 (October 1970), 30-41. For more specific information about the Bahamas platform see Henry T. Mullins and George W. Lynts, "Origin of the Northwestern Bahama Platform: Review and Reinterpretation," *Geological Society of America Bulletin* 88:10 (1977), 1447-1461, and Norman D. Newell, "Bahamian Platforms," in Arie Poldervaart, ed., *Crust of the Earth* (Geological Society of America Special Paper 62, 1955), 303-316. Also, there is a brief description of the geologic origins of the Bahamas in David G. Campbell, *The Ephermeral Islands: A Natural History of the Bahamas* (London: Macmillan, 1978), and an excellent explanation of plate tectonics in the Caribbean (which does not include The Bahamas) in Neil Sealey, *Caribbean World: A Complete Geography* (Cambridge: Cambridge University Press, 1992).

One of the truly beneficial results of the Quincentenary of Christopher Columbus' voyage was that it focused attention on the native Bahamians who were the first Americans to make contact with Columbus. In 1987 a conference—Bahamas 1492: Its People and Environment—was held in Freeport, Bahamas, which brought together most of the scholars with knowledge of the Lucayan Indians, and some very interesting papers were presented. Unfortunately, these have not been published. In 1992 several new books appeared. The most useful is William F. Keegan, *The People Who Discovered Columbus: The Prehistory of the Bahamas* (Gainesville: University Presses of Florida, 1992). Also published in 1992 was Irving Rouse, *The Tainos: Rise and Decline of the People who Greeted Columbus* (New Haven: Yale University Press, 1992), and D. J. R. Walker, *Columbus and the Golden World of the Island Arawaks* (Kingston: Ian Randle, 1992. Anyone studying the period of contact between the Europeans and native Americans should read Alfred W. Crosby, *The Columbian Exchange: Biological and Cultural Consequences of 1492* (Westport: Greenwood, 1972). For a report regarding recent digs in Abaco see George A. Aarons et al., *Prehistoric and Historic Archaeological Field Research in Abaco, Bahamas: 1988-1991* (Decatur, IL: White Sound Press, 1992).

The single most important collection of primary sources for the early years of the history of the Bahamas is British Colonial Office file number 23 (CO 23). It includes 324 volumes of official correspondence between the Bahamas and Britian during the period from 1696 to 1943. The documents are available to researchers in London, and a microfilm copy is available at the Bahamian National Archives in Nassau. A valuable guide to a portion of this file was prepared by D. Gail Saunders and is titled *Bahamas Original Correspondence*. This list and index of CO 23 covers the period from 1767 to 1786, which includes part of the period of loyalist settlement in Abaco, and is available at the Bahamian National Archives. Another valuable source of primary documents was *Book B*, available at the Lands and Surveys Office in Nassau. It includes the land grants made by the crown in Abaco during the period from the late eighteenth to the mid-nineteenth centuries. Correspondence of Sir Guy Carleton, the British Commander-in-Chief in New York City during the 1780s, as well as other documents relating to the loyalist settlement of Abaco can be found in the British Headquarters Papers at New York Public Library.

Some additional documents from the loyalist period which were useful and are not to be found in any of the above collections are:

Blanchard, Cornelius. Petition to James Edward Powell. New Providence, 6 April 1785. Copy at Albert Lowe Museum.

Dumaresq, Philip. Letter to Sylvester Gardiner. Marsh Harbour. 6 March 1785. Copy at Wyannie Malone Historical Museum.

Survey Report, 1784. Copy at Wyannie Malone Historical Museum.

Wilson, John. Manuscript Report on the Bahama Islands, 1784. Includes instruction of Robert Morse to John Wilson, 14 July 1783. Copy at Boston Public Library.

Also, *The Royal Gazette*, a newspaper published in New York City was useful for information concerning the loyalists before they departed from New York for Abaco in 1784.

Information concerning Abaco during the early nineteenth century was found in the series of reports titled, simply, *Colony of the Bahamas*. These were published each year and are popularly called the "Blue Books." They are available at the Bahamian National Archives. Précis of reports by the Resident Justices and Assistant Resident Justices stationed in all the Out Islands, including Abaco, during the late nineteenth century appear in *Bahamas: Votes of the Legislative Council*, which were published annually. A most valuable source is Governor Rawson W. Rawson's very complete report on the Bahamas which was prepared for the year 1864. Governor Rawson placed his information in perspective rather than simply reporting the facts and statistics for the current year. His report was published in London in 1866, and is available in Nassau as well as in London. Also, the *Annual Colonial Reports, 1881-1907*, were useful for this period.

The originals or carbon copies of the reports of the Assistant Resident Justices and Commissioners (after 1908) stationed in Abaco for many, but not for all, years from the 1890s through the 1950s are available at the Bahamian National Archives. These are filed by district (i.e.- Marsh Harbour, New Plymouth, Cherokee Sound).

Several accounts written by visitors to Abaco provided useful information (listed in chronological order):

McKinnen, Daniel. *Tour Through the British West Indies in the Years 1802 and 1803*. London: J. White, 1804.

Ives, Charles. *The Isles of Summer*. New Haven: by author, 1880

Powles, Louis Diston. *The Land of the Pink Pearl*. London: S. Lowe, Marston, Searle, & Rivington, 1888.

Shattuck, George B., ed. *The Bahama Islands*. New York: Macmillan, for the Geographic Society of Baltimore, 1905.

Bell, Hugh M. Bahamas: *Isles of June*. New York: R. M. McBride, 1934.

Rigg, J. Linton. *Bahama Islands: A Boatman's Guide to the Land and the Water*. New York: Van Nostrand, 1949.

Wadleigh, G. R. *We Called it a Vacation*. New York: J. Felsberg, 1950.

Helweg-Larsen, Kjeld. *Columbus Never Came*. London: Jarrolds, 1963.

Five personal memoirs written by twentieth-century residents of Abaco were useful:

Albury, Haziel. *Man-O-War: My Island Home*. Hockessin, Delaware: Holly, 1977.

Cottman, Evans. *Out Island Doctor*. London: Hodder and Stuoughton, 1963.

Ford, Jack. *Reminiscences of an Island Teacher: Life on Green Turtle Cay in the Bahamas, 1948-1953*. Decatur, IL: White Sound Press, 1992.

Gottlieb von Sanden, Owanta. *Angel Stand by Me*. Marsh Harbour, Abaco: Daybreak Publishing, 1987.

Johnston, Randolph W. *Artist on His Island: A Study in Self-Reliance*. Park Ridge, New Jersey: Noyes, 1975.

The best general history of The Bahamas is Michael Craton and D. Gail Saunders, *Islanders in the Stream: A History of the Bahamian People* (Athens, GA: University of Georgia Press, 1992). This is volume one of a projected two-volume set and covers from aboriginal times to the end of slavery (1838). Craton and Saunders succeeded in writing a new kind of national history—one which describes the lives of the people of the Bahamas rather than documenting the political trials and tribulations of the colonial Governors. More traditional general histories are Michael Craton, *A History of the Bahamas*, third edition (Waterloo, Ontario, Canada: San Salvador Press, 1986), and Paul Albury, *The Story of the Bahamas* (London, Macmillan, 1975). A history emphasizing the role of the African-Bahamian is Harley Cecil Saunders, *The Other Bahamas* (Nassau: Bodab Publishers, 1991).

Various other published and unpublished works were useful. These include:

Barratt, Peter. *Grand Bahama,* second edition. London: Macmillan, 1989.

Bethel, A. T. *The Early Settlers of the Bahamas* Nassau, 1937.

Bethel, Parick J. *The Economic, Physical and Social Growth of the Town of Marsh Harbour,* unpublished typescript, no date.

Bethel, Patrick J. *Growing Up In Cherokee Sound: 1935-1950,* unpublished typescript, no date.

Bethel-Daly, Paulette Anne. *Uneven Development in The Bahamas: Past and Present,* Ph.D. Dissertation, University of Massachusetts, 1980.

Brown, Marjorie W. *From Sand Banks to Treasure Cay.* 1977.

Dodge, Steve. *The First Loyalist Settlements in Abaco: Carleton and Marsh's Harbour.* Hope Town: Wyannie Malone Historical Museum, 1979.

Collinwood, Dean, and Steve Dodge, eds. *Modern Bahamian Society.* Parkersburg, Iowa: Caribbean Books, 1989.

Durrell, Zoé C. *The Innocent Island: Abaco in the Bahamas.* Brattleboro, Vermont: Durrell Publications, 1972.

Evans, F. C., and R. N. Young. *The Bahamas.* Cambridge: Cambridge University Press, 1976.

Fawkes, Randol. *The Faith that Moved the Mountain.* Nassau: Nassau Guardian, 1979.

Hughes, Colin A. *Race and Politics in the Bahamas.* New York: St. Martins, 1981.

Johnson, Doris. *The Quiet Revolution.* Nassau: Family Islands Press, 1972.

Johnson, William R. *Bahamian Sailing Craft.* Nassau: Explorations Ltd., 1973.

Johnson, Howard. *The Bahamas in Slavery and Freedom.* Kingston: Ian Randle, 1991.

Moseley, Mary. *The Bahamas Handbook.* Nassau: Nassau Guardian, 1926.

Rodgers, William B. III. *The Wages of Change: An Anthropological Study of the Effects of Economic Development on Some Negro Communities in the Out Island Bahamas,* Ph.D. Dissertation, Stanford, 1965.

Peters, Thelma. *The American Loyalists and the Plantation Period in the Bahama Islands,* Ph.D. Dissertation, University of Florida, 1960.

Riley, Sandra. *Homeward Bound: A History of the Bahama Islands to 1850 with a Definitive Study of Abaco in the American Loyalist Plantation Period.* Miami: Island Research, 1983.

Saunders, D. Gail. *The Slave Population of the Bahamas, 1783-1834,* M. A. Thesis, University of the West Indies, 1978.

Saunders, D. Gail. *Bahamian Loyalists and Their Slaves.* London: Macmillian Caribbean, 1983.

Siebert, Wilbur H. *The Legacy of the American Revolution to the British West Indies and Bahamas: A Chapter out of the History of the American Loyalists.* Columbus: Ohio State University, 1913.

Taylor, Sir Henry. *My Political Memoirs: A Political History of the Bahamas in the 20th Century.* Nassau, no date.

Wilder, Robert. *Wind from the Carolinas.* New York: 1964.

Newspaper sources were valuable for recent events. *The Tribune* and *The Nassau Guardian* are the two Nassau dailies. Since 1986 articles in these two newspapers have been indexed in *The Bahamas Index and Yearbook,* an annually published reference work. Also, *The Bahamas Handbook,* an annual publication of Dupuch Publications, is a valuable source of current information about The Bahamas.

Further investigations of materials about Abaco and The Bahamas should begin with Paul Boultbee, compiler, *The Bahamas,* World Bibliographic Series, Volume 108 (Oxford: Clio Press, 1989). This is the only published bibliography devoted exclusively to The Bahamas.

Index

British Imperial Lighthouse Service, 62
Brown, Thomas, 43, 48
Buckley, William F. 209, 217

calcium carbonate, 5
Canadian Imperial Bank of Commerce, 100
Caribs, 11
Castro, Fidel, 100
cassava, 13
Cat Island, 27
Caribbean Sailing Yachts (CSY), 141
Carleton, 39-40, 42-45, 97
Carleton, Sir Guy, 33, 38-39
Cave Cay, 52
Cedar Harbour, 85, 115, 192
Cedras, Raul, 158
Charles III, 33
Charleston, 31, 37, 59
charter sailboats, 140-141
Chase Manhattan Bank, 100
chenille bug, 44
Cherokee Sound, 52, 74, 81, 97, 122, 138, 169, 194-201
Christie, Perry, 165, 167
churches, 159-161
Civil War (U.S.), 61, 63-66
citrus, 69, 70, 148
Coco Plum Creek, 40, 49, 74, 84
Columbia, 227
Columbus, Christopher, 14, 16, 19-20
Commission of Inquiry, 165
Conch Inn, 170
Cooperstown, 85, 115, 118, 161, 185-191
copper, 51
Cornish, John, 48
Cornish Cay, 41
Cornish Town, 52, 93
Cornwall, 85, 86
de la Cosa, Juan, 20-21
cottage tourism, 139
Cottman, Evans W. 105-107
cotton, 43-44, 209
Council for a Free Abaco, 120, 123
crawfishing, 89, 90, 96, 147-148, 201
Criminal Investigation Department (CID), 131
Crockett, J. B., 96, 101
Cross Harbour, 85, 86
Crossing Rocks, 52, 74, 122, 194-201
Crown Haven, 53, 115
Cruden, James, 48
Cuba, 100
cruises, 143
cucumbers, 102, 148
Cyrano, 209, 217

Day, Adrian, 128
Dean, Ernest, 200
Deborah K II, 170, 195

depression, 90
Dole, Sanford, 66
Donald Roberts, 231
Donnie VII, 183
Doris Davis, 103
drip irrigation, 149
drugs, 150-154
Dumaresq, Philip, 44, 46
Dundas, C. C., 93
Dundas Town, 93, 94, 118, 169
duhos, 12
Dunmore, Governor, 46-48
Dupuch, Etienne, 112
Duvalier, Jean Claude, 102
Duvalier, Papa Doc, 102

eco-tourism, 139
Edgecombe, Medius, 188
Edwin's Boatyard, 183
Eight Mile Bay, 41, 43, 52
Elbow Cay, 90, 155, 179, 202-205, 218
Elbow Reef Lighthouse, 62
elections,
    (1956), 114
    (1962), 114
    (1967), 115
    (1968), 116
    (1972), 118-119
    (1977), 164
    (1987), 165
    (1992), 167
electric service, 87, 171
Eleuthera, 24, 27, 66, 209
Empire Day, 186
England, 22-24, 116
Esquire, 132
Exuma, 27, 157, 234

Fair Abaconian, 42
Family Islands, 163
Fawkes, Randol, 113, 114
fiberglass boat construction, 26, 235
Fisher, Henry Augustus, 227
fishing, 97, 200, 211
Florida, 32-33, 43, 47, 58, 70, 86, 102, 193
Fox Town, 115, 147, 193
France, 22
Free National Movement (FNM), 117, 118, 119, 133, 158, 161, 168, 190, 204
Freeport, 85
freight service, 87, 170
Friends of Abaco, 126
fruit-growing, 46

Gansevoort, Captain, 65
General Asembly, 48
general strick (1958), 113
George III, 31
Georgetown, 234-235